the Do-Over

A Memoir of
Work and Love

Amanda MacKenzie

Published 2017
Printed in the United States of America
PRINT ISBN: 978-0-9988141-0-0
E-ISBN: 978-0-9988141-1-7

Cover and interior design by Tabitha Lahr
For information, contact: www.amandamackenzie.com

For my sister Darlington,
the biggest star I know

I dwell in Possibility—
—Emily Dickinson

Contents

Prelude

In my twenties I was in a hurry to figure out the details of my life. To get there, I made some pretty big decisions based on what I thought I *should* do, as if there were a map for life and following it would lead straight to everything I pictured: a lifelong career, a marriage, a house, and finally children. This approach worked. Sort of. By twenty-eight, my life looked good on paper: a respectable career, a handsome husband, a house in the suburbs decorated like Martha Stewart had done it—albeit on a budget. But in my rush to figure out life, I'd ignored my inner compass—letting other voices drown out my own and making choices that didn't really fit with my heart.

To say that I woke up one spring morning at age thirty and found myself living a life that didn't feel like my own would be an exaggeration. But only slightly so. The seeds of discontent had sprouted and had been growing for a while, but I'd ignored them as a gardener overlooks the first weeds of the season: tiny, delicate—how harmful could they be? As usual that morning, the view from bed was easy on the eyes—my dark-haired husband asleep beside me in a bedroom we'd painted a cheerful yellow, in a house we'd picked out together—but still, I lay there and thought,

This doesn't feel right, and I felt sick inside. Not the sort that comes from an upset stomach or having too much to drink, but the sort from feeling like your life is out of whack. And once I admitted this truth to myself, I couldn't take it back.

I'm not usually a decisive person, but I became one. I mobilized all the courage I could muster and said good-bye to life as I knew it—the cheerful yellow walls, the shared bed, the house in the suburbs that held it all. By summer's end I'd moved out and told my husband I was pretty sure I wanted a divorce.

And then it was just me—in a studio apartment, on a single mattress on the floor, staring up at plain white walls. Now what?

And so I began again. This time, though, I let go of how I thought I *should* be, of outdated ways of thinking about myself and life, of burying my dreams, of putting others first all the time. I stopped judging my actions by a self-imposed standard of "rightness" (How does this look to the outside world?) and instead asked, "How does this make me feel?" In short, I practiced putting myself first.

I was late to the party, but I finally figured out that it feels *good* to let go. To throw out the map. To say "Yes!" because it feels right, even if you don't know exactly where yes will lead. To lose track of time because you're in love with what you're doing. To choose yourself.

Of course, this shift—letting go, listening to my inner wisdom, following my heart—didn't happen overnight. I had to befriend patience, and as a result, I became pretty good at enjoying the journey instead of trying to figure it all out. Now, nearly ten years since that spring morning, I've grown into a better listener and bigger believer in myself and everyone else around me—discovering, though it's hardly a secret, that life is all about change, which means it's all about beginning again. Not once or twice. Not only in those big moments of transition. *Every* day brings a chance to start afresh. To loosen up, let go, and allow life to surprise you with her beauty.

And she will, too.

Part One: Deciding

And now we welcome the New Year,
full of things that have never been.
—Rainer Maria Rilke

1. Now What?

In late summer of 2000, when I was about to turn twenty-four, with no prospects of work or love on the horizon, I moved back home with my parents. The only things they asked of me were that I cook dinner once a week and figure out my life. They didn't put a timeline on the latter, which was pretty generous of them; they seemed to have faith that I would figure things out in good time. But I wasn't planning to stay long anyway. I loved my family and the house I grew up in in the suburbs of Boston, but living at home in my mid-twenties was definitely *not* how I imagined my life unfolding. I was in search of the next Big Thing, and just as soon as I discovered what that was, I'd be off.

As late summer turned to fall and I was no closer to figuring out the next Big Thing, I patched together a collection of odd jobs to fill the time between now and then. I was a babysitter, substitute teacher, and farmhand, none of which made me feel very good about myself or my future prospects—and compared to my friends who were moving ahead with work or school, putting their education to use our second year out of college, I felt like a professional loser. Deep down I knew I had as much potential as they did; I just didn't know where to direct any of it.

And then in dark December, just before the shortest day, an unexpected hint of light peeked out from the horizon.

Jonathan called.

I'd met Jonathan when I was a junior in high school, seven years earlier, when my family started going to church down the hill from our house. It wasn't my family's first foray into Sunday services: my parents had met as members of a church choir in nearby Cambridge, and had continued to take us to that city church until family life—I'm the oldest of three—called for a closer church with a cozier feel. The most logical choice, because of its proximity to our house and its denomination, was Pilgrim Congregational Church—"Pilgrim" because our denomination traced its roots back to the religious dissidents on the Mayflower, and "Congregational" because that was the name of our denomination today, a theologically liberal tradition in which individual congregations made their own decisions, like whom to hire as minister.

Jonathan was our minister, and he called me that December day to ask if I would speak in church the following Sunday. I didn't consider myself particularly religious, but growing up in the church had given me an appreciation for community, and in this time of transition, Pilgrim Church was another familiar "home" I'd returned to—a place where everybody knew my name, my family, and my life story so far. The previous year the congregation had wowed me with their generosity, too—donating thousands of dollars and bags of winter clothes for the refugee camp in Hungary where I'd spent the first year after college volunteering (when I wasn't teaching English, which was my official reason for being in Hungary). Now, a year later, Jonathan asked if I would thank everyone for last year's great gift, which would hopefully encourage their generosity once again this Christmas season, this time for a more local cause.

Though I was happy to speak, I couldn't help but compare my life now to what it had been a year ago. Then, I'd felt strong, confident, and full of potential—my life in Hungary had been a grand adventure, full of meaningful work, weekend travel around Eastern Europe, and boys. Now life felt like a watered-down version of what it had been, and I felt like a one-act wonder, brought back to talk about the interesting things I *used* to do.

✳ ✳ ✳

"We're going to be late!" my little brother Silas yelled upstairs to me as I finished writing my remarks Sunday morning just before church, incurably last-minute as usual.

"Coming!" I hollered back, throwing on a black velvet top, a skirt, and flats, and pulling my dark blond hair into something meant to resemble a French braid.

Silas was waiting at the back door. Tall, skinny, blond, and dressed in a pair of dark green sweatpants that were almost too short because he was growing so fast, Silas was fifteen and a freshman at a nearby boys' school, to which he had to wear a coat and tie every day; on weekends he lived in sweatpants and T-shirts, accented with a shark's tooth dangling from a string around his neck. Luckily ours wasn't the sort of church where anyone cared much about appearances.

"Jonathan asked me to speak today," I told Silas as we walked down the hill to church.

"Oh, cool! Are you ready?"

"Yep! Just finished writing something. It's no big deal; I don't really get nervous speaking in front of people."

"Me either. Can we practice driving after church?"

"Of course! Let's ask Johanna too."

On Sunday afternoons I gave Silas and a church friend lessons in the elementary school parking lot in my red Volkswagen stick shift. It was a bright side to living at home, this chance to connect with my brother; since he was nine years younger, I'd always thought of him as a little kid, but now we felt more like equals, one of the many benefits of aging.

Inside the church—a classic New England sanctuary with

white walls and tall windows that let in the light—we settled into a back-left pew, our usual spot. Sometimes Silas passed notes during church; he was funny, and I had to remind myself to stifle my laughs.

"You're up, Sis!" he said, nudging me, as Jonathan invited me up front and everyone turned toward me expectantly. I smiled at my parents as I walked down the aisle; they were sitting up front next to the organ, dressed in maroon robes with the rest of their choir friends. Taking my place behind the lectern, I smiled out at everyone, spoke for a few minutes, and then it was done.

Pilgrim was not a clappy sort of church. On the rare occasion that people put their hands together in a worship service, it was usually for something cute the kids did or a particularly grand piece on the organ. But I must have tapped into something that morning, because when I finished speaking, the congregation actually clapped.

For me? I wondered, caught off guard. After four months of feeling lame, like I was wasting my potential, all of those hands coming together felt like an affirmation of who I was, reminding me that I was good at something.

But the applause wasn't the only thing that surprised me that morning.

"Have *you* ever thought about becoming a minister?" my friend Luke asked me, standing in the sanctuary after the service. Luke was in divinity school and doing his minister internship at Pilgrim. He was also single, at twenty-nine, and, according to Jonathan, a few of the church ladies thought we'd make a cute couple. I had a sneaking suspicion my mom was in that group. Earlier that fall, she'd invited Luke to the house for dinner without telling me. That afternoon, I just happened to check my email and saw a note from Luke saying he was looking forward to dinner at my parents' house that night.

Tonight? Dinner? I'd thought to myself, confused.

"Mom!" I yelled up from the basement office where the

family computer lived. "Did you invite Luke the student minister to dinner?"

"Oh! Yes. I must have forgotten to tell you," she called down from the kitchen.

As if. It wasn't the sort of thing my mom would forget to mention. More likely she'd "forgotten" to tell me because she knew I'd see through her generous invitation to the matchmaking endeavor that it was. If I'd grown up in Bangalore instead of Boston, my parents would have married me off by now. Cultural heritage had saved me from that fate, but my mother wasn't above a bit of low-grade interference in my dating life. Scott, my first serious boyfriend, happened to be the son of one of her best friends, also from church. Our first date had been a holiday ball at which both of our families were present. I knew my mom had good intentions (my happiness), but sometimes she seemed overly interested in my dating life—or, at times, bothered by the lack thereof.

This time, though, her machinations lined up with my interests—I already *had* a small crush on the student minister, not that I would have admitted as much to my mom—and once I got over my annoyance at her scheming, the evening was quite nice, actually. Sitting in front of a roaring fire with your parents, kid brother, and a student minister wouldn't be everyone's idea of fun, but my dad poured generous glasses of red wine from a one-liter jug of whatever had been on sale, and the conversation flowed too, straight through cocktail hour and into dinner.

That had been a month ago, and since then my mother the matchmaker hadn't brought up Luke's name again, as if she had done her part and was now standing back to see what might unfold. From where I stood now, it looked like Luke was more interested in my career goals than my marriageability.

Had I ever thought about becoming a minister?

This was actually an easy question to answer: of all the things I had ever thought about becoming—and it ran the gamut from Miss America (age ten) to park ranger (age twenty-two)— being a minister had never even crossed my mind.

Jonathan was standing nearby. He smiled at me in a knowing way, as if Luke had just told a joke, and now Jonathan would explain the punch line. But instead of "Haha, just kidding," Jonathan put his arm around my shoulder and said, "We should talk. Let's have lunch."

Becoming a minister? No joke. They were serious.

✳ ✳ ✳

Jonathan was a laid-back guy who put people at ease with his casual approach and sense of humor. Sometimes from a distance I mistook him for my dad—balding, wire-rim glasses, quick to smile—but since he was ten years younger than my dad and not *my* parent, though he had a wife and three little kids of his own, Jonathan was easy to talk to about all sorts of things. When I was in high school, he'd led our small but close-knit youth group that met on Sunday nights to eat pizza, play games, and talk about thoughtful topics. I knew most of the kids from school, but at youth group we felt like family, with Jonathan as our fun-loving but responsible uncle. He told funny stories from his own teenage years, talked to us like equals, and won our trust easily.

But when Jonathan and I met for lunch a few days after I spoke in church, the fun-loving minister was all business. He really *did* think I should consider divinity school and ministry, and he told me why:

"You're a natural in front of people," he reminded me, "better than a lot of actual ministers. You don't get nervous or try to be something you're not. You're just *you* up there, and people listen. You're inspiring! And you're great with words too. What you say is clear and moving."

I knew I was a good speaker, and a good writer too, but surely that wasn't enough material out of which to make a minister.

Jonathan wasn't done yet.

"When I went to divinity school twenty years ago, most

of my classmates were my age, just out of college. But today there are fewer young students and more middle-aged ones— they've had professions in another field and now, later in life, feel 'called' to ministry as a second career. They might have lots of life experience, but some are experiencing church for the first time. What you've got going for you is that you already know the church *and* you're young. Churches will love that. It's a great combination!"

Jonathan was starting to make sense. Still, I noted some glaring omissions from his growing list of my qualifications.

"But I'm not particularly interested in reading the Bible," I confessed.

"There are all types of ministers," Jonathan said, brushing off my concern. "And some are more 'scholarly' than others. You'll learn what you need to learn about the Bible in divinity school."

Compared to other ministers I knew, Jonathan was definitely on the less "scholarly" end of the spectrum. He was more likely to tell amusing or heartwarming stories in a sermon than wrestle with theological conundrums. I remembered the last time I'd tried to engage him in a theological conversation; I was home from college on winter break, and Jonathan was driving a few of us up to New Hampshire for a youth group reunion at a lake house. As my friends joked around in the backseat, I decided to pop the question that had been on my mind.

"Do you think God is a man or a woman?" I asked Jonathan.

As a newly declared women's studies major, I was starting to notice the preponderance of male language in church, even a liberal one like mine, and it frustrated me.

"Neither," Jonathan told me. "God's beyond gender."

"So why is God always referred to as He?" I pushed back, because once I started paying attention, He showed up everywhere. Just like when you're buying a new car and start noticing your favorite model at every stoplight, where before you only saw cars. Familiar hymns, the Lord's Prayer, even the comforting doxology (short hymn) that we sang after the offering each week—

they all bugged me with their "Fathers" and "Lords." Whatever happened to "Mother" or "Lady God"?

But this didn't seem to bother Jonathan.

"It doesn't really matter what terms you use. God is bigger than our human descriptions," he offered. And then he changed the subject.

I wasn't particularly satisfied with his reply. I thought language *did* matter and influenced how we thought of things. He made me think of Michelangelo's God on the ceiling of the Sistine Chapel, touching fingers with Adam at the moment of creation. Picturing God as an old, gray-bearded man is fine if that image works for you. I had nothing against old, gray-bearded men— there were some in my family whom I loved—it just wasn't an image that helped me feel any closer to the divine. So for now, until the rest of the church changed their approach, I was self-censoring, silently bleeping out any masculine references to God: "Our [bleep], who art in Heaven . . ."

As I thought back to this example during my lunch with Jonathan, it showed me two things: One, Jonathan wasn't really interested in theological conversations about God's gender, but he was still a great minister. So maybe it wasn't such a big deal if I hadn't warmed up to the Bible yet—or didn't even think of myself as particularly religious. And two, maybe I *did* have an interest or two when it came to theology; after all, I'd clearly thought about God's gender. Maybe, as long as I had these other gifts, and a willingness to learn, it wasn't such a crazy idea to think that I could follow in my minister's footsteps.

Out in the parking lot after lunch, Jonathan put his arm around my shoulder again. "Think it over," he said. And then, as he opened the door to his sporty silver car, he looked back over his shoulder.

"And talk to Luke!"

Then he was gone.

✳ ✳ ✳

Alone with this newborn idea, I held it gingerly, getting used to how it felt, and was surprised that it didn't seem as strange as I'd expected. Like Jonathan said, I was at home in the church, and when I began to picture the shift from layperson to minister, I imagined it would feel like a natural progression, as when a camper becomes a counselor, a student a teacher, a daughter a mother herself. It wasn't such a leap to think that now it was my turn to care for a church. I mean, how different could it *really* be from sitting in the congregation every week? And besides, there was already one minister in our family—my mom's cousin Bob, in upstate New York—and plenty of other lifelong churchgoers in my family circle to give me advice.

Since moving home four months earlier, I'd felt as if I was hanging out on the sidelines, waiting for a sign that it was my turn to get back in the game of life. Now, finally, it felt like someone was waving to me from the field: "Come on! You. Yes, YOU! It's your turn. Get in here, girl. Come play with us!" Though I'd never been a natural athlete, I knew the rules to playing the game of church, and it seemed like I might have what it took to really shine. Still, it had only been a week since Luke asked the question, and less than that since my lunch with Jonathan. There was more digging to do.

Christmas Eve fell on a Sunday that year, and after church that day, when I followed Jonathan's advice to ask the eligible student minister if he'd like to grab a coffee and tell me about divinity school, I was pleasantly surprised by his, "Great! How about today?"

Luke and I walked the short distance from church to a Starbucks in the center of town, chatting easily along the way, ordering coffees, getting a table. And it wasn't until the movement stopped and we sat across from each other that I felt butterflies in my stomach, suddenly conscious that this was the first time we'd been together alone, without church people or my parents between us. I was bursting with questions! And not just about divinity school. What about his life outside of church? His family? His dreams? His *dating* life? But this was supposed to be more informational interview than date, and I had no idea what Luke thought of me, so, for now, I curbed my enthusiasm for personal details and stuck to professional ones.

For his part, Luke warmed to this subject easily, talking about his classes at a nearby seminary called Andover Newton Theological School. Though many divinity schools are attached to big universities (Harvard, Yale, Duke), this was a freestanding graduate school that had been training Protestant ministers since the mid-1800s.

"I'm in my third year," Luke explained, "and living on campus in a studio apartment."

"Well, I'd probably live at home. To save money. But three years? That's a long time to be in school again."

And live at home, I added to myself.

"Well, actually, I'm taking four years to finish the program, but if you take your time like that, you can work part-time as a minister, like I'm doing at Pilgrim."

"That's the part I think I'd like best, more than the classes," I confessed. "I'm not sure how scholarly I am when it comes to theology."

"I love it!" Luke said. "This is what I'm reading right now." He held up a black book as large as a dictionary. "It's Karl Barth, a German theologian."

"For what class?"

"No class, just for myself."

I flipped through the thin pages with their tiny font and Luke's notes in the margins. If Jonathan was on the less-scholarly end of the minister spectrum, then Luke was his polar opposite. I could tell that he liked to wrestle with ideas and had a straightforward, open approach to talking about religion. He was not at all shy about alluding to God and how He or She (Luke called God "She"!) might be working in our lives. His openness, and this conversation, was all a bit overwhelming and refreshing at the same time, like when a giant wave crashes over you and you stand up, dazed and invigorated, both at once, and then go back in for more.

Looking around Starbucks I wondered if other people over-heard our conversation. Would they think we were weird for having a chat about God? Though I'd grown up around churches, I wasn't used to talking about God in public. Was that even allowed here in our liberal, intellectual corner of New England? I was still getting my sea legs when it came to religious talk; Luke was leaps and bounds beyond me, and although I couldn't imagine getting excited about a book by Barth, I liked that Luke did, that he was smart and intellectual—he'd gone to Harvard, like my father and grandfather, and before that the same boys' school where Silas was. But more than that, I liked his enthusiasm—for school, for ministry, even for this conversation. "Interesting!" he said after almost everything I said, and I could tell he was really listening. Across the table I admired his soft brown hair, which was poking out from underneath a winter cap he hadn't taken off. I looked down to his broad shoulders and solid chest, then back up to his hazel eyes, and thought, *I could look into those clear eyes for the rest of my life.*

Of the hundreds of millions of thoughts we have in a life-time, isn't it interesting how some are burned in our memory and never leave? This was one. Perhaps that's because it surprised me, how enthralled I felt by this man who seemed like me and yet so different at the same time. And though I felt a bit silly that my thoughts were racing ahead of reality—this wasn't even a date—it certainly was pleasant to imagine a lifetime with Luke, *or some-one like him,* I added, just to be realistic.

Okay, back to the topic at hand, I reminded myself, *Luke the student minister and what I can learn from him. Not Luke the boy-friend and what it might feel like to wrap my arms around him. But he's just so appealing.*

I know you can't judge a book by its cover, but if I'd seen Luke on the street, I wouldn't have thought he was a minister. "He's so handsome and personable," a middle-aged woman from church had once said. "He looks like he could be a senator." Dressed in a navy blazer, a Brooks Brothers button-down, and khakis on Sunday, with his athletic frame, dark hair, sparkling hazel eyes, and easy smile, Luke did look like he could fit in anywhere, and I was surprised that this handsome looks-like-a-senator man had ended up here, studying to be a minister at a little-known seminary.

"My dad passed away just after I graduated from college," Luke began by way of explanation, "and I was a mess. I didn't know what to do next, but my grandfather was really there for me. He's a retired minister who had a long, amazing career, and we had lunch every week and talked about life and God and the church."

Already I wanted to meet this grandfather of his.

"Along the way I took up meditation and qigong, and I read a lot of spiritual stuff, and eventually all of that led me back to the church. I hadn't been much since I was a kid, but I started going to a big church in Boston and from there to studying at Andover Newton."

I knew from Sunday mornings at church that Luke was a gifted preacher, and that people were drawn to him, but hearing him talk now it was clear that, beyond the skills, he felt very drawn to this work, to wrestling with the big questions of life, serving, and making the world a better place.

And that's just how I wanted to feel: drawn to something.

"Whatever comes next for me, I want it to feel right," I confessed. "In the same way that going to Hungary after college just felt right. I didn't have a connection to Eastern Europe, or plans to teach, but even so, I *just knew*, as soon as I heard about the opportunity, that I wanted to do it. No matter how it turned out, I was sure it would be a huge learning experience."

"Interesting!" Luke said, nodding along.

"Am I asking for too much, to feel that rightness again? Am I being too particular?"

"Those are great questions!" Luke said, and he nodded again and gave me a thoughtful smile. "I totally don't want to sound too suggestive or anything, but maybe God *is* calling you. No rush, though; sometimes it takes a little while to figure it all out."

As our conversation wound down, it seemed like maybe

I wasn't the only one who'd been thinking deep thoughts about something other than divinity. Luke admitted that he didn't know me very well, but even so, he said, "I think you're amazing!"

✳ ✳ ✳

On my walk home from coffee, I pondered some inevitable thoughts. Did Luke think of me as someone he might like to see outside of Sunday? Like a girlfriend? I was flirting with a minister and ministry, and I didn't know if either might be a right fit. Walking through a small patch of woods—a shortcut to my parents' house, which sat on a quiet dead end—I remembered a scrap of wisdom from my cousin Barbara.

At seventy, Barbara still worked full-time alongside her husband, Dwight, my mom's first cousin, on their small farm. I'd worked there briefly as a farmhand that fall. Barbara knew I was impatient to figure out what came next, and like Luke she didn't shy away from God-talk.

"Do you pray about it, kid?" she'd asked one afternoon in September, sitting at the picnic table next to her farm stand. I liked how she called me "kid"—it made me feel young and taken care of—but I didn't have much of an answer to her question. My prayer life could be summed up by the medieval theologian Meister Eckhart, who said, "If the only prayer you ever say in your whole life is thank you, it will be enough." I said thanks a lot, but I wasn't in the habit of asking God for help when I needed it.

"Why not put your hand in God's?" Barbara suggested.

Holding hands with something divine sounded sort of comforting, and I imagined a strong, old hand, soft to the touch, its skin showing the marks of time. Like my grandmother's hand, only much, much bigger. Holding on to a hand like that, I'd feel safe, but more than that, I'd feel strong. And that's how I wanted to feel going forward—like the strongest, truest version of me.

Would this path bring me closer to a stronger, truer me? Could I expand my picture of what a minister might look like to include me too? Jonathan and Luke seemed to see it. Maybe I just needed a little more faith in the unseen, to trust that things would always work out for me.

I emerged from the woods and headed down the road toward the house I'd grown up in—a colonial with brick steps leading up to a dark green door decorated with a simple evergreen wreath, and candles in the windows, smoke in the chimney—and I put aside the unknowns about the future and opened the door to familiarity. To me, Christmas Eve was the most magical night of the year, and I already knew what I'd find inside: my mom in the kitchen; my sister Emily, home from college, baking something chocolate and playing DJ with Christmas carols; and my dad and Silas behind closed doors, wrapping presents last-minute in newsprint. We'd eat in the dining room, at my great-grandparents' table, and after dinner my parents would leave early for church to practice with the choir, while the three of us "kids" killed time until the candlelight service at eleven o'clock. It was the best church time of the year, and though it was always a struggle for an early bird like me to stay awake after the big dinner, stay awake I would.

Around ten thirty, Emily, Silas, and I bundled up then grabbed our old-timey wooden lantern and lit the candle, the perfect accessory for the night's walk. Even though we were in different stages of life (high school, college, and then there was me), the three of us were close, and in moments like this, walking through the woods on a snowy night as we did every Christmas Eve, I was grateful to put aside decisions and rest in the grace of the moment right now. We walked briskly through the woods and down the hill, toward the center of town and the white steeple atop the brick church that was Pilgrim, light streaming out its tall windows, beckoning us inside.

As if by magic the double front doors opened as we walked up the pathway, and two middle-aged men in the same plaid trousers and red blazers they wore every Christmas Eve welcomed us in.

"It's the MacKenzie children and their lantern!" they observed, as they did every year.

"Merry Christmas!" everyone greeted us as they handed out candles for later, and we found an empty pew not too close to the front, as my brother *did* have that habit of passing notes and *sometimes* I nodded off even though it was my favorite night. I'd certainly have to work on that if I was going to lead one of these services myself.

We knew the words to all the carols by heart, and the three of us belted out each hymn as it came, but my very favorite part of the service came at the end, when we picked up the candles we'd been given on our way in. Ushers walked down the center aisle with brass candle lighters, stopping at each pew to light the end person's candle, and we passed the light down the row until everyone in the sanctuary held a tiny, flickering flame. By then the chandeliers in the sanctuary had been dimmed, so it was just our candles lighting the room, and then we started to sing. Even though I'd already heard it a hundred times that season, "Silent Night" sounded most beautiful on Christmas Eve. In our hymnal the words to the carol were printed in English and German, the original language of the tune. A few people were singing that version, and as I heard their *stille nacht, heilige nacht* mixed with *silent night, holy night*, I remembered an old story I'd heard as a child.

Nearly a hundred years ago, a few months into the war to end all wars, on the Western Front in Belgium, German and British soldiers had an informal agreement that this night would be different. They came out of their trenches on Christmas Eve, shook hands, sang songs, removed their dead from the no-man's-land in between the two camps, and, according to some accounts, even played a soccer game. Some Germans had placed small Christmas trees above their trenches, which were close enough to the British trenches that they could hear each other when they shouted, and certainly when they shot, but that night they sang instead: patriotic songs, Christmas songs, and "*Stille Nacht*," too—the Germans in their language, the British in theirs—and in that corner of the war guns were silent; it was peace for a night and into the next day: the Christmas Truce.

That was a century removed and a thousand ways different from where I stood singing, but on a night like this I could understand the power of an old song—feel the peace, the break from everyday concerns, even ordinary ones like mine. Maybe this peace was what it felt like to hold hands with the divine.

The lights went up and the spell was broken; quiet time ended as all around me people started to shift, blowing out their candles and standing up to sing the finale, "Joy to the World." I stood up too and looked around. My heart skipped a beat! There was my college boyfriend, sitting a few rows back and across the aisle. I shouldn't have been that surprised—Scott was from my hometown, and his parents went to church here (he was the same one with whom my first date had been a holiday ball, our families in tow). I hadn't seen him since the night we broke up—a couple of years ago, when I was a senior—and last I'd heard he lived in the Midwest. *He must be home for Christmas*, I figured, and my mind went back to the Christmas Eves our families had spent together.

Once upon a time I'd really loved Scott and imagined we might get married. It had been a long-distance relationship—he went to the Coast Guard Academy in Connecticut, and then was stationed in Alaska after graduation, while I was still in college in Virginia—but I'd pictured the day we'd live closer, and it *almost* happened. After Alaska he was sent to Maine, but just before the move he broke up with me for an Alaskan girl and brought her east instead. I'd tossed all of his letters in the trashcan and hadn't looked back.

Until tonight. I wished I had the courage to walk right up to Scott, fling my arms wide open, and give him a big, friendly hug—as if to say, *No hard feelings, life has moved on, and I'm happy to see you*. Instead, I felt awkward, and that held me back. What to say after all these years? I hoped I might sneak by.

But Scott saw me.

"Amanda!" he called, flinging *his* arms wide open and giving me a big, friendly hug and a kiss on the check. "Merry Christmas!" he offered. As simple as that.

"Merry Christmas!" I offered back to him.

My own Christmas Truce.

I stepped out of the sanctuary and into the foyer, where Jonathan and Luke were standing in their long black robes, shaking hands with the congregation before we ventured into the cold night air.

"I have something for you," Luke said as I shook his hand. He led me to the side and handed me a slim paperback.

"I know this might seem a little weird. I wasn't planning to give you a Christmas present ahead of time. But after our conversation this afternoon I came home and remembered this book, and I wanted you to have it. It's a book of prayers, written by another minister."

I looked down at the cover. I wasn't sure what to make of the title: *Guerillas of Grace: Prayers for the Battle*. But I knew right away that I would read it and like it, because it was from Luke.

He gave me a big hug then. I could tell he felt awkward about it, since we were in church and around a bunch of people, but I was glad he did it.

It was my second big hug from a handsome man that night. Joy to the world!

At home in my single bed, snuggled under flannel sheets in the minutes before sleep wrapped me up in its arms for the night, I opened Luke's book of prayers. Inside he had written a message: *"Just in case God is calling you . . ."*

I wasn't sure what I thought of this inscription or of God speaking to me, but I loved the way he'd signed it: *"Merrily, Luke."*

It had been a silent night, and then a joyful one. And now, as I turned out the light and drifted to sleep in the early morning hours, it was a merry Christmas.

2. A Path

Just out of college my dad taught Latin for a couple of years, which meant that when I started Latin in middle school, I had my own personal tutor at home. He was the one who taught me that vocation comes from *vocare*, Latin for *to call*—so one's vocation is work to which one is specially drawn or called. In the case of ministry, it's God who calls. This was a new way of thinking for me. What if God *was* calling me, as Luke had suggested? How would I even know it?

On stage a few days after Christmas, I peered out from beneath my bonnet at a full house; the Gothic hall at Harvard, carved out of wood like the inside of a ship, could hold a thousand people, and tonight the floor, mezzanine, and balcony were full, the definition of cozy, as people crammed shoulder to shoulder on wooden benches, while onstage fifty of us stood in front of a replica of an Appalachian cabin flanked by evergreens.

My family had been going to see *The Revels* every December for as long as I could remember—a seasonal performance that celebrated the winter solstice with singing, dancing, and storytelling, each year set in a different period and place. When my dad, who loved the stage and was a regular in the cast, had suggested I audition with him back in September (I had time on my hands and a decent voice), I'd gone for it, and now it was the end of the season, the last of eighteen performances set in old-timey Appalachia—my final night in a bonnet, shawl, calico dress, and apron.

Toward the front of the stage a robust black woman in a costume like mine stood up, and that was our cue; I stood too, moving downstage with the rest of the cast, as she began to sing in a deep, resonant voice:

A-ma-zing . . .

She started slowly, stretching out the first word, until a few more voices joined in:

Amazing grace . . .

And then the rest of us:

. . . how sweet the sound, that saved a wretch like me!

I knew that the "wretch" in the hymn referred to its composer, a minister and abolitionist named John Newton who used to captain a slave ship before he was "saved" by grace. But there was something in his words for me too; I might not be a wretch searching for salvation, but I was searching for a meaningful place in the world.

I once was lost, but now am found . . .

I looked over at my dad, his arm around his stage wife. He was an accountant by day but was so clearly at home making music on stage. Before crunching numbers, around the time he taught Latin, he also built harpsichords. Then I came along and he had to make a better living, but he'd always found ways to weave music into his life; after my mother, it was his true love, and I thought his world was brighter for it. What was my true love, the thing that would make my days brighter? We kept singing:

. . . was blind, but now I see.

I looked to my right at six old men standing center stage, their deep voices discernible over the rest of ours. These gospel singers, the unofficial stars of the show, had been making music together for fifty years, and when they opened their mouths it carried you away. One had trouble walking, so he ambled onstage leaning on his friend's arm and sat on a stool while they sang. I watched the strong old men and wondered what they had seen in life.

As the last verse approached, the lights in the hall went up so the audience could see the words in their program and sing along.

When we've been there ten thousand years, bright shining as the sun . . .

And now it was everyone on stage plus a thousand people in the hall singing this grand old song. Each had been saved by something, whether they called it God or grace or music or love.

And that's when I felt it: an unusual, sweet feeling welling up inside of me, a deep-seated sense of peace in the pit of my belly.

Where is this coming from? I wondered as the music wove its way around me. I felt secure in its arms, surrounded by a thousand voices and just as many stories.

My mind wandered to the possibility I'd just begun to consider—of being a minister in a church like the one I'd grown up in—and I realized that this new idea was actually starting to feel comfortable, like sitting in front of a fire on a cold winter's day. Maybe, finally, a way forward was making itself known. Maybe this peace in the pit of my belly, this whisper of contentment from within, was a sign that I was on the right path. Decision-making had always involved the head and the heart for me—the thoughts I could put into words and the deep-down feelings I couldn't. This, then, was the heart part of it, a deep-down feeling of contentment that trumped my thoughts while I sang, while I soaked up the warmth of this moment.

Looking back, if I had to pinpoint a moment when I felt "called," it was then. I didn't hear a loud voice or see anything out of the ordinary; no burning bushes for me. I wasn't even in a traditionally holy place like a church, but on a stage in a university hall filled with singing people celebrating winter. *What if God is calling me, as Luke suggested?* I'd wondered. *How would I even know it?* As it turns out, I knew it by a deep-down sense of peace, as if all the moments from the last three weeks—the seed of an idea, the encouragement, the conversations, my own thoughts—had met up in this one instant so that I was standing in a spotlight of big, bright feeling and offering a pleasantly surprised but contented "yes" to the possibility that had found me. And in that moment, I didn't feel quite so lost anymore.

I carried it with me, that feeling—after the song was finished, and the applause had died down—out into cold night air and whatever came after that; it was a memory of contentment, a sense that this could be my calling.

✳   ✳   ✳

The last day of the old year arrived on a Sunday, leaving a trail of snow in its wake. Inside I stomped the frozen chunks from my boots, and then took off my boots to dry, though the room was so chilly I kept on my jacket. The building had been full of life this morning, but now we were like two church mice with the place to ourselves, and despite the cold in Luke's office, I couldn't believe my good fortune—that a spontaneous lunch after church had turned into a walk in the woods, and now it was late afternoon and we were still together, on the last day of the old year, sitting on the floor since there was only one chair.

"So I've been thinking about us dating," Luke said.

Dating! My ears perked up as if I were a dog and Luke had just said, "Treat!" I could tell we liked each other, but I hadn't guessed he would bring up the state of us so soon; it was only our second Sunday outing, but Luke wasn't shy.

"I've actually talked to my grandfather about it—he's the retired minister—because I want to make sure it's not inappropriate for us to start something since I'm the student minister at your family's church. I mean, we're both single, and we'd step into this as equals, but still I wanted his take on things."

I was pretty surprised that Luke was *telling* me all of this, bypassing the guesswork that usually makes up early dating.

I wasn't used to such candor, but clearly Luke played by his own rules, and I liked his openness, even if I couldn't quite match it.

"Grandfather said that I should trust my heart, that you sounded wonderful . . ."

Thank you, Grandfather!

"And that I'm sensible and thoughtful, and I wouldn't be considering anything with you if you weren't really special, which you are. So anyway, I'm not sure we want to announce this to the whole church . . ."

The church ladies would love it! I thought.

"But I figured we'd tell Jonathan because he's like my boss, and we're both close to him, and obviously your parents."

He's thought of everything.

"I mean, all of this is only relevant if you're interested in dating me, that is—"

"Yes!" I jumped in. "I mean, I don't know where all of this will lead, but I like you too, and it feels good, and, ah . . ."

Luke was looking at me encouragingly with those clear hazel eyes, as if he expected me to share more, so I came up with a compliment—that was always easy for me.

"You're really good at saying what you think. I'm not quite used to sharing so much right away. I guess I hold my feelings close to my chest. I mean, once it took me two hours in the passenger seat to work up the courage to say, 'I'll miss you,' to my college boyfriend before he left for school."

"Well, I just think it's really important to talk about things," Luke offered. And in that moment, I was very glad we were talking too, because just like that, it appeared we were trying this on.

Five hours later, after one of those epic conversations that characterize the early days of dating, we stopped talking long enough to notice that it was dark outside, and the clock confirmed that we were just a few hours away from a New Year. We pried ourselves off the floor and, having established that neither of us had plans for the night, drove into Harvard Square for a drink. It wasn't hard to find a bar in this college town, and over drinks our conversation was more laid-back. Neither of us were big drink-ers, but Luke admitted to his share of parties in high school and college. I watched as he pushed the lime wedge into his Corona, stuck his thumb in the glass bottle, turned the bottle upside down, and—voilà!—the lime floated to the bottom without a spill of beer. It was my first Corona, and I wasn't so smooth, but I liked that Luke was. He could talk about relationships *and* knew his way around a beer bottle. A modern-day Renaissance man.

In the early hours of the New Year, we walked back to Luke's Subaru, waiting for us on the roof of a parking garage overlook-ing Harvard Square. Luke ran toward a patch of ice and glided across it for a few beats before slipping, and I admired that he wasn't afraid to run and fall and look a little silly in the process.

Standing side by side at the edge of the roof, we looked down at the view before us: the campus lights twinkling and the Charles River beyond them winding its way toward an ocean just out of sight. Overhead was a star-filled sky.

Luke whispered in my ear, "You're utterly charming."

And then he kissed me for the first time.

It was excitement and peace wrapped into one moment.

✳ ✳ ✳

The first month of the New Year is named after Janus, the Roman god of beginnings and transitions, gates, doors, passages, and endings, often depicted with two faces—one looking back to the past, the other toward the future. There's something so refreshing about standing on the cusp of a New Year—we can gaze back if we choose, but the past doesn't own us as we turn our faces toward a future inevitably "full of things that have never been," as the poet Rilke says. That January, looking back at an autumn of indecision, it appeared that I had arrived at a new beginning: a boyfriend, and, if not work, then the start of a plan before me. I'd have to decide what divinity schools to apply to, but I had a month before the applications were due, and some distance might bring perspective on next steps. So I decided to go out of town and visit Emily at college in Virginia. On the drive home, I took a detour through upstate New York to see my cousins.

My mom's first cousin Bob was a minister in his late fifties. On the "scholarly" spectrum of ministers, my cousin fell somewhere between Jonathan and Luke. At first glance he appeared serious and studious, a slight, balding man who wore bow ties under wool sweaters, but he loved practical jokes and had put on magic shows for us when we were kids, after which his pretty wife Jean would amuse us with balloon art. Jean had been an accountant but left that profession to embrace her traditional role as minister's wife. Whether by choice or necessity they were a frugal couple—family lore said that Jean ran her finger around the inside of the ketchup bottle to get out the last bits—but as frugal as they were with their resources, Bob and Jean were generous with their love and laughter, and I wanted to tell them in person about the new beginnings in my life. Bob would be retiring soon, and since they didn't have children of their own, I knew he'd find it meaningful that someone in the next generation was taking up the profession.

Sitting around the dining table after dinner in their house full of family heirlooms, I admitted that I was falling in love with a minister, and was thinking about becoming one too. Bob and Jean had a sweet and steady relationship, and I hoped to be as in love with my husband after thirty years as they were with one another.

"How do I know if Luke is that one for me?" I asked them. "I really like him, but he's five years older, and it seems like he might be more ready to 'settle down' than I am, but still, I *really* like him, and—"

"Why don't you pray about it?" Bob asked, sounding reminiscent of Barbara on the farm with her "put your hand in God's" suggestion. "And then, after you've prayed," he continued, "just trust God, and your own feelings too."

I had a vague sense of God somewhere up there watching over me, but I didn't feel particularly close to God, and seeking divine wisdom when I had questions hadn't occurred to me. Even if it had, I would have dismissed it as something only really religious people did. Like Bob. And other ministers. Other ministers like . . . me?

The next morning, before I left, Bob handed me a Bible with a stiff black leather cover and pages trimmed in red. It smelled old when I opened it, and when I looked at the first page there was an inscription saying it had belonged to my great-grandparents. Tucked between the pages I found slips of paper with citations in my great-grandmother Christine's handwriting. I'd never seen her handwriting before, or even met her, since she died before I was born, but I'd heard she was a tiny, devout woman with a good sense of humor. Were these notes about her favorite passages?

I flipped to the verses, hoping they might speak to me, but they didn't. While I liked the symbolism of a family Bible being passed down, in reality I didn't look at this book and feel very connected to it. If I was going to make a go of it as a minister, or even just develop my spiritual side, I couldn't rely on someone else's inspiration. I'd have to do it in my own way. Starting with my own words.

So on the rainy drive home to Boston, I took Bob's advice to pray. Starting the most natural way I knew how, with *thank you*, I listed aloud things I felt grateful for, whatever came to mind: *Thank you for my red car, my sister, her chocolate cake, going to Virginia.* The longer I kept at it, the more it flowed: *I'm grateful for the rain, the sun, driving on this open road.* Like a faucet that hasn't been used in a while, what started as a trickle began to gush: *For Luke, and how he kisses, for Pilgrim Church, and Jonathan, my great-grandmother, my cousins.* Sometimes I challenged myself to list ten things I was grateful for—or, if I had more time, a hundred—but that morning I lost count as my gratefulness unrolled like a giant, unedited thank-you note to God.

But I *did* have some questions too, and those I was less practiced at sharing with God. It was like speaking a new language, one that didn't feel like home yet, and I felt self-conscious addressing my worries to God for two big reasons:

Would people think I was a weirdo for praying like this?

And more important, what if I didn't like God's answers?

The "people" I was worried about weirding out, like my friends, were nowhere in sight; I was alone in a Volkswagen on a highway miles from home. But I was so oriented toward what others thought of me that I made up judgments where none existed—*not* a particularly helpful practice when you're trying to figure out your own path in life. Besides, everyone is usually too busy thinking about themselves to worry about what you're doing, and even if they have an opinion about your affairs, *yours* is the opinion that matters most.

As for the second hesitation—what if I didn't like God's answers?—well, I realize now that's not how prayer works. God doesn't hurl down responses like an overbearing parent: *Do this, or else!* At least, that's not how God was talked about in the church I'd grown up in. In fact, my one and only personal experience of the divine was when I'd had a vision of God sitting beside a fire, looking like a large Native American lady. In my momentary vision She'd held my head in Her lap and said, "You are beautiful and greatly loved, just as you are." That's how I believed God worked: *I see you just as you are, and I love you for it.* And whatever "answers" might follow our questions, they emerged from within.

Of course I wasn't thinking all of this as I drove down that rainy road by myself. I just knew that I felt a bit self-conscious praying aloud. But I kept going anyway, starting in with the questions:

"How do I *know* if Luke is The One?" I asked aloud. "I mean, we've only been dating for a few weeks, but we spend so much time together, and I feel as if I love him! As if we could get married. But that's crazy, isn't it? I'm only twenty-four. I feel so young. I still live with my parents. I'm still figuring out my place in the world. And I worry that I'll get so caught up in this relationship that I'll neglect my best interests. Like, what if I apply to a divinity school far away, and I get in? Should I move even if it jeopardizes my relationship with Luke? Maybe I'm getting ahead of myself, but I just *really* want us to work out, and I know he does too. Luke says I'm the right woman at the right time. How do I know if he's that for me?"

For an hour I wondered aloud like this. Was I praying? Or simply talking to myself? All I know is that I imagined someone listening and that felt comforting; even though I *was* alone I didn't *feel* alone.

Eventually, I stopped talking.

And it. Was. Quiet.

I'd emptied out my mind, tossing all the words I could come up with into the void that was my car, and now I would wait and see what might emerge out of the clearing.

What did I hear?

Well, I didn't hear the immediate reassurance that I might have wanted, a Hallmark card from on high: *Dear Amanda, Luke is just right for you. Everything will work out between you two. No doubt about it! Have faith. Love, God.*

Not that I would have trusted such a cheesy wrap-up to my heartfelt prayers anyway.

I didn't hear a prophetic warning, either: *Repent! Turn around. You're too young, going too far too fast.*

But black-and-white pronouncements, that's not usually how prayer, or life, works, is it?

This is how life works: You quiet down, and then you wait. Eventually, you will see or hear or feel something. And if you don't, well, that's something too.

In place of any grand pronouncements, I heard only the whoosh of the wipers; I saw only the road ahead. But I felt something: at peace with where I was. Like how it feels to watch the sunset over water: you don't worry about where the sun's going; you just enjoy how it looks right now, sinking below the horizon, sending out an encore of color as it disappears from sight.

Contentment was the encore my prayers sent out, like a silent blessing from the here and now, a reminder that:

Here and now is your life.
  And right here, right now, you are greatly loved,
just as you are.

To that I said, *Amen*. And I drove home feeling lighter.

✳ ✳ ✳

I'd narrowed my list to four schools—Harvard, Yale, Duke, and Andover Newton, where Luke went—and now it was time to visit each on my own terms, to see how this new idea felt outside the familiarity of family and friends. Since Duke was down South, I decided to save a visit for later that spring, if I got in, and in the meantime I visited the others. Andover Newton, only twenty minutes from my parents' house, was the outlier in the group; since it wasn't connected to a larger university like the other divinity schools were, it had a more flexible academic plan. This meant that, as Jonathan had told me, it attracted older students returning to graduate school years after college, hesitant to jump in full-time, as well as those who had full-time jobs and liked the flexibility. At Andover Newton, full-time grad students in their twenties like Luke and I were the exception.

I noticed this on my first official visit to campus as I looked around the circle of prospective students seated in the Admissions Office; out of a dozen hopeful seminarians, all were older than I, except for a willowy brunette who looked about my age. But it wasn't just my age that separated me from the other candidates. As we went around the circle and said why we were there, who or what was "calling" us to divinity school, it seemed like everyone else—mostly middle-aged women—had been considering the possibility of divinity school for *years*, but life circumstances, or their own fear, had kept them from saying yes. Until now. Here they were, finally taking the plunge.

"Hi there. I'm Laura," the willowy brunette introduced herself in a voice like dripping honey; she seemed like one of those people who took her time with everything she did. "I'm from the Christian Science tradition, and my church doesn't actually have ordained ministers, so I'm here to further my own spiritual journey. I'm not exactly sure what I'll do with a degree from divinity school, but I love to learn. And sing—especially gospel."

Her answer made me feel a little better; at least I knew what I wanted to do with this degree.

As Laura finished up, everyone turned toward me, smiling, but still I felt out of place. My call wasn't big and dramatic, it was little pieces of a puzzle adding up—encouragement from those around me, looking back over my shoulder at my journey so far, and my own feeling of contentment right now. And while I would end up writing that sort of thing in my application essay, there was no eloquent way to say all of it here, in the midst of strangers, even if they did seem particularly kind.

"Hi! I'm Amanda," I started, with as much cheerfulness as I could muster. "And I'm here because my minister suggested that I think about becoming a minister myself. And four weeks later I'm still thinking about it, which is four weeks longer than I've considered any other job. So, here I am!"

After the session, languid Laura came over to me. "I think your honest, laid-back approach is cool!" she admitted. And I appreciated her positive outlook, especially because I was worried about my answer being so different from everyone else's. I had begun to think that I could make a good minister—Jonathan, Luke, and cousin Bob seemed to think so too—but compared to the rest of the prospective students there that day, I felt like a fake because I didn't think of myself as particularly religious. I couldn't even mention God's name, outside the comfort of my own car, without feeling somewhat self-conscious. Even with their different styles of being ministers, Jonathan, Luke, and Bob seemed comfortable with religious language and ideas, and apparently my fellow prospective students were, too. Would divinity school teach me how to be more religious? Did I even want to be?

✳ ✳ ✳

I wasn't the only one who wondered if I was religious enough to become a minister, as it turned out. My college roommate Molly, visiting from the Midwest, in the midst of a PhD in neuropsychology, couldn't believe my plan when I told her.

"But we made fun of the religious kids in college!" Molly reminded me.

"Amanda's not *that* kind of religious," Kelley chimed in. Kelley, our other roommate, lived just an hour away in New Hampshire, and had visited Pilgrim a few times, so knew it was a pretty open-minded church compared to the conservative brand of Christianity we'd met in college. Like many campuses, ours was pretty quiet on Sunday mornings, but those who *were* vocal about their beliefs often had a Bible-as-the-literal-word-of-God approach and focused on evangelization.

Coming from traditional Catholic and Protestant backgrounds on the East Coast, the three of us had never experienced this conservative brand of Southern Christianity and had been particularly surprised when it knocked on our door one Sunday afternoon as the three of us were sitting around our campus apartment doing homework—or, in my case, procrastinating.

Knock knock.

"Are either of you expecting company?" Kelley asked.

"I'm not."

"Not me."

Knock knock.

Molly, who was closest to the door, left her perch at the kitchen table to peer out the front window. "I don't recognize them."

"Open the door," suggested Kelley. From back in the living room, she and I heard the door creak, and then Molly's tentative, "Hello?"

"Hi, we're from Campus Crusade for Christ, and we'd like to invite you to our meeting tonight."

"I can't imagine knocking on a stranger's door and inviting

her to my church," I whispered to Kelley. "I mean, I like the church I grew up in, but it seems like an invasion of privacy, or worse, trying to foist my beliefs upon someone else. As if *my* way is the right way."

"Well, it might be the right way for you, but that doesn't mean it's right for everyone else," Kelley amended. She really was quite sensible.

We turned our attention back to the conversation out front, just in time to hear Molly's letdown.

"Ooh, I'm sorry, but we're not really religious right now."

"Maybe you'd like to give it a try?"

"We all went to church growing up, so nothing against religion, it's just not where we are at the moment."

Molly didn't say that our friend Nicole had just been dumped for Jesus—her boyfriend said he wanted to spend more time with the Lord—or that her own ex-boyfriend was headed for the Catholic priesthood, or that Kelley was dating an avowed atheist.

"Well, could we just leave this CD for you then?"

"Sure, free music!" They had her at "free." Molly was on a frugal kick. "We promise to listen! Thank you! Ta-ta!"

The door shut.

"Look, ladies . . ." Molly began, heading back toward the living room where Kelley and I were waiting on the couch. "It's Christian rock! Shall we crank up the stereo?"

To our surprise, one of the songs had a great beat, and a curious lyric about a missionary "shoveling elephant dung," and we danced around our living room singing along, mimicking a shoveling motion whenever the chorus came up. It didn't necessarily bring us any closer to God, but we had fun (and God, I like to think, likes us to enjoy ourselves).

But dancing to the song about elephant dung was the closest I'd come to anything religious in college. It was the first time in my life that I didn't go to church every Sunday. And the one course I took in the religion department I dropped after a week. I just wasn't interested.

So I wasn't surprised that Molly was surprised when, two years later, I confessed that I was applying to divinity school.

"But here's the thing," I explained. "My sort of church couldn't be further from the kind that knocks on doors and thinks everything in the Bible is true. For one thing, I don't know anyone at Pilgrim who takes the Bible literally, or even talks about their religious beliefs outside of church. And for another, the Congregational tradition, which is the type of church I belong to, was the first church in the United States to ordain an African American, a woman, and an openly gay person. I'm mean, I'm actually sort of proud to belong to such a progressive church, one that would ordain me even if I were an African American lesbian. And love me all the more for it! And finally," I said, "being a minister is more about helping people in a setting I like than furthering any religious agenda. I'll still be me," I assured her (and myself). "Just me with a job in a church. But don't worry, I won't become some religious nut. Remember Dave? He was a minister, and he was pretty normal."

✳   ✳   ✳

Dave was the counterpoint to the conservative Christianity I met in college. But before I called him Dave, I knew him as Dr. Burke.

Dr. Burke was a first-year professor my senior year of college and, though I never took a course with him myself, when another professor recommended me to be his teaching assistant, I jumped at the chance to help the young professor teach a course on leadership. That spring, when I wasn't dancing to the "elephant dung" song or procrastinating on my thesis, I was swooning over Dr. Burke. He was thirty-one, single, and the first man I knew who called himself a feminist, which, as a double major in leadership and women's studies, made him my equivalent of star quarterback.

But there was more. Between college and his PhD, Dr. Burke had gone to divinity school and was an ordained minister who preached occasionally at a nearby church. Okay, so this wouldn't be every college girl's fantasy, but a man feminist *and* the first minister I'd ever met who was close(ish) to my age and actually cool? Be still, my beating heart.

A week before graduation, when classes had officially ended, Dr. Burke offered to take me to a diner I loved, as a thank-you for my help that semester. The diner was an hour away in Charlottesville—a *whole hour* in the car with the star quarterback! I couldn't believe my good fortune. After dinner we walked through campus—Charlottesville is home to the University of Virginia—and ended up in a walled garden that smelled like lilacs. Dr. Burke wrapped his arms around me from behind and whispered close to my ear, "I'll miss you next year."

Which was when Dr. Burke became Dave.

Dave met my family at graduation a week later (and told his colleagues, my former professors, who were happy for us). We dated through the summer and into the next year, when I moved to Hungary to teach English. Living in a small village on the other side of the world from anyone I knew, I had a lot of free time on my hands, and when I asked Dave to send me some light spiritual reading, suitable for a beginner like me, he didn't disappoint. My favorite was a slim paperback by a theologian named Frederick Buechner. Like a dictionary, *Wishful Thinking: A Seeker's ABC* was organized alphabetically, and it redefined 150 religious terms in everyday language that appealed to a lukewarm questioner like me. Scary religious words like *sin* or *salvation*, words that I associated with that conservative brand of Christianity, were described in a less judging, more open way. Sin, for example, wasn't a laundry list of "immoral" activities, but instead it was broadly described as, "what you do, or don't do, that widens the gap between people." Not that I was planning to add "sin" to my everyday lexicon—"Look at that sinner! He didn't return my smile as we passed on the sidewalk!"—but I appreciated this way of looking at sin because of what its converse implied, too: that whatever brings people closer (like, perhaps, sex) is not a sin.

As for *salvation*—which I associated with the unappealingly narrow slogan "Jesus saves!"—Buechner described it as losing yourself in something you love (music, fun, a breathtaking sight), and in the moment of losing yourself, you find that "you are more fully yourself than usual." Beautiful everyday things, then—like a kiss, a good book, watching a sunset—can save us.

Years later I learned that Buechner had been the minister at the boarding school in New Hampshire where my dad was a student in the sixties. In his free time, my dad learned to play the organ in the campus chapel and was a regular at Sunday services too, which meant he'd heard plenty of Buechner's sermons. "Coincidence," Buechner writes, is "a whisper from the wings that goes something like this: 'You've turned up in the right place at the right time.'" That my dad's minister from high school had landed in my tiny apartment halfway around the world at the inspiration of my professor-minister-boyfriend? A whisper of coincidence indeed.

As for that young professor-minister-boyfriend, partway through my year abroad it became clear that Dave was ready to settle down—he was nine years older, after all—and so we parted ways, not *particularly* smoothly, and a decade passed before we saw each other again and I got to say thank you. When Dave sent me those books I didn't know I'd later feel a tug toward the ministry. I simply had time on my hands and the desire to read something meaningful. Buechner wrote that *faith* is "not being sure where you're going, but going anyway. A journey without maps." It was only in looking back that I could see how the points on my mapless journey connected—how Dave's example, and the books he sent, nourished the soil for the seed of minister to sprout and take root.

✳　✳　✳

In the end I decided to become a minister in spite of the fact that I wasn't particularly religious. In an inclusive church like mine, I figured there must be a place for a young woman who didn't consider herself traditionally devout—who liked to use everyday words to describe theological ideas, who'd had a vision of God as a large Native American lady, but who had the skills and gifts to make a good minister anyway. And there was this urging, too: my memories from growing up in the church, a place where I'd felt loved and special outside my family, and where my most vivid rememberings centered on people, not doctrine. Like the time I baked pies with Alan.

Alan was the minister for most of my growing-up years before we switched to Pilgrim. The church he led in Cambridge, where my parents had met singing in the choir, was a serious, intellectual community committed to social justice (there was even a homeless shelter in the basement), and Alan was a serious, intellectual guy. A few weeks before my Confirmation at age thirteen—the Sunday when I became an official member of the church—Alan invited me to the parsonage, the grand yellow house that the church owned and lent to Alan and his family as part of his compensation. The rest of my Confirmation class had been invited too, but I was the only one who could make it, and while nowadays a minister wouldn't be allowed to invite a child to his house alone, back then there was nothing weird about it. Except this: When I arrived, Alan, who usually dressed in a suit or black robe, was standing at the back door in an apron. He led me into the kitchen, where piles of rhubarb, strawberries, and dough lined the counter, and we got right to it, rolling up our sleeves and baking half a dozen strawberry-rhubarb pies.

We might have talked about religious matters while we worked, but if we did, I don't remember it. What I do remember are the pies. Alan showed me how to cut strips of dough and weave them one over another to create a lattice pattern over the deep pink piles of fruit filling each crust. My mom was a great baker, but even she never took the time to weave stripes of dough atop her pies. I had no idea that this serious, intellectual man whom I heard every Sunday, preaching sermons I didn't understand, knew how to bake such beautiful desserts.

Now, at twenty-four, I wasn't much more experienced at talking about God than I had been at thirteen. But making someone feel welcomed and loved, as I had always felt in the church? Surprising a child on the cusp of her teenage years with a lesson on how to craft beautiful food? Teaching that anything that brings people closer is good . . . that faith means it's okay not to have a road map for life . . . that the beauty we lose ourselves in is the same as what saves us? *These* were beliefs I could get behind, gifts worth sharing. And that's how a not-very-religious girl found herself on the path to becoming a minister, and believed that it might actually make some sense.

3. Choices

The first time my grandfather, Beau, proposed to my grandmother she said yes, but then she changed her mind and gave him the ring back. Beau put her on a bus and gave her the fare home, a dime. Which seems pretty generous, considering. But he was a steady sort, seven years older, a Lieutenant in the army stationed in North Carolina, where she, Jinny, was a student at Duke. With his model good looks and plenty of confidence, Beau wasn't in a rush—a loyal lab to this social butterfly whose nickname was the Blonde Bomber, for her bright hair and, I suspect, her even brighter personality. Jinny was one hot ticket (on the original Pearl Harbor Day, family lore says she had three dates), but eventually my grandfather's patience paid off, and they got married in her family's church in rural Pennsylvania and then moved closer to his family outside of New York City, where they stayed for life.

I thought of this as I drove toward my grandmother's petite red house where she lived now, minus my grandfather, who had passed away a few years earlier. Theirs was an enduring love; my grandmother still wore a gold medallion around her neck, a gift from my grandfather. In French it said:

Je t'aime plus qu'hier moins que demain.
Or, *I love you more than yesterday, less than
tomorrow.*

I came from a long line of enduring lovers, and that was
what I imagined for myself, what I hoped Luke and I were on the
way toward, that our love wouldn't just remain constant, but grow
as we grew old together.

I pulled myself back from my thoughts and looked at the
clock, surprised that it was already midafternoon, which meant I'd
been driving for four hours. The warm August air blew in through
the front windows, which were rolled all the way down, and my
hair was probably a tangled mess, but I didn't really care since
there was no one in the car but me and, if all went according to
plan, the only other person I'd see today was Jinny. According to
the highway signs whizzing by, I'd just crossed into Pennsylvania
and would be to New York by early evening. I assumed my grandmother would be home, but I hadn't actually told her I was coming. No one knew where I was, or what I was doing, and that made
this feel like a G-rated version of being on the lam as I drove north
on I-95. Earlier that Saturday morning I'd been a divinity student
at Duke, about to start my first week of classes, and now I was
driving away from it all. It wasn't illegal, but it was certainly out of
character, and the fact that I'd just up and left without telling a soul
felt like . . . what *was* this unfamiliar sensation? As if I'd veered off
the grid for a day and had no one to answer to but myself.

Free. That's how I felt. And lighter, as if I'd shed a sense
of obligation and was taking a crack at life on my own terms. I
hadn't done anything truly wild, like sold all my possessions and
bought a plane ticket around the world. Just the opposite: my car
was full of stuff, and I was heading home, but still, this choice felt
liberating.

I pulled over at a payphone (this was 2001), dialed, and took
a deep breath; hopefully the first call would be the easiest.

"Hi, Grandma. It's Amanda."

"Hi, honey! How's Duke?"

"Well, actually, I left. I'm driving home, and I'm almost in New York. I wondered if I could stay the night?"

"But your mother said she took you down to Duke last weekend, and helped you move into your new apartment, and . . ." she paused, "are you okay?"

"I'm fine. I'll tell you about it when I get there. I just wanted to make sure you're home tonight."

"Yes, of course, I'm here, sweetie, and you can stay the night. I'll have a martini waiting." Jinny was a much more accomplished drinker than I was, but the thought of something strong sounded good.

"Great. Thank you, Grandma. Oh, and one more thing," I warned her, "I haven't told my parents where I am. I will, but I want to wait until I get to your house, so please don't call them."

"Your secret's safe with me!" she assured me. And she signed off.

My secret. It had taken me almost a quarter century, but I'd actually made a major decision without consulting a single soul but my own. Was it the practical decision? Did I *know* it would all work out the way I hoped? No, because this was a journey without maps, alongside faith: trusting my path would work out because I was listening to the still, strong voice inside me, the one that had told me, earlier that morning, to give in, to turn around, to go home.

✳ ✳ ✳

Five months earlier . . .

Duke, my top choice, the school I'd imagined going to in fifth grade, had just accepted me, had even offered a full academic scholarship, and a three-month summer internship in a rural church. After my parents, Luke was the first one I wanted to tell.

"Wow! That's amazing. I'm so happy for you!" Luke said over the phone, and I could tell he really was, even though a southern migration would bring changes to our relationship.

"Now that I'm accepted, I should visit. I haven't been to Duke since I stayed with a friend in college there. Do you want to come too?" I asked, hoping he'd fall in love with the place too, that he'd offer to move to North Carolina when he finished divinity school in a year, and that we could start a life down there together.

"I'm not sure what the point of my visit would be."

"To see the school. And maybe you'd really like North Carolina too."

"I just don't know that it makes sense for me to move down there. I know you love the idea, but my life is here—my family, the lake house."

Luke's mom and stepfather lived in Boston, but they also had a sprawling-but-still-cozy house two hours north, on a lake in New Hampshire, an oasis of calm where his family gathered for lazy days and bountiful meals. I loved it there too.

"Well, *both* of our families live in Boston, so of course we'd come home often. And they could come visit us."

"But all my church connections are here too. And it's important that I get a good job after graduating. That's my priority."

"But there are Congregational churches in North Carolina too. My mom's friend knows a minister from Boston, she's about our age and went to divinity school at Duke, and now she's a minister down there. Maybe you could meet her? She could give you a sense of how their church culture compares to New England, what the job scene is like . . ." my voice trailed off. I was not-so-secretly hoping that a talk with the young minister would sell Luke on southern living.

"I can't imagine a life down there, but I'm open to visiting and seeing how it feels," he said.

It wasn't a giant yes, but it was a step, and I would take it. I hoped the South would work its springtime magic on Luke, and that North Carolina might look like more of a possibility than he imagined, but this wasn't the first conversation we'd had on the subject. It seemed like he wasn't really considering a move to join me in a year, and he wasn't thrilled at the idea of a long-distance relationship either.

Which meant: Our relationship might very well end if I moved. But I didn't *want* it to end!

We'd been dating only four months, but during that time I had grown to love Luke with a sureness that surprised me. There was something magical about him; he was so completely himself, without pretension, genuine and eager, and we fit into each other's worlds so well. Much like that autumn evening six months ago, when my mother had invited Luke to dinner unbeknownst to me, and we'd sat around the fireplace talking easily with my parents and Silas, the past few months had been filled with easy companionable moments like that, as if we were floating downstream together.

Should I give up my dream of going to Duke, if it meant Luke and I would work out?

✳ ✳ ✳

Two weeks later, I was walking around Duke's campus, picturing myself at class in these stately Gothic buildings, hoping that Luke was enjoying his meeting with Carrie, the young minister from Boston, a cheerful blonde who loved her life down South. They were going to talk about churches in the area, and while it still didn't sound like he ever saw himself moving and working down here, I *hoped*, just maybe, he'd hear about a church that would pique his interest, and that a seed would be planted.

I plopped myself on a bench at our meeting place and watched for Luke and Carrie.

I'm in love with this school, I thought to myself. *And with Luke.*

When they came into sight, I joined them, and we all talked easily for a few minutes. Luke was his usual enthusiastic self. He didn't have many friends, but he could if he wanted to. People always warmed up to him right away.

After Carrie left, the two of us wandered through the gardens on campus, down a meandering pathway where extravagant rhododendron blossoms elbowed their way onto the trail. Springtime was my favorite season in the South—it came earlier and lasted longer than it did in New England, and all of that green felt like an affirmation of life, mirrored the sense of possibility I felt.

We drifted toward another bench and sat down.

"It's beautiful here," I said.

"It *is* pretty."

"I think I'm in love with this school. I could picture myself going here, and the possibility feels exciting."

"That's great," Luke paused. "But I can't picture living here. It doesn't make sense for me."

"But I like the idea of creating a life for myself someplace new and different, pretty and warm, and of having my own apartment too. Not that I don't love my parents and Silas, but it's been nearly a year, and I'd love to set up my own space, have friends over, and feel more independent."

"And I get that," Luke said, and I knew he really did hear me. "*You* should make the decision that feels right for you. But just because it's right for you doesn't mean it's right for me."

"But what about us? If you came it would be an adventure for us together. We would make new friends, and explore a new place, and our families could come visit."

"Amanda, you're not hearing me. That's your dream, not mine. I'll come visit you next fall. And we can see how things feel long-distance. But I have to say, I'm not excited by the idea of it; a long-distance relationship is not really what I want now."

And then he added: "It seems like our relationship is not the top priority, not *the* focus, for either of us right now."

I knew he was right, even though I was hesitant to admit it. I really *wanted* us to work out, but if *we* were my focus, would I even be considering Duke?

If a relationship is further along than ours was, if you've committed to staying together for a bunch of beautiful reasons, chances are you make big decisions together. But our partnership wasn't actually much of a partnership yet, more like two individuals leaning toward each other, a collection of strong feelings and fun times, that hadn't developed roots yet. We'd only been dating four months; I had to stand on my own feet, make this decision alone, and for the first time in my life I wanted two things that seemed to conflict with each other—Luke and Duke—and I had the feeling I'd have to give up one or the other.

Life is full of choices, but this one seemed more black-and-white than I was accustomed to: the perfect man against the perfect school. Not that I couldn't find a great school in Boston, or a new relationship in North Carolina, but like a child stamping her feet, crossing her arms, I wanted what I wanted: the faraway school *and* the nearby man and, frustrated that Luke wouldn't consider the alternative, didn't try to picture a happy life for us in another state, I wanted to shout at him: "Follow me! And trust that it will work out."

Wasn't that how love was supposed to unfold? You loved long and deep, more than yesterday, like my grandparents, and made decisions on behalf of your love, partners on the same team. Or was that just some fairytale fantasy of a relationship? Because oftentimes it felt like Luke and I were playing for opposing teams, each rooting for our own interests above the relationship. Which totally makes sense from where I sit now—we were young, and just starting out in our careers, and while we appeared to have similar dreams on the surface (marriage, kids, careers in the church), if I dug a little deeper, I had a restless, spontaneous impulse that Luke didn't, while he had an intensity and depth that I lacked. But I couldn't articulate all of that from the bench. I just felt frustrated, disappointed. His resolution led me to realize something important, though: you don't have control over what feels right to someone else, no matter how much you love him or her. To the contrary, the more tightly you hold, or try to sway, the more you push away. I couldn't alter how Luke felt about moving. He seemed resolute in his decision not to leave home, and that was his decision to make. Now, I had to figure out what felt right to me.

✳ ✳ ✳

If a deadline's getting closer and you still don't know what to decide, I'd suggest an hour in the company of peace, quiet, and trees. Out of the stillness you're bound to catch a whisper of wisdom from within. If nothing else you'll hear your breath, perhaps a bird or two, leaves rustling in the breeze, and all of it will be a reminder that whatever you decide, life carries on, and you will too. What's up ahead doesn't hang on this one decision, however big it seems at the time, because what's up ahead are many more choices.

I leaned back against an oak and closed my eyes. Like I had on the rainy drive home from New York, I started with *thank you*, grateful that I had choices, even if I wasn't sure which to pick. The peace, quiet, and trees around me were nestled in a large park-like cemetery, all rolling hills, ponds, and an impressive collection of conifers. I imagined that most of the people underground in this old place hadn't had options like I did, not only a chance at graduate school, but also a choice of where. With a nonchalance that surprises me now, I'd tossed Harvard and Yale out of the running pretty quickly because of their academic focus (I wanted to be a minister, not a professor) and their cost, and now it was Andover Newton (where Luke went) versus Duke, between staying close to home or moving south, between a future with Luke or not.

I'd always dreamed of going to graduate school down South, but now that the chance was actually in front of me, was it really what I wanted in the here and now reality of my life?

Can your dreams change? I wondered. Could you truly want and imagine one thing for your future, and then life unfolds differently than you "planned" and so your dreams adjust too?

I knew that Duke would mean big changes in my relationship with Luke—that we'd be long-distance, and there was the very real possibility that he wouldn't move, and our relationship wouldn't last three *years* of long distance, which was how long the program was.

I thought back to conversations we'd had since our visit to Duke, conversations Luke described as "painful," which was not how I wanted our relationship to feel. I wanted to be the one who made his life happier, easier, not painful, and I felt guilty for causing him to hurt.

I tried to quiet my mind, listening for some sort of wisdom from above me:

Hello there? God?

Or maybe below:

Spirits of wise dead people! Is anyone listening? Surely one of you must have something to say.

A bird sang. Some leaves shivered.

I'd figured that because I was praying about *divinity* school, the signs would be bigger, brighter than in "regular" life. Not so. As usual, figuring out what came next had more to do with the still voice inside me than any outward signs—the voice that had told me "Peace" in the car, and "Yes" onstage.

After an hour or so I got up, shook out the old quilt I'd been sitting on, and knew that I would go to Duke.

I couldn't say no to the opportunity before me. Well, actually, I could, but I didn't want to. It felt like it was the most exciting choice on the menu when it came to school. As for my relationship, I told myself to have faith, to trust in the mapless, unseen possibility that if I did the right thing for me, my relationship with Luke would work out too.

✳   ✳   ✳

I moved to Durham, North Carolina, at the end of August, into my very own one-bedroom apartment over a professor's house, just a five-minute drive to campus. My mom drove south with me, in my red Jetta, just as she had during college. We hung a few pictures, covered the bed with a patchwork quilt I'd just finished sewing, bought me an iron, and then when there was nothing left to do but get started with my new life, my mom flew home.

And there I was alone with the very things I'd craved a year ago—my own apartment, a clear and respectable career path that was starting out at a beautiful school, and a boyfriend too. The only problem was that Luke wasn't actually here, and I ached inside.

Buck up, Amanda! I told myself.

I thought about the plane ticket Luke had to visit me in two weeks. That was something to look forward to.

I started orientation and tried to get into the discussions in my small-group seminars, but, not surprisingly, it seemed like everyone felt more comfortable than I did with God-talk and group prayer, and I felt out of place. Suddenly I missed not only Luke, but also everything else familiar from back home—my family, my non-churchy friends, Pilgrim, and Jonathan's laid-back approach to religious matters.

I commiserated with a new classmate from the Midwest who felt out of place too. We complained about our more conservative peers, but I didn't want to turn into someone who hung out with people on the edges and couldn't appreciate where she was. What's more, it seemed like this classmate might have a crush on me. Compared to Luke he seemed young and bland, and the thought of dating anyone besides Luke made me feel sick inside.

The worst of it was that when I talked to Luke on the phone, he sounded different—not like the enthusiastic man I'd come to care for, but more serious, resigned, distant. Even though he'd encouraged me to do what was best for me, I knew he was hurt I'd decided to leave, just as I was hurt he didn't promise to move here next year. Was this an adjustment period for both of us? Or was it the start of the end?

Now that I was down here in North Carolina, trying to settle into my new life, the reality felt very different from the dream, and I realized that I wanted Luke and me to work out more than I wanted to go to my "dream" school.

On Friday night a few days into my "new life," I went to

a basketball game with some of my classmates. I tried to enjoy myself, but my heart felt like it was someplace else. That night when I fell asleep, I dreamed that I hadn't decided where to go to school yet, that the decision was still mine to make, and I chose Andover Newton. I woke up early Saturday morning feeling more peaceful than I had in months; I was going to Andover Newton.

And then I opened my eyes, and the unfamiliar view from bed reminded me that I had actually picked Duke. I felt nauseated. It was only seven in the morning, but I had to do something, or my unsettled thoughts would make me crazy. I called my cousin Bob, the minister in New York.

"I've only been here for five days, but I feel so out of place," I confessed, "uncomfortable, and sad, not at all excited for the semester ahead, and I miss Luke, but not just Luke, everything else at home too."

Bob tried to reassure me that my feelings were normal.

"It takes time to get used to a new place and a new phase of life," he reminded me. "And divinity school is a different sort of place, full of big questions and new ideas. It's an adjustment for *everyone* at first."

After we hung up, I didn't feel any better. So I put on my sneakers, hoping that some movement would relieve my uneasiness. I walked down the quiet residential street in my new neighborhood, trying reassure myself:

Listen, Amanda, this isn't the first time you've moved to an unfamiliar place where you don't know anyone—the same was true for college and the year after in Hungary. And yes, at first you felt homesick, you're prone to it, but eventually the sick faded and just the feeling of home remained. You thrived in both places. It just took some time.

As much as I tried to reassure myself that I would feel better eventually, this felt different. At college and in Hungary—even though I was homesick and lonely at first—I didn't doubt that I'd made the right decision. I had faith that I was in the best place for me, even when it felt hard. That I wasn't in a serious relationship made it easier to take a risk, to sail away from the safe harbor; there were no one else's feelings, or reactions, to consider. But this time I felt it in the pit of my stomach—an unsettled sense that maybe I had *not* made the "right" decision for me. I had thought that Duke was my doorway to independence, the next great adventure. Now that I was actually here, I didn't care about the open door ahead; I was focused on the closed door behind me, and I wanted to turn around, open the door, and walk back through it, to return to Luke and my familiar life.

I remembered an email I'd received earlier in August from Laura—the willowy brunette gospel singer I'd met at Andover Newton when we were both prospective students. We'd kept in sporadic touch, and she'd decided on a divinity school in New York City. In her latest email, sent a few weeks before I left for Duke, Laura updated me that she had changed her mind, taking back her "yes" to the New York school and asking Andover Newton to reaccept her instead.

I was envious that she'd changed her mind, since I didn't think that was an option for me. I'd made the smart decision, the expected one, the one I was proud to make. The notable school. The independent life. So many things were already in motion before I left for Duke: I had that full scholarship. I'd signed a lease for an apartment in Durham. I'd put myself, and Luke, through countless hours of emotional conversations. My parents were so excited for me.

Besides, second-guessing my decisions wasn't something I did, and so far that approach had served me well.

So far.

But now, I remembered something my childhood friend Elizabeth had said to me the year before divinity school and Luke came on the scene, when I was still searching for the next Big Thing. Sitting in a darkened movie theatre, waiting for a film to start, I admitted that I wasn't excited for the future, that it felt like life was just happening to me.

"You know," Elizabeth said simply, "you actually have a lot more control over your life than you realize."

And then the screen flickered to life, and the soundtrack cut off any doubts I might have voiced. Elizabeth got the last word, and her reminder that, no matter what situation we find ourselves in, we always, always have choices, made a dent in my pattern of thoughts.

I kept wondering as I walked.

I might like to *think* of myself as someone who didn't second-guess her big decisions, but I couldn't deny it: a whole lot of second-guessing was going on here. I now had to ask: What was I going to do about it? How was I going to take control of my life? Was I going to make up my mind to make the best of it? To settle into Duke and wait and see what happened between Luke and me? Or was I going to . . .

Change my plans.

There. I'd let myself say it.

Was I going to give up this particular plan, and surprise everyone, including myself, by turning around, opening the door, and walking back through it, toward home again and all that was familiar? Deciding to walk ahead by going back? I felt like Janus, that two-faced god of beginnings, looking ahead and back, both at once.

I kept walking. I crossed over a stream. I paused.

And then I turned around.

✳　✳　✳

I walked back to my apartment like I was walking on hot sand. I was going to do this *now*. Before I got cold feet. Before I second-guessed my second guess. I wasn't going to consult anyone first. Not my cousin Bob, not my parents, not even Luke. I didn't want any of them trying to talk me out of this, as I guessed they would.

I unmade my bed, folded my patchwork quilt, dumped it in

a large tote. I un-hung my pictures from the wall, packed my iron, filled a box with all the new books I'd bought for classes at Duke. The bookstore was closed on Saturday, so I'd have to mail them back. I carried all of that, and rest of my belongings in bags, down the fire escape that doubled as my entrance to the outside world and tossed them into my backseat.

All that was left upstairs was my steamer trunk, a large wooden chest with pretty metalwork that my mom had rescued from a friend's attic and refinished for me as a Christmas present. It was heavy, awkward to carry, and full of stuff, and a few days earlier my mom and I had struggled together to get it up the fire escape and into the apartment.

Not today.

Today I carried that steamer trunk all by myself, down the fire escape, across the driveway, and lifted it into the trunk of my Jetta. I wouldn't have believed it was possible, that I was strong enough to do it, if I hadn't lived it. I was just that determined to leave.

Now that everything was tucked into my car, there was just one more thing to do.

I tapped on my landlady's door.

"Hello!" said the middle-aged gray-haired professor. "How's it going?" Had she noticed me piling my life into my car? It didn't appear so.

"Hi. So this is a bit sudden, but I've actually decided to leave. Right now. And I know that's unexpected, and a hassle for you, and I'm sorry." I was embarrassed. I'd never backed out of anything this big before. But I couldn't worry about what she thought of me.

"Well, that *is* a surprise. It will be tricky for me to find a new tenant with such short notice, since the semester has already started. If I can't find someone to replace you, you'll have to keep paying your monthly rent until I do."

I hadn't thought of that, but it was a cute apartment, and a great location, and I felt pretty sure she'd find someone.

I jumped in the car, looking back just long enough to reverse out of the driveway, and then I drove forward.

I drove without stopping until I had crossed the Mason–Dixon Line into Pennsylvania. And that's when I stopped to call my grandmother.

Even though she'd graduated from Duke and was excited that I'd be going to her alma mater, I knew Jinny wouldn't judge me for leaving. After all, the Blonde Bomber had changed her mind about marrying my grandfather. Twice. In fact, she would probably only listen to half my story before launching into one of her own—she talked *a lot*—and tonight that was just fine with me.

That evening, settled into my grandfather's faded maroon armchair, where he used to sit and solve the *New York Times* crossword every morning, I felt safe and cared for. Best of all, I didn't feel judged for what I'd done. I knew it would be a different story at home, that my parents would be disappointed in me for changing my mind and leaving Duke. I took a tentative sip of the martini she'd promised me.

"There's plenty more where that came from!" Jinny offered; she had an amazing tolerance. I took a second sip and wondered if I was drunk already. My grandmother, quiet for once, came and sat next to me as I dialed my parents' number.

"Hello?" It was my dad who answered, and I was grateful for that; he'd be less emotional, more practical.

"So what's your plan?" he asked as soon as I told him that I'd left Duke and would be home tomorrow.

"Don't worry, I have one," I assured him. Which I did, sort of: to beg Andover Newton to reaccept me.

"Hmm," he sighed, resigned to my autonomy. "All right then. We'll see you tomorrow." And then, just before hanging up, he added an obvious forewarning: "I don't think your mother will be very pleased with this change of events."

✳ ✳ ✳

When I was eight, and Emily was four, our mother signed us up for two weeks of day camp. Silas was a newborn, and I was sick at the thought of leaving my mom and baby brother for a *whole day*. The first morning of camp, little sis skipped down the woodsy trail toward a new adventure, while I hung back alongside our brown station wagon until, finally, I worked up the courage to take a step forward.

And I threw up in the bushes.

Now here we were, sixteen years later, and I was coming home, again, just as Emily was leaving for a semester in Northern Ireland. At least I hadn't puked. Yet. But there were still my parents to deal with, and that Sunday afternoon, as my Jetta, steamer trunk, and I rolled into my parents' driveway, Emily bounded down the back steps with another warning: "Just so you know, I'm the *only one here* who's happy to see you."

Which was a slight exaggeration, since Silas was always happy to see me too, but she was right that my parents weren't. My dad's pretty good at looking forward, not back, as long as you have a plan, but my mom's cold shoulder took me by surprise.

"I can't *believe* you came back," she finally admitted as we passed in the kitchen a few days later.

Usually my mom said kind, supportive things, but when she criticized, her ideas were like tiny annoying splinters that sat under my skin and festered. I couldn't help but feel their impact.

She kept going.

"I can't believe that you gave up a great opportunity for Luke. He should have been willing to move south for you, after he graduates." She shook her head at me. "You shouldn't have come back just for him."

"*I* chose to come back, Mom. Luke didn't ask me to. I didn't tell him until I got here, and he was just as surprised as you."

Which was true. When I'd called Luke from my parents' house, he'd been completely stunned at my change of course, and *I* was surprised that he wasn't as excited as I thought he'd be. Sure, he was glad to have me back, but after months of intense conversations about my move, and an emotionally draining summer, I think he was still a little hurt by my decision to leave in the first place, and it would take a few weeks for things to feel "normal" between us.

At least he wasn't angry with me. Like someone else.

My mom kept going.

"It's not that I don't like Luke, I do, but why should you have to change your plans for him? If your relationship is as important to both of you as you say it is, why wouldn't you wait it out for a year? And then he could join you down South? That's not too much to ask. I think he's selfish, and that you felt bad so you came back."

No matter how eloquently I tried to explain myself, my mother was set in her way of thinking. She liked to be in control, was accustomed to her life and her children's lives working out the way she imagined, and this—her oldest giving up a scholarship and great school for, it seemed, a "selfish" boy—wasn't how she'd raised me to act. For my part, I wasn't used to her disapproval; we'd never had a real fight before, and now every time I was in her company, I felt the urge to plead my case. I *wanted* her to understand and respect my decision. But hers wasn't my mind to change.

Years later, Silas gave me a book, *What You Think of Me Is None of My Business*, the liberating premise of which was this: It doesn't matter what other people—even the ones you live with— think about you and your decisions; what matters is how *you* feel. You are the one who wakes up every morning to your life; you are responsible for your own happiness. Though I still cared deeply what my mother thought of me, I knew that I would rather wake up in New England, even if, for now, that meant the single bed in my childhood bedroom, under my mother's roof, than a cute apartment down South.

By leaving Duke, I gave in to the part of me that craved comfort and familiarity, and I gave in to the love I felt for Luke. I had a hunch our relationship probably wouldn't survive if I stayed away. Should that have been a sign that we weren't meant to be? At the time I just thought I was being practical; I never expected to find great love at this young age, imagining instead that it'd take a while for me to find someone who fit. But here I was, feeling such a connection in my mid-twenties, and I wanted to see where it might lead.

* * *

A week after I arrived back home, I had my appointment at the admissions office at Andover Newton. I stood in front of my closet and picked out a pretty white linen top that Kelley had given me a year earlier but which I'd never worn. I had a habit of saving new clothes for months (or a year, in this case) until the "right" occasion came along. Today seemed like a fresh start, a morning momentous enough for a new shirt, which I paired with some tan linen shorts and sandals; it was hot out, and Andover Newton was a casual sort of place.

As I sat in the same room where I'd met Laura at the open house for prospective students last January, I felt like I was eating a slice of humble pie. Gone were the big-name schools, the full scholarship, and the summer internship. Instead I was looking at three to four years at a little-known, under-funded theological school where the average student was nearly twice my age. But it had a reputation for turning out talented ministers, and it was nearby to all that I loved best. With any luck, Laura and I would be starting classes together the following week.

The head of admissions—a kindly middle-aged woman named Margaret—remembered meeting me back in January, and she still had my application materials from the spring.

"So, Amanda, tell me why you're back," she began.

I couldn't convince my mom that I'd done the right thing, but if I had a hope of getting reaccepted to Andover Newton, I had to convince Margaret.

Omitting the part about Luke—Margaret would have known him as a student at the school, but talking about your boyfriend in an interview felt a little unprofessional—I confessed that I'd made a mistake, that in leaving home I'd realized familiarity was the very thing I craved as I began this new journey.

At the end of our meeting, Margaret gave me a hug and told me that Andover Newton would be honored to have me.

"Thank you, God!" I cried out.

Well, not really. Despite recent shifts, I hadn't changed *that* much, but I did buy myself a Frappuccino to celebrate, and as I sipped slushy coffee through a green straw I felt very grateful for this chance to begin again, to right my course. I remembered my grandmother's yes, then no, then yes again to my grandfather's proposal, and how well that had turned out. Maybe changing your mind wasn't such a bad thing after all. If life is always changing, doesn't it make sense that minds, and the decisions that get made in them, are changing too? I certainly felt more settled inside than I had for months.

On the drive home I stopped at the post office to mail my textbooks back to Duke; that, along with an email from my former landlady that she'd found another tenant, wrapped up all the loose ends down there. "You've just made some pretty big decisions that will shape your life," Jonathan's wife had said to me at church on Sunday, and I agreed—changing my mind, coming home, giving Luke and me another shot, I thought of these as BIG decisions that would set my course for life, forever and ever, amen. And they *were* big, and they *would* shape my life, but not necessarily in the ways I had imagined.

We don't live in a static world; it's dynamic, always changing, and so are we. Every day a slightly altered you wakes up, from the hairs on your head to the thoughts inside it. Every day there are new decisions to make, and the Big Thing you figured out yesterday brings another set of decisions today. Like picking a college. It seems like a life-changing decision at the time, and it's big, maybe the biggest one you've made so far, but once you get there a whole new slew of decisions awaits—what to study; who to hang out with; who to sleep with (or not); how to spend your free time, internships, summer vacations—so that what you thought was *the* big decision becomes just the first of many, as life sails ahead.

The thing is, you just don't *know* where one decision will lead, or what your options will look like once you get there. So you guess, listening to your inner wisdom, making the best decision you can at the time, and then you throw off the mooring and set sail. Sure, there will be waves you could not see at the start, and they might take you off course. Or fog will roll in, and you'll lose sight of shore. But then the water calms, and the sun comes out—it always does—and you'll find you're right where you meant to be. Even if you didn't end up taking the exact course you imagined traveling to get there.

As August turned to September in 2001, I was living with my parents again. But this time around, on the cusp of turning twenty-five, I had prospects—in work *and* love. And I was determined to see them work out.

Part Two: Trying

It is not down in any map; true places never are.
—Herman Melville

4. Love the Questions

Jake was the first boy who liked me enough to kiss me. This didn't happen until I was sixteen, but in my imagination I'd been kissing boys since I read my first romance novel at eight years old. In real life, though, I was self-conscious around boys I liked, more likely to turn away than smile, which could easily have been mistaken for snobbishness and certainly didn't attract any of my crushes. Now I realize the power of something as simple as a smile to draw people to you, but back then I thought my problem was that I wasn't pretty or fun enough for the average guy.

Until Jake.

Not that Jake was a crush to begin with. I was actually sort of embarrassed that he liked me. He was a different style than my friends—more townie than preppy, he wore a mesh ball cap on top of his crew-cut and a thin gold chain, and he had a pretty noticeable splash of acne across his face. He said things like "dude" and wasn't in the "smart" classes with my friends and me, and he didn't play sports, though he *was* in the marching band. But when our mutual friend Erik introduced us on the playground one summer night, where Jake was hanging out with some of his shorter, scrawnier sidekicks, he made me laugh.

As the weeks wore on, and it became clear that Jake had a crush on me, I edited my picture of the type of guy I could imagine kissing. Beneath that acne he had kind blue eyes, and beneath his tough-talking veneer, a generous heart. Jake wasn't someone I would have picked out of a crowd, but I felt like a happier, prettier, smarter version of myself when I was around him, and that brought me a sense of confidence that I wasn't used to feeling around a boy. Over the years I've seen that love often comes in unexpected packaging; that the ones we end up loving best aren't necessarily the ones we might have imagined for ourselves; that when someone makes you *feel* the way you've always wanted to feel—like the best version of yourself—then how he looks, or what he does for work, seems less important than you thought it might. But at sixteen it was a revelation that someone who seemed so different from me could make me feel so good.

Jake and I were in the woods at the end of my dead-end street when we kissed for the first time, sitting on a big rock for two, lip-to-lip, when Silas, age seven, discovered us.

"Mom and Dad told me to come find you," my brother announced. "It's past your curfew."

"I have a curfew?" I marveled aloud. I knew I was out later than usual, but I'd never had an official deadline, since my friends and I didn't usually stay out late. That I was out with a boy made all the difference, though, and despite the fact that my parents clearly knew where I was, they didn't want me to get too carried away.

"You're supposed to come home. You might be in trouble," Silas added. And then, having delivered his message, my parents' little henchman hurried home.

I was grounded for a day or two, during which time Jake couldn't help but stop by with a present for me, and my parents liked him enough that he was allowed to enter. We sat in the back garden under the crabapple tree, on a stone wall that encircled my mom's vegetable garden, and he presented me with a paperback copy of *Cinderella*.

"You aren't the first princess who had to rush away from her Prince Charming, and back home to her 'wicked' parents," he joked. It was silly, but my laughter was genuine, and we kissed again.

Even though I liked how it felt to kiss Jake that first time, and all the times after—warm and a tinge of excitement down below—at sixteen I didn't imagine that we would do much more than kiss. My mom liked to gossip about boys with me, but she didn't seem comfortable talking about sex, or anything related to it. The one thing she had told me clearly was that sex was special enough that she hoped I'd wait until I was married to have it, as she and my dad had waited. When she told me this at thirteen, it sounded quite reasonable. I was still awaiting my first kiss; to my early teen mind sex seemed like Africa—a very distant territory of which I'd heard, but I had no idea what *really* went on there and I didn't feel the inclination to visit anytime soon. And then, when my first kiss came, I was just so excited to be kissing that I didn't yearn for much more than that. While I *had* noticed that the few times Jake's hand wandered below my waist, pants on, it felt good, I also noticed a twinge of guilt, as if I shouldn't be feeling this sensation yet. That was as far as things with Jake went.

We broke up after a few months, and Jake starting dating the woman who would become his wife. Years later I saw her at the market, pushing two boys in a grocery cart who looked like tiny versions of their dad, and I was struck by the urge to whisper in their little ears as I passed by, "Your dad taught me how to kiss, but even better than that he made me laugh." But of course I didn't. Instead I smiled to myself, and felt grateful for my first kisses, and the surprising packages that make you smile.

✳ ✳ ✳

After Jake I didn't kiss anyone for two years, until the end of high school when, the summer before senior year, my outdoorsy friend Becky convinced me to spend a week on the tallest mountain in

Massachusetts. Becky was a petite brunette burst of energy who'd had many experiences that I hadn't, like cycling down the West Coast for one and, even more impressively to me, getting drunk *and* having sex, though not at the same time. I admired Becky's outgoing, adventurous approach to life, and when she asked if I wanted to spend a week in the wilderness as a part of a volunteer trail crew, I bought my first pair of hiking boots and pulled myself away from a good book to spend a week shoveling dirt in western Massachusetts.

It was one of those experiences when you surprise yourself by saying yes, and though you're a little nervous at first, you couldn't be more glad you did something so seemingly out of character, because the beautiful thing is, you end up feeling more like yourself for having done it. Though my parents had taken us hiking and camping, nature never really spoke to me until that summer. Digging a trail up the side of a mountain, the smell of earth, pine, dirt under my nails, all of it made me feel stronger. We ate our meals at one long table and slept in bunks in a 1930s stone lodge on top of the mountain, and by the end of the week I loved how I felt when I laced up my boots every morning—like a sturdier version of myself, like I could handle more than I realized.

Our last night on the mountain we celebrated with a trip into town, to catch a minor-league ball game with the rest of our trail crew and a few of the staff from the lodge. As I slid down the aluminum bench next to Becky, I was surprised when the cutest boy on staff slid in next to me. Riles was a dark-haired, green-eyed college boy from Vermont, whose smile revealed dimples and a perfect set of teeth, and when we got back to the mountain after the game, he asked if I'd like to stay outside and look at the stars.

I felt a flutter in my belly. The cutest one never picked me.

Would he try to kiss me?

This seemed like the perfect backdrop for it—atop a mountain on a warm summer's night beneath a pitch-black sky. I hadn't kissed anyone since Jake nearly two years before, and a hookup like this felt like a rite of passage for a girl on the cusp of turning eighteen.

Riles stood next to me, our shoulders touching.

"Do you see that one?" he asked, pointing up at a gathering of stars that all looked the same to me. "It looks like a flattened W. That's Cassiopeia."

"Oh, yes, wow," I said, pretending the scattering of stars looked like something to me, but really I was too distracted by Riles's warm body to concentrate on sky details.

As the rest of our group drifted inside, Becky appeared beside me.

"Don't do anything I wouldn't do," my friend whispered in my ear, and then she winked and ran after our trail leader, a lanky college kid who had a little crush on her. For the first time in my life I was alone with an almost-stranger—a very handsome almost-stranger I would actually pick out of a crowd for his good looks—and I had the feeling he wanted to kiss me.

I could have shouted for joy. I felt so excited, so *normal.*

Riles and I walked over to a stone tower that stood nearby, the most prominent feature on the mountaintop aside from the lodge. He sat down, leaning his back against its base, while I nestled myself between his legs and leaned back, resting on his chest.

"After a week on this mountain, you smell so good," he whispered, stroking my hair.

Really? I hadn't showered that day, and I was still wearing trail clothes, but I decided to bite my tongue. Maybe he really *did* think I smelled good, or maybe it was just a line, but whatever, it was working. I smiled to my good-smelling self and then, trying to be as natural and go-with-the-flow as I could, I turned around, and we started kissing.

Inside I felt as warm and relaxed as the mid-August air around me. I almost couldn't believe this was *me*—in worn-out clothes and boots, kissing a hot stranger on top of a mountain, as if I had done this many times before. Who knew I would be so *good* at hooking up? Go me! I was born to kiss! This felt way better than reading a book. So good I bet I could keep it up all night.

Riles stopped.

My eyes flew open. Had I done something wrong?

"Hey," he whispered, his lips brushing my ear. "Do you want to go back to my trailer and have sex?"

I froze.

Come again?

I pulled back slightly, looking a bit confused, and Riles, sensing a question in the making, tried to anticipate it.

"Don't worry," he assured me, "I have protection."

Protection?

My mind was slowly registering. Condoms. *He has condoms. In his trailer.*

But what happened to kissing? I wanted to ask.

This was only my first hookup! I was still mastering the art of French kissing; sex was still like Africa to me, that unknown continent I had yet to explore, of condoms and, apparently, doing it in trailers.

I looked at the lovely boy still beside me, expectantly waiting for a response. It seemed like he actually thought I might say yes, but I didn't even consider it.

"Uh, no thanks," I replied instead.

Just like that, the spell was broken; after a few more minutes under the stars, my first hookup came to its natural conclusion.

I was flattered that I seemed attractive (and good-smelling) enough that someone as cute as Riles could actually imagine having sex with me in his trailer. Or maybe he was just desperate after a summer on the mountain. In any case, I couldn't imagine it. Now that I had been faced with the choice to have sex or not, it seemed so obvious: I would wait until I was married. Not every teenage girl turns her back on premarital sex, and those who do, do so for different reasons. Growing up Catholic, my friend Theresa remembers the priests at school preaching "a pat on the back and a hearty handshake" as the only acceptable form of physical contact before marriage. It was clear what her religious leaders and, by association, God thought about sex before marriage, but I hadn't been taught to think about God in relation to my intimate life. I figured that She had enough to think about, without wondering if I was doing it. If anything, God wanted me to be true to myself, to do what felt right to me, and to me sex seemed like a BIG DEAL. It could lead to babies, and disease, two overwhelming possibilities, and even if I was using protection and minimized the risks, it was such an incredibly intimate act that I wanted to feel confident and sure about my decision to have it. I didn't want my first time doing this special thing to be overshadowed by guilty feelings, or awkwardness because I was doing it with someone I didn't know well. In a trailer! The easiest way to ensure that I felt confident in my decision was to wait until I was married, safe in the arms of someone I knew well.

The summer before my eighteenth birthday in September, I hoped that Riles was the second in a long line of boys I would kiss. But I imagined a very short line, of just one, in which stood the man whom I would sleep with. I didn't know who that one would be, but I was content to wait and see.

✳　✳　✳

When I met Luke six years later I was still holding fast to the ideal of no sex until marriage. I was twenty-four by then, and I knew that waiting until marriage marked me as an odd duck, at least among my circle of friends, and that most of my boyfriends had had more experience than I had, but to his credit, Luke received my position without question, though it probably helped that I wasn't shy about other forms of intimacy. And Luke, for his part, was pretty open to talking about all of it.

"Do you want to tell me one of your fantasies?" he asked one winter night as we were lying next to each other in his single bed on campus, a year into our relationship, and a few months after I started divinity school.

Of course! I had lots to choose from. Like Luke proposing. Our beautiful wedding. A pretty house. Three children. Now which one should I actually share aloud?

"A fantasy . . ." I said, stalling for time. "What kind of fantasy are you thinking?"

"A sexual one."

Oh. *That* kind. I fell silent, scouring my mind. I peered in the corners. There must be one hiding out someplace. There! Found it. I shook off the dust.

"Well sometimes I've imagined . . ." I spoke tentatively, unused to this sort of intimate sharing, "having sex in a field."

There. I had said it.

"And?" Luke asked.

He wanted more?

"And . . . we don't have any clothes on."

He looked at me expectantly.

"And . . . we're lying on a quilt?" I asked.

I was going to have to start making this up on the fly if he expected any more.

"And . . . that's as far as I've gotten. What about you?" I asked, eager to take the focus off me.

"I guess I've had a bit more practice at this than you have," Luke told me. "I've been having fantasies since I was a teenager. Maybe it's more common for guys."

And that was all he said. Maybe he thought it would be too much for me to handle one of his fantasies—and he was probably right. Unless you counted lying naked on a quilt or kissing a cute guy, I'd never had a sexual fantasy, and honestly I didn't really see the point in having them or talking about them. I wasn't interested in adding other experiences to my sexual toolbox. Making out, oral sex, and masturbation were all accounted for. The only thing missing was intercourse, and I'd put that in a box labeled Marriage and set it on the top shelf, out of sight, where it would gather dust until I saw a gold band on my ring finger. But here's the thing: you can't open your box after ten years of it being tightly closed up and expect everything inside to function without flaw.

At least I couldn't.

But I wasn't thinking any of that that winter night. In fact, I wasn't really thinking about sex at all; I didn't consider myself as a very sexual person, but looking back it's more like I hadn't developed that side of my personality. My friends and I didn't talk about sex much; my siblings were younger; there weren't other older role models in my life who might teach me something. In fact the first person who encouraged me to develop my sexual side was my therapist, but Bonnie was still a year away.

That night I was just relieved that our foray into fantasy land was over, and my feelings of embarrassment dissipated, turning into something more gentle and sweet as I curled up next to Luke and thought about how nice it would be to fall asleep next to his warm body every night.

That was the sort of fantasy I liked to dream up.

✳ ✳ ✳

Even though I dreamed about falling asleep next to him every night, and had come back from Duke to give our relationship a shot at the future, when Luke brought up the *actual* possibility of engagement that winter, I wasn't sure if I was there yet.

This bothered me, that I could love someone so much, and yet not feel ready to officially say, "Yes! I'll marry you." *What's wrong with me?* I wondered, wishing I could just flip a switch inside and be ready to take the next big step, that my thoughts would hurry up and catch up with my heart. I knew I had to figure out what this hesitation was about, or else Luke might get tired of waiting for me to make up my mind and leave. He had said as much; he was thirty to my twenty-five and was looking ahead. He'd be graduating from divinity school in another semester and was thinking about jobs for that June, and he was concerned that I wasn't in the same place when it came to thinking about us. I had to agree—even though I loved spending time with Luke and fantasized about us being married, with a pretty house, three kids—something inside gave me pause.

So I decided to seek out wisdom in the form of a cheerful middle-aged sage called Jory, a family friend from church, who was also the mother of my college boyfriend Scott. This meant she knew me, and my family, quite well, and she knew Luke too, since she went to Pilgrim, where he was still the student minister. Unlike my parents' cut-and-dried approach to emotional conversations, Jory was happy to engage in long, winding discussions about feelings. On one memorable occasion she'd invited my entire family over to take the Myers-Briggs, a personality test of which Jory was a devotee, and talk about our results. This wasn't the sort of navel-gazing that made my family tick, but we all dutifully filled out our forms and then actually had fun talking about ourselves for the evening. Jory's open way made it easy. And a few bottles of wine didn't hurt either.

That January afternoon I slipped off my shoes, nestled into the corner of Jory's big soft couch, took a sip of tea, not wine, and scanned the room for new pictures of my old boyfriend.

"So!" Jory said cheerfully, bringing me back to the present moment. "What's up?"

I looked over to the rocking chair where she sat smiling, round face and glasses framed by shoulder-length brown hair, and knew I could tell her anything.

"Luke and I have been talking about getting engaged," I started out.

"Ooh, that's exciting." Jory clapped her hands together.

"Well, yes, sort of. For the past year I've imagined us getting married, but now that we're seriously talking about engagement, it seems like he's ready, and I'm not. I don't know *why* I'm resisting, and I want to just figure it out *now*."

I paused, but Jory didn't say anything, so I kept going.

"My dad thinks I'm still being formed through divinity school, and not ready to 'hitch my wagon' to someone else's wagon. And my mom is still angry that I came back from Duke for Luke. She thinks I passed up a great opportunity for him, and that he should have been more supportive. And Luke thinks that I don't communicate enough in our relationship, that I need to become more comfortable sharing my feelings, but now that I'm actually communicating, everything feels heavy and unclear!"

I came up for air. Jory smiled over at me.

"And what do *you* think, Amanda?"

"I don't know. That's why I'm here."

"What does your heart say?"

I waited a few seconds. I could feel it pumping in my chest, but what was my heart *saying* to me? I listened harder; still I didn't hear anything, sort of like when I was in the cemetery and prayed for a clear answer about where to go to school—my heart didn't say yes or no, do this or that. But there was, in place of a clear answer, a feeling—it felt like a warm wave washing over me. The feeling caught me by surprise, as waves can do, but felt like comfort at the same time. I even tasted saltiness on my lips, and I noticed that tears were running down my checks. Jory handed me a tissue.

"My heart tells me that I love Luke so much," I admitted to Jory.

And it was true: I loved Luke so much. I had never met anyone like him, and he said the same about me.

I thought about a print I'd bought at a museum in Hungary, a black-and-white drawing of two zebras intertwined so that you couldn't see where one ended and the other began. Sometimes that's just how it felt when I was with Luke; we fit together as two neighboring pieces of a puzzle, or a couple of zebras from Hungary.

Then what was with my hesitation? What was the niggling sensation in the pit of my gut that held back my "Yes!" whenever Luke brought up engagement? I'd always imagined that I would just *know*, without a doubt, when I met the one I was going to marry. I had even written a letter to him my senior year of college, then put it in an envelope addressed to "Someone." It said:

I don't know who you are or where you are, but tonight I'm thinking about you. It's okay that we haven't met yet because I've got my own plans right now, and it's really important to me to follow them, wherever they take me. But sometimes I get lonely, and then I think about finding you, and I feel a little

calmer, and a small smile creeps across my face,
because already I know you can make me laugh.

Back in college, between boyfriends, I'd been so sure that Someone was out there and that we would meet when the time was right. I hadn't doubted that it would be clear to both of us that we were the other's Someone. And in the beginning things *had* felt that clear with Luke; it was a large part of why I'd come back from Duke, because I'd wanted us to work out.

But now that we were actually talking about marrying each other, my feet felt cold because I knew that, in addition to all of the love and connection, there was this—things felt hard with Luke in a way that I hadn't experienced with anyone before. Underneath our similar backgrounds and interests, we had pretty different ways of experiencing the world.

"Life is hard," Luke would tell me repeatedly. "That's what I've learned."

"But I don't think it has to be," I would counter. "Sometimes it feels to me like you make decisions harder than they need to be."

"It's not my opinion. It's true," he would say. "You just associate that truth with me because I'm the first person who's told you that life is hard, but you will come to see it's true too."

And I did; in many ways life felt beautiful with Luke by my side, but it also felt harder, in large part because our ways of being in the world were different. He wanted me to communicate more about my feelings and everyday decisions, and I wanted him to talk less about all of that, not get mired down in the dirt, but enjoy life.

Not that he didn't have his fun, light moments, and not that I didn't have my deep ones, but the rub came in what we needed to feel connected. I needed more lightness and laughter. Hadn't I learned that all those years ago when an unexpected townie on the playground had made me laugh? And remembered it again when I wrote a letter to my future Someone knowing he would make me laugh?

"You don't communicate enough!" Luke would tell me.

Everyone else in my life thought I talked a lot. Like, too

much. But I wasn't used to talking about my feelings in a relationship context, especially with someone who was so adept at it. If I wanted us to move forward, though, I felt like I'd have to become more comfortable processing my emotional life with Luke.

I looked around, but my friends and family didn't seem to model this kind of interaction.

Kelley didn't have these sorts of challenging conversations with her fiancé. They had their own hurdles—Gerry was an Irishman awaiting his visa to move to the United States, where he'd then have to find a job—but they both *knew* they wanted to marry one another.

My parents certainly didn't have these sorts of gut-wrenching conversations. They bickered about trivial things, like driving.

"Turn right here!"

"Not yet."

"Yes! This is it."

"No! It's too early."

"Just do it."

"You're so annoying."

"But I was right."

"This time."

This was the sort of "conflict" I was used to, not drawn-out emotional conversations about feelings, like the sort Luke needed to feel connected to me. Sometimes Luke even shouted or wept when he was overcome with emotion, and I did *not* know how to respond to that. I wasn't a yeller, I didn't come from a family of yellers, and to me yelling was "out of control" behavior, and I liked to be in control.

"Luke seems like an emotionally needy person," my dad had said in recent conversation. "And you need someone who's less emotional."

"I think he makes things too hard for you," my mom had added. "Like all that struggle over coming home from Duke. He should have been happy for your great opportunity, and promised to help make your relationship work long-distance."

"You're young, and still in school," my dad said, "being formed and shaped, and it's not the right time to hitch your wagon to one person."

"But, Dad," I reminded him, "you were twenty-three when you got married! Isn't that a little funny to call me too young? I'm older than you were."

"But my personality was more set than yours."

I looked at him quizzically.

"What I mean is that I was done with college and wasn't planning on grad school like you are. I had already been formed, and was on a career path, and I was who I was. But divinity school is a life-changing sort of experience, and you're still figuring out who you are and where you're going, and Luke is too."

Their words made an impression on me that I couldn't shake. I'd always been close to my parents and, maybe because I was the oldest, sought their approval more than my siblings had, especially my sister Emily. In college she started going by her middle name, Darlington, pierced her nose, took up belly dancing, and now, in her junior year, she was dating a Canadian and making plans to live with him in Toronto for the summer while she pursued modeling. Darlington didn't let anyone else's opinions stop her from following her compass.

In the fall just before meeting Luke, I'd taken an orienteering course in the White Mountains and learned how to use an actual compass. It was just a simple plastic device dangling from a red string, but I remembered how satisfying it felt when the arrows lined up and showed me exactly where to go, and I yearned for the voice inside me to speak so clearly. What I've learned is that it always does, in time. Clarity can't be rushed, though, and if you're more committed to making a decision *right now* than making a decision *right for you*, then you might miss it.

Looking back on it, my parents seemed to be saying *slow down*. What was the big rush to figure out my life all at once? I was young, only twenty-five, just wading into adulthood, and a sea of possibility spread before me. *Slow down* and enjoy the view.

Sure, I had questions about my relationship that were perfectly normal. "Be patient toward all that is unsolved in your heart and try to love the questions themselves . . ." the poet Rilke said. My questions weren't a sign of immaturity, but a message from my heart, and if I'd been patient with them I would have heard clarity. My parents, and even wise impartial friends, didn't have answers for me, but I did—deep inside was a clear voice that had been with me since the beginning, my own internal compass. Guiding me toward the right path for me. Sometimes it was hard to hear that inner wisdom amidst the strong voices surrounding me, and contradicting each other—

My parents said, "Luke makes things *too* hard."

But Luke said, "Life *is* hard!"

My parents said, "Slow down."

While Luke said, "Let's figure this out!"

But if I practiced patience, as Rilke said, and loved where I was, questions and all, I would eventually hear my inner voice, which always is, after all, the one that matters most.

I longed for this clarity, but in my longing I forced it, making things harder than they needed to be. My mind was a jumble of thoughts, but instead of slowing down, letting go, and enjoying the journey, confident that clarity would come, I pushed through the mess to emerge on the other side, as if I were hiking off-trail, fighting my way through brush, tripping over tree trunks. Looking back, what I want to tell my younger self is: *Slow down, sit on that stump, find your compass, line up the arrows, and only then start walking. Take your time, and you'll see the trail ahead, and you'll know the way to go.*

I had been taught that I could have what my heart desired—a career, husband, and children—and that's not an unreasonable assumption, over time; it's where many of my friends have ended up now, in their late thirties, in the midst of motherhood, marriage, and meaningful work, but it took time for these details to emerge, and they're still emerging. Like a canvas partially painted, life is a work in progress whatever age you are—colors and details are always being added that enhance the overall picture, and one can't possibly know at twenty-five what her canvas will look like at thirty-five. But oh how I wanted to! And I painted as much of my big picture as I could in my twenties. But in my rush to *figure it out*, I hushed the questions, instead of loving them, and when I did that I hushed my own inner wisdom too.

In the short run it's easier to ignore doubt, to continue down the well-worn trail you're already on because you know where it's going, and there must be good reasons you were on it to begin with. But eventually, ignoring your inner compass takes you further from who you really are, and further from the things that make you happy.

It takes a lot more courage to slow down, sit on that stump, and listen to the still, small voice inside whispering, "Now wait just a minute . . ." And yes, sometimes it *really* complicates life in the short run to change directions. It upsets people you love, makes things awkward or sad, for a time—but it's nothing you cannot handle, and I know this: when you truly listen to your inner compass, and follow where it leads, life is beautiful. But no one told me this when I was twenty-five. Or if they did, I wasn't listening.

✳   ✳   ✳

"You do know that I really want to be with you," Luke confessed, looking into my eyes with such obvious love that I felt a swell of emotion in return.

We'd been sitting in his car for an hour talking about the state of us, and it looked like we might have landed somewhere. The past month had been full of words—with my parents, Jory, alone with my journal, and most of all with Luke. I was so ready to move beyond indecision. Out of the mess of words inside my head, I was searching for *just* the right ones to float to the surface, the words that would make everything all right, ending the drawn-out conversations and carrying us forward. Together.

I remembered what I'd felt on Jory's couch.

"My heart just tells me I love you so much," I confessed to Luke.

And it was true.

"And the scariest thought is that I might lose you," I added.

Which was also true, though not necessarily for the reasons I imagined then. What I didn't realize at the time was that buried beneath the love was fear of the unknown. If not Luke, then who? What if I let go of our relationship, in the hope of finding a more perfect-for-me match, but never met him? What then? Would I end up a single minister living with her parents? The mere thought made me shudder. (And would have made my mother shudder too.)

When I imagined a future without Luke, the only possibilities I saw were bleak, for both of us—loneliness, no kids of my own, and lame dates with big dorks for me; and for Luke a heart so broken that he'd give up on love and, maybe, join a monastery. Did I say bleak? I meant downright depressing, but I never even encouraged myself to imagine other possibilities. I was stuck in my way of thinking, and I wanted the search to be over. Luke and I might not sync up as seamlessly as I wished, but I so wanted him to be my Someone that I insisted to myself that it was so. It was easier, and more secure, than listening to the still, small voice inside whispering, "Now wait just a minute . . ." Who knew where that voice might lead?

And so, armed with my great love, Someone by my side, and the newfound awareness that life is hard, I chose to continue down the trail I was on.

Looking back, I can see another truth—that because I believed something to be true, I attracted that energy. Until then I hadn't thought that life was hard, and it wasn't. But once I began to take on the mantle that life is hard, well, wouldn't you know, it would become just that. Not right away, but slowly, over time, until eventually the easy, full-of-light-and-laughter life that I'd known disappeared, and I felt like a dried-out husk of my former self.

But I couldn't have seen that back then. As January came to a close, I was just so relieved that I'd finally figured out I wanted to marry Luke and that life could go back to comfortable.

5. Life Is a Journey

From my perch partway up the mountain, I watched the lake below. Across the water I could just make out the speck that was Luke's mother's house, where we were staying for a few days on a late-May vacation before Luke started his new church job and I took a summer class.

From up here you could only see the big picture: lake water, trees, and a few houses scattered along the shore; the world below looked old-fashioned in its simplicity, tidy and peaceful, and being up here I felt peaceful too.

"I love you," I said easily to Luke sitting next to me on a big rock.

"I love you too," he beamed. "And I want to marry you!"

"Okay! I want to marry you too," I smiled back.

"Well, do you want to make it official?" he asked. "I have a ring here," he said as he reached into his pocket.

A ring! I'd guessed that Luke would propose soon-ish, but this afternoon caught me by surprise.

He held out a black velvet box. "Will you marry me?" he asked, in his sweet, earnest way, and I saw genuine love in his sparkling eyes and could tell he was little bit nervous, which made him seem even more endearing. As he passed me the velvet box, there was only one answer:

"Yes! Of course, yes!"

We hugged and kissed, admired my new-to-me ring—a generous sapphire-and-diamond hand-me-down, in the best sense of the word, from Luke's mother—and took a few pictures, our bright smiles far outshining our scrubby hiking clothes.

As Luke drove us home from the mountain to the lake house, I rolled down my window.

"I love Luke!" I shouted from the passenger seat, out the window to the trees as we whizzed by.

"We're engaged!" I hollered to cars speeding by us in the opposite direction, and I waved my hand out the window, showing off my ring.

"And I'm sooo happy!" I shouted to everyone who could hear, which was just Luke. And he smiled, happy too.

It was like I'd crossed from one landscape into another—emerging from the expansive-but-sometimes-overwhelming forest of Dating, with all its what ifs, wondering, and prolonged heart-to-hearts, and into the sunny pasture of Engagement, where promises of stability and surety swayed gently in the breeze. No longer would I wonder, *Who am I going to marry? Or, Will Luke and I work out?* The question I'd been dreaming about since I was ten, when I wrote myself a letter to be "opened on my wedding day," would finally be answered: It was Luke. Looking back on my mountaintop proposal, from where I sit now, I remember the details of how it happened, and the happy feelings that followed; from the outside it looked just right. But if I'm completely honest with myself, I also remember that, buried beneath all of that happy inside me was a little something else.

In the moment Luke handed me the black box, I registered a sensation inside of something contrary, a sliver of a feeling so tiny I might have missed it, except that it stood apart from all of the big happy feelings washing over me, and so I noticed it for its otherness. At the time I didn't know to translate the feeling into words, or if it even mattered. Ninety-five percent of me was joy; 5 percent was this "other" sensation, as if a bird perched on my shoulder was chirping, *Are you sure? Are you sure?* It was such a tiny chirp, but even so, I felt disloyal for feeling it. I had expected to feel 100 percent "YES!" But maybe that was unrealistic. Maybe I was being simplistic in my expectation of *complete* clarity. This tiny chirp circled, even as I said yes, admired my ring, and loved my fiancé. And though I noticed it hovering there, I hoped it would fly away if I didn't pay it any more attention; it was, after all, a minority in the midst of a happy majority.

In all the stories I'd read or heard about proposals, a woman says yes or no, but never "95 percent yes!" When it comes to big-picture moments like this, isn't life supposed to be clear, like the view from the top of that mountain, so old-fashioned in its simplicity that it calls forth a deep-seated feeling of peace? I still wonder how this might feel—to have complete clarity in the moment that someone asks if you'd like to spend the rest of your life with him or her. I realize it's not a given, that plenty of people never meet someone with whom it's such a clear yes. And so they say no. Or, like me, say yes even so. But from my perch now, I wouldn't say yes again unless I felt it completely, because here's the thing: the shortcut to the peak, the easy yes, might get you there faster, but in your rush to the top you're bound to miss all sorts of treasures along the trail—birdsong, new growth, detours more beautiful that you can imagine. And when you do arrive, determined and out of breath, the view from the top might not feel quite so satisfying as you imagined.

That May day, however, I noticed the chirp, and then, because it was so tiny after all, I willed it to fly away, and I let myself dwell in the happy majority, where there was so much to celebrate, where life felt easier, more comfortable. At least for now.

✳   ✳   ✳

We'd kept our relationship discreet around Pilgrim Church. Luke was the student minister, and I was a regular church member, and we didn't want people to feel uncomfortable about our connection. We were playing it safe, but in reality I suspected most people would be happy for a love connection at Pilgrim, and many had probably guessed already.

Luke's last Sunday at Pilgrim was in early June, a few days after we got engaged, and we decided to share our news. He was preaching that morning, sitting up front beside Jonathan and the choir, including my parents.

"Does anyone have any celebrations or concerns they'd like to share?" Jonathan asked toward the end of the service, just after Luke's sermon. This chance for people to share what was on their minds happened every week; usually I didn't say anything, but today my hand shot up.

"Amanda," Jonathan called on me, smiling from his position in front of the church. Had he guessed what I was going to say? A hundred heads turned and looked at me as I stood up, and I remembered and then repeated the words Luke and I had decided on the night before:

"My mother once told me that if I went to church I might meet a nice young man," I started out. "And I am happy to say that my mother was right. As many of you know, I've met a wonderful young man here at Pilgrim, and it's Luke. We've been purposefully discreet about our relationship, but we're happy to be less discreet today as we announce that we're engaged!"

As if it were one giant wave of joy, the room erupted in applause. Luke stood up from his seat in the front, smiling, and looking slightly overwhelmed but happy. Across the aisle from me, two women rose as they clapped, and then everyone else followed, until the whole congregation was on its feet and clapping. It was a standing ovation for our engagement, and though I felt self-conscious at the attention, I was also relieved to be spilling our secret, grateful for the warm reception it received.

Downstairs after the service, the church had put together a

celebration for Luke's last Sunday. After they'd thanked him and given gifts, it was Luke's turn to speak. He took the microphone.

"Wow. Thank you!" He shook his head in disbelief. Standing there in his flowing black robe, Luke was handsome and charming in front of the crowd, but he also had an endearingly humble side, as if he couldn't quite believe that he had arrived at such a joyful moment—a church that loved him, another one awaiting his arrival, a fiancée by his side, and a roomful of people cheering him on.

"After three years, I'm sad to be leaving Pilgrim," he admitted. "Maybe I'll just keep on talking so this day doesn't end!"

Everybody laughed.

"Did you see my new stole?" he asked the crowd, stalling for time, pointing out the scarf-like vestment that was draped around his neck, a generous parting gift from the church.

"Isn't it beautiful?" he continued.

And then he gestured toward me. "And isn't Amanda great?"

Everyone laughed again.

"Cut the cake!" someone shouted.

There was a chocolate cake, our favorite, to celebrate Luke's last day, but as he handed over the microphone and walked toward the cake table, someone else shouted, "Amanda should help you! It will be good practice."

"If only we had a miniature bride and groom for the top!" someone else joked.

As I made my way to the cake, I felt a hand rest lightly on my arm. I turned to see Sophia, a petite woman, tan and wrinkled in her late seventies, always dressed in bright yellow. Even though she was very slow, Sophia walked a lot and could often be seen shuffling along the main street through town in her trademark shade of sunny.

Sophia called herself an astrologer, although I didn't know when or where she practiced, and she almost always had a serious concern to share in the Sunday service, but today it was all celebration.

"I just knew it!" she whispered to me as I paused beside her. "Remember I told you months ago that Luke was so handsome, and that I had a feeling you two would make a wonderful couple? I was right!"

I remembered, and I smiled back at her.

From all sides people were congratulating me, and it felt as if we were part of something greater than the two of us—a wide flowing stream of people who knew us and loved us; many had been married for years and others were still looking for their someone, but wherever they were on their journey that day, they celebrated ours. It was as if we'd grown up in the same small town and now the town was celebrating that two of its own had chosen each other. In the midst of this community our relationship made sense. We were two thoughtful, eloquent seminarians who loved each other and the church. Surrounded by all of this support, the less-comfortable aspects of our connection faded into the background; it was easy to forget the tiny doubts and hard conversations with such a community buoying us up.

One might think that, in the years to come, I would remember that Sunday and the hundred people who had celebrated us, and feel pressure to live up to their great expectations for our happily ever after. Had I been raised in a more conservative religious setting, with an emphasis on "traditional" values, it might have felt like that. But instead, I was blessed with a community that taught me that love, not rules, is at the heart of Christianity, and that that love includes not just love for others, but for yourself, too. And so I would remember that day—Sophia's whispering, Jonathan's big smile, and countless other family friends—for all the ways in which it felt like people were rooting for love, wherever it leads.

✳ ✳ ✳

Luke meditated regularly, read spiritual books in his free time, and practiced qigong every day. I'd never heard of qigong before I met Luke, and even though it didn't look like much to me (Luke stood in one place, gently swinging his arms from side to side), apparently there was a lot going on inside. In Chinese, *qi* means "life energy" and *gong* is a skill developed through practice; through the holy practice of breathing, meditation, and movement, one can balance the energy flowing through one's body, which made such a difference in how Luke felt that he almost never missed a day of his hour-long discipline.

We were yin and yang when it came to that; though I'd dabbled in yoga and taken one meditation class to see what Luke was up to, I didn't practice anything regularly. I *wanted* to be the kind of person who meditated, though. My thought patterns could probably have used a makeover. If minds were shops, mine would be an antique store—not the minimalist, tasteful kind, but one teetering with so much crappy stuff you want to turn around as soon you open the door. Not that there weren't some gems hiding within, but you had to pick through the detritus first: piles of needless worry, stacks of judgment, corners where envy hid out, and a whole section devoted to out-of-date ways of looking at the world: Change Is Bad, Conflict Is Worse, and The Best Thing Is To Make Other People Happy. This way of looking at life held me back from embracing the here and now, but I rarely made time to sit still, clear my mind, and make space for new material.

I *wished* my mind resembled a shop more like Marmalade, the cheerful boutique in the center of my hometown, full of useful items like cookbooks, candles, and pretty cards with positive messages. A bell jingled as the door opened, as if to say, "Welcome, friend! Good things live here," and I always felt uplifted when I stepped in. A mind full of useful and positive thoughts would be a nice change, but no one had ever told me how to cultivate one. I wondered if meditation might help, and when I noticed that a professor at divinity school was offering a two-week summer course on spiritual practices, I registered right away. It sounded practical and uplifting, and, having just finished my first year of divinity school, it was about time I had my very own spiritual practice. Maybe I too could find the discipline to sit (or stand) for an hour every day. Okay, I'd settle for fifteen minutes—even five—if it would transform my mind from a second-rate antique shop into a cheery boutique like Marmalade.

Spiritual Practices for Healing and Wholeness was the full title of the course, but I brushed over the bit about healing and wholeness. I'd leave those touchy-feely words to some of my older classmates, who seemed to blossom in emotional settings. I'd known going into Andover Newton that the majority of students were older than me, but a year into things, I was surprised at how disconnected I felt from my classmates. Among the students my age, there was a cohort of religious partiers (who loved to pray as much as they loved to drink and smoke pot), and then some pretty nerdy types, but no one who seemed middle-of-the-road like me. The largest contingent of students were middle-aged, recently divorced women who were into women and treated seminary as one big therapy session, taking everything very seriously and using every opportunity to overshare about the hard things in their past. Ugh! I didn't consider myself hurt or broken, and my own life experience felt miles away from theirs. On the contrary, at the start of this summer I was much happier than I'd been the previous June, when I was planning to go to Duke and unsure of my future with Luke. Now I was dwelling in the happiness of my engagement, living in a familiar place, and eager for life ahead.

Spiritual Practices met in the meetinghouse, a one-room clapboard building with big windows and a front porch with rocking chairs; if I had to pick a favorite building on campus, it would be this quaint one. Not that there was much competition. Though Andover Newton lived on a twenty-three acre hilltop overlooking Boston, there was an air of neglect around campus now—chipped trim on its nineteenth-century brick buildings and a few "newer" buildings from the seventies that hadn't been updated since. Clearly the school lacked the resources of divinity schools connected to universities, and though it trained its students to be great ministers, this also meant that most of its alumnae would never be particularly well-endowed. Once upon a time, when Protestant churches were thriving in New England and the school had had more resources, the meetinghouse had been a gymnasium, but nowadays the old gym was used for art exhibits and less-traditional classes like Spiritual Practices. Because it was just one big open room, without furniture, class was held in a circle on the floor, and we'd been instructed to wear comfortable clothes, as we'd begin each session with twenty minutes of yoga. Sitting cross-legged on my purple yoga mat, I scanned the room and wasn't surprised that most of my twenty classmates were middle-aged women. The exception was a girl about my age who I recognized as Marraine (rhymes with *terrain*), an outdoorsy blonde from Maine who seemed like she might be on my wavelength; we smiled at each other from across the room.

Our professor was a kindly middle-aged woman named Gretchen, who dressed in loose-fitting linen, sat cross-legged on the floor with us, and was known for taking students on service trips to Central America. Today, though, we'd be exploring lands closer to home: our minds. As she handed out packets on each of the spiritual practices we'd cover, it read like a list of exotic possibilities: centering prayer (*Sounds so holy!*); lectio divina (*What is that?*); and lamentation (*Hmm, that doesn't seem very uplifting*). Our first assignment was to choose a "spiritual companion," a classmate we'd meet with during the two-week course, and then continue to see throughout the summer, so we could hold ourselves accountable to our new practices. "Choose a spiritual companion" sounded an awful lot like "pick a partner," and even at twenty-five those words still made my stomach drop, as if I were a kid again, afraid to be the last one standing, with no one for a match. I brushed away that dusty old thought, more antique than boutique, and when Gretchen announced a break, I caught Marraine's eye. She smiled at me as I walked over and asked, "Do you want to be spiritual companions?"

"I was just thinking the same thing!" she said.

Hallelujah! My first-ever spiritual companion. And along with that came the reminder that looking someone in the eye and assuming she'd like to be my partner felt a whole lot better than passively *waiting* to be asked. Maybe I could apply that to all sorts of social settings where I usually hesitated to make the first move—like walking up to a stranger at a party and starting conversation. The new-and-improved Boutique Me would not only meditate on a daily basis, clearing her mind of out-of-date thoughts, but also ease gracefully into conversation with complete strangers. Just call me Marmalade!

✳ ✳ ✳

Marraine and I became fast friends, talking easily on the front porch of the meetinghouse about our preferred pronoun for God (She) and more secular subjects (men). Marraine was the first person I knew to try online dating, and I was fascinated by her stories *and* the easy way she talked about sex, which I still wasn't in the habit of talking about, much less at divinity school. So far, after a year of school, Laura, the willowy gospel singer, was my only good friend, but now it looked like I had a second friend, and perhaps a spiritual practice as well. Lectio divina, which means *divine reading*, had captured my attention when Gretchen explained it; reading was my second-favorite activity after eating, and I wondered if this timeworn discipline first established by monks in the sixth century might be The One for me. The purpose of lectio divina was to enter into a conversation with God and cultivate contemplation, a four-step process: read, meditate, pray, contemplate.

If class had ended there, with lectio divina, I would have been content; I had a new friend, and a potential practice. But the second week of Spiritual Practices introduced me to the Wailing Wall and lamentation, and from there a dark cloud descended. The proper name for the Wailing Wall is the Western Wall, and it's the only surviving piece of an ancient temple in Jerusalem that was destroyed two thousand years ago. For nearly as long, the site has been the holiest of holies for Jewish people, a place to offer prayers upon arrival in the Holy Land, where it's tradition to write notes to God and stick them between cracks in the wall, transforming two-thousand-year-old stones into whispers to the divine.

The June morning when I first heard of the Western Wall, I was sitting on the floor in the meetinghouse, sunlight streaming through its big windows, making the stones in my engagement ring sparkle. Just back from being resized at the jewelers, the thick platinum band with its sapphire and two diamonds fit perfectly, and it was starting to feel like my ring, not just on loan from my future mother-in-law. Best of all, when I looked at it, I felt happy; it was a beautiful, sentimental piece of jewelry, but more than that, I loved what it stood for: my connection to Luke and our future.

I looked up from my ring.

Gretchen was describing the Western Wall and how it led us to our next discipline, which was lamentation, or the spiritual practice of weeping. There's a whole book in the Old Testament called Lamentations, and many of the Psalms are laments too, heartfelt complaints to God from the depths of the writer's soul. Unlike lectio divina or meditation, lamenting isn't something one strives to practice regularly, but a spiritual resource that enters the scene at the most sad, painful, or unbearable moments in our lives. Here in the meetinghouse, Gretchen explained, we were going to build our own mini-version of a wailing wall, and then write lamentations (complaints to God) to stick into the cracks in the wall. We could even read our lamentations aloud, if we liked.

I did not like.

I shut my eyes and rolled them so no one could see. I did *not* want to write a complaint to God, and I certainly didn't want to hear my classmates complain aloud. It wasn't that I didn't like the idea itself. It was just the sort of hands-on, symbolic activity that I'd do with my students when I became a minister. In fact, a few years in the future, I'd lead a group of fourth graders in constructing their own mini-wall, where they collected rocks in the woods outside the church, stacked them up, and then wrote prayers on tiny slips of paper that they stuck between the stones. It was sweet. But the thing is, I didn't tell them what sort of prayer to write. That sunny morning in the meetinghouse, I would have been happy to write a prayer of gratitude or celebration, but I didn't want to dwell in the depths. I didn't want to lament. It felt like I was being forced to think hard or sad thoughts, when life actually felt quite good.

I looked back down at my ring, sparkling in the sunlight.

Come on! I urged myself. *Tap into some primal feeling of grief. Think of something to feel down about!*

Maybe I needed to turn my mind to thoughts of the world. Surely there I would find *something* depressing to complain to God about.

What about hungry children?

Now that *was* sad.

I wrote down a petition about hungry children. But it didn't feel genuine. Not that I didn't *genuinely* want all children to go to bed well-fed—of course I did—but it felt as though I was coming up with a lament just for the sake of it, and instead of it bringing a sense of release, I felt annoyed.

As I sat and listened to classmates read aloud their laments, it was apparent that they didn't share my resistance to the assignment. On the contrary, many of their laments were filled with so much rough stuff and raw pain that it felt like group therapy, not a graduate class, and even though I had signed up for this elective of my own free will, I resented the fact that I had to linger in these depths.

Looking back on this creative assignment, I see that it was just an exercise, no big deal, but the activity stands out as representative of the bigger picture—a feeling of heaviness that developed for me around being a minister. Before divinity school I thought church was enjoyable: diverse, friendly people; familiar music; inspiring messages. But divinity school was an intense place, and in my training I was being asked to look at the harder sides of life: injustice, sacrifice, sickness, death. I figured that one day in my life some of those would come calling, but I didn't want to dwell on them now.

I thought back to an old story my mom liked to tell, about a trip to visit her college roommate Tricia in Kentucky. Tricia had a son, Stephen, about my age, and when we were toddlers, our moms dressed us up in matching wool coats and hats (pink for me, blue for him), then sat me down on his lap in the stroller and took a picture.

"Stephen, what do you think of Amanda?" his mother asked in her perky southern drawl.

"*Heavy*," little Stephen grunted from beneath me.

Heavy, that's how today felt, as if I were being asked to carry a weight I didn't want to hold. In fact, that's how a lot of school felt, with its overarching focus on the deeper, more intense stuff of life. This shouldn't have been surprising; I was being trained to be a minister, after all. Among other things, pastors are supposed to preach prophetic messages, visit hospitals, and bury people. It's a thoughtful sort of profession, to say the least. But oftentimes I felt weighed down, not uplifted, by what I was studying, as if I were wearing a bulky wool overcoat, black, not pink, and five sizes too big. I compared myself to Luke, who seemed naturally drawn to spiritual practices, theological texts, and deep discussion, and felt shallow in comparison, as if I were bobbing on the surface of the sea, when I *should* be deep down below exploring its depths.

What I know now is that life is not about where you *should* be at a given time, but where you feel most yourself, most at home in your own skin. No one tells recent college graduates, "Follow the herd!" or "Give up your dreams for the greater good!" Rather, you're encouraged to find something you're passionate about— do something you love, and that you're good at, and you'll actually *enjoy* your work. Maybe not all the time every day, but plenty of times it will feel like joy. As I studied how to be a minister, I didn't feel much joy, but I figured that would come with the job itself, once I graduated. I wanted to get through *learning* how to be a minister, so that I could enjoy *being* one. If I could pour a

pitcher of words over my younger self until she was soaking wet
with their wisdom, I would shower her with a stream of:

Life

is

a

journey,

not

a

destination.

I imagined that where I was going would feel so much better than where I was. But if divinity school didn't feel particularly
engaging, more like an obstacle to overcome, wasn't it possible
that being an actual minister might not feel like such a great a fit
either? And likewise, if dating Luke felt hard, wasn't it possible that
marrying him would feel that way too? If the journey felt out of
sync with my soul, how did I expect the destination—even more
formal commitment in the form of ordination and marriage—to
feel so much better?

To give my younger self some credit, I wasn't completely
clueless about the connection between journey and destination.
I wrote in my journal that I thought marriage to Luke would be
hard, and I admitted to myself that ministry didn't always feel like
a natural fit either. But like the bird on my shoulder chirping, *Are
you sure?* neither of these feelings was enough to halt my forward
progress, to consider a detour, much less a do-over. I preferred
the feathered nest I knew to the wide-open sky.

Later that year, I would admit some of my doubts about
ministry to a pastoral counselor who was evaluating my psychological fitness. (Seminarians in the Congregational tradition had
to go through an evaluation, before ordination, to assure we were
healthy enough to be someone's spiritual leader.)

"Sometimes I just want to be the minister's favorite layperson," I confided in the counselor, "an involved church person, like

my parents and their friends, maybe the head of a committee, or a Sunday school teacher, but not the religious leader herself. I really love the church, all of that community, music, traditions, and quiet time. I'm just not sure that I love being one of its leaders."

I was crying as I confessed this, for confession is what it felt like, something that I had to get off my chest in order to move forward. What a relief it was to say aloud. To admit that being the one in charge of a church wasn't feeling like a natural fit, at least not yet.

"I won't include that in your report." The counselor smiled kindly at me.

I was grateful for her subtle omission, but more so for the fact that I'd spoken my worry aloud, that I'd admitted this unease to a professional and she hadn't seemed particularly surprised. Maybe this sort of doubt was normal. I was only partway through divinity school, after all, and I figured it would just take another year or two to get used to my new role. That these were growing pains, and the work of being a minister would eventually feel more comfortable. Truth be told, though, I never grew out of this discomfort; it followed me throughout divinity school, and even though I grew more accustomed to the robe and sense of authority, I never felt fully like me in the shadow of my unease.

Despite the discomfort, I never considered dropping out of divinity school. My practical side reminded me that the end goal (minister) fit my skills, and around each corner I encountered positive affirmation for my gifts. Beyond that, I was comfortable being on a clear path. The unknown intimidated me. If not minister, then what? And just as I couldn't imagine a partner other than Luke, I couldn't imagine a job other than minister. Or rather, I didn't try to. I had come this far; I didn't want to change my mind and find myself right back where I had started two years before. I was twenty-five already, privileged recipient of two decades of solid education. It was about time I made something of myself.

This was the voice of reason, singing its practical song. It didn't sound unlike my parents' advice to me, but the tune was so familiar, its lyrics so ingrained in my head—*I should I should I should*—that I can't attribute it to them alone. What it was not was a song of passion or excitement. Neither Duke nor Andover Newton felt like a natural fit; my classes felt heavy; and now the idea of being an actual minister did too. But I chose to soldier on in spite of the unease. Our family friend Stew had dropped out of divinity school in the sixties, and another friend, Jory's husband, had graduated but had chosen another career path. These were two of our closest family friends, but I never even thought to ask them why they'd changed their minds. I just chugged on. *I should I should I should.*

As for the spiritual practices, well—I intended to keep up lectio divina, but by the end of the summer, my infatuation with sacred reading had faded, and it felt more like a chore than an eye-opening connection to the divine. In the coming months I kept looking for my match. For a few weeks I practiced my own version of centering prayer—clutching a tiny globe in the palm of my hand, I prayed for hungry children and the rest of the world. When a portable labyrinth came to campus, one that mirrored the circular design on the floor of Chartres Cathedral in France, I walked the winding path to its center and out again, trying to feel something in the meditative movement—my peers, waving bright scarves in the air and moving their lips in silent prayer as they walked, certainly seemed to—but all I felt was like was a fish out of water, trying too hard. I belted out spirituals and tried to clap and sway in sync with Laura and the rest of the gospel choir on Wednesday afternoons. I even spent a semester practicing Taizé worship, meeting in the campus chapel before sunrise to light candles and chant hymns in the tradition of monks from Burgundy.

None of it felt like a natural fit. I wanted my connection to God to mirror some of the joy and contentment I felt in everyday life, not to feel like work. But maybe I was going about it backward. Maybe the one I really needed to connect with, to honor, was myself, and then I would feel more joy and contentment in my relationship with God and the rest of the world.

Could it be, I wondered, *that how ancient or traditionally "holy" a practice seems isn't actually as important as how it makes you feel inside?* If that was so, then there *was* one spiritual-ish thing that felt good every time I did it, though I hadn't really considered "walking in the woods" serious enough to be my spiritual practice because it came so naturally and felt so easy. On a trail by myself I always felt calm and centered inside, and somewhere along the way I usually found a rock in the sunshine, where I'd sit and list all the things I was grateful for. Without even realizing it, I usually began my list with, "Thank you, God for . . ." which probably meant I was praying, right? And when I got up five or ten minutes later, I could almost hear a still, small voice inside whispering, "Peace."

Emily Dickinson wrote, "Some keep the Sabbath going to Church – / I keep it, staying at Home – / With a Bobolink for a Chorister – / And an Orchard, for a Dome –" To listen to birds, or tip your head back and gaze at treetops; to walk about in a natural spot, feel warm sun on your face, and say thank you—today I wonder, What could be more spiritual than that? But in the midst of divinity school, and being engaged to another seminarian, perhaps it's not surprising that I was caught up in a more traditional, less earthy way of defining holy. It's not that domes and choirs aren't pathways to the divine, but they don't hold a monopoly on what is sacred. Stew knew this; he was our family friend who'd left divinity school years ago. As it turned out, his great love is birds, and though he's never preached a sermon, when you hear him describe the wren, or make the call of a great horned owl, you can't help but love those creatures as he does, if only for a moment. They are the content of his "sermons," his conduit to the divine.

I thought I had to become some holier version of myself, when all I really had to do was plant my behind on a rock and listen to the birds; in other words, just do what came naturally to me, be myself. This was a lesson I would learn over and again, as I navigated how to be a minister in my own way. From the beginning, I knew I was a different sort of candidate; I didn't have the same sort of religious zeal or even curiosity that many of my classmates did, but still I believed that I was called and gifted, and it was affirmed by people around me. The challenge was how to grow into the role in a way that felt authentic. I preferred walking in the woods to meditating, gratitude to petition, bobbing on the surface to exploring the depths. I didn't consider changing directions, but I'll give my younger self some credit for trying to follow the set path in her own way.

When you are strong in yourself, grounded in who you are, you can appreciate another's way of being without feeling like you need to be that way yourself. This is what I would remind myself as I tried to carve out my own niche. The holiest of holies is a cracked wall filled with notes, an orchard for a dome, a rock in the sun, the hoot of an owl on a cold winter's night; it is wherever you find yourself standing, or sitting, or kneeling on the ground, to offer your thanks to the world in one of a thousand ways.

✳ ✳ ✳

"There's something I need to talk about," Luke admitted as we hiked up a modest hill outside of Boston. It was the end of the summer, Spiritual Practices had finished up, and I'd just returned from a two-week hiking trip with my mom. My stomach dropped as I anticipated an overwhelmingly emotional conversation. Not the happy reunion I'd pictured.

"I don't feel connected like I want to," Luke went on.

"You mean because I've been away for two weeks? Or is it something bigger than that?"

"Bigger. Like right now I'm going through stuff, and having feelings about us, and it feels like you don't even want to hear about them."

Well, he had a point. I *didn't* really want to hear about his conflicted feelings. I wanted to have an ordinary, not-emotionally-strained conversation about what we'd been up to the last few weeks. I wanted to hear all about his new job and tell him about my trip. Ordinarily Luke was a great listener, able to summon genuine enthusiasm about almost any topic under the sun, and I loved that about him, but today he had other things on his mind. And so he continued:

"You make me feel bad for having feelings and wanting to talk about them, but that's who I am. I *need* to process my emotional stuff. It's healthy. It's what people *do* in relationships."

"O-kay," I responded, taking a deep breath, but I felt slightly sick inside, like I might throw up—that's how unsettling these conversations felt to me. In the antique shop of my mind, conflict was still bad, and this was starting to sound like one of those talks we'd had last winter, before getting engaged. But where was all of this pent-up frustration coming from now? I thought things were fine, better than fine.

And then Luke said it.

"Sometimes I wonder if we should even get married."

Oh God.

I wanted to scream at him, and fall down on my knees crying at the same time. (Maybe I had a good lamentation in me after all.)

"But we're engaged!" I blurted out, tears starting to fall. "We've decided!" I insisted.

At twenty-five I didn't know anyone who'd called off her engagement. I was only the second in my circle of friends to actually get engaged, and it certainly hadn't been some fly-by-night decision we'd come to lightly. Now that he'd asked, and I'd said yes, now that we were committed and making plans, doubt wasn't supposed to creep back onstage and steal the show. In retrospect, I realize that a broken engagement, while painful, can be a lot less messy than the alternative, a broken marriage, but a thought like that never crossed my mind back then. Broken marriages were things that happened to other people; no one in my immediate circle of friends or family was even divorced.

In my heart of hearts, even after Luke flung the words out there, I didn't really believe we were headed toward a broken engagement. I was used to the fact that sometimes, in the heat of the emotional moment, he said extreme things. Even so, I felt shallow and foolish. I'd spent the past ten days cavorting through the Spanish countryside with my mother, happily telling the middle-aged ladies in our hiking group that I was engaged, eager to stretch out my hand and show off my ring when they asked, enjoying their attention, and feeling secure in my relationship—all while my fiancé was back home doubting our future. I was in love with Luke, but I was also in love with the idea of settling down, of the clear path before me.

Perhaps I was so in love with this idea that I was afraid to speak up and admit that part of who Luke was—his intensity, his way of processing everyday life, his tendency to delve deeply into big issues—made me feel uncomfortable and didn't fit with who I was in the world. To Luke this sort of conversation might feel like a natural part of a relationship, but to me it felt *heavy*. Was I wrong to want things to feel lighter, easier? I didn't think so. Where I *was* wrong was hoping Luke would become more like me when it came to our relationship; it wasn't realistic, or fair, to expect my way to work for him. Perhaps this was a giant sign that this wasn't a right match for either of us. Which is what Luke seemed to be saying, after all. But I didn't want to hear it. Like a horse with blinders on, I could only see straight ahead. We had agreed upon this course, and I would not be distracted.

Oh God, I thought again, midway up the modest hill. Where was the still, small voice inside, whispering "Peace," at a moment like this?

Years later, while teaching a course on world religions, I would come across a line from the ancient Chinese philosopher Lao Tzu: "A good traveler has no fixed plans, and is not intent upon arriving." In my car, cruising down an open road, being in the moment came so naturally to me, but when it came to being married, I was decidedly less Taoist in my approach, all fixed plans and intent upon arriving. I had thought that being engaged would make things feel settled between us, that our questions would disappear, and emotional conversations would be exchanged for practical ones, like, "Who should we invite to dinner?" But even though we had taken this big step, and announced it publicly, it didn't erase Luke's tendency to ask big questions about "us" and my unease when he did. Now I looked toward marriage itself for those settled feelings. It was as if there, just up ahead, over the next hill, and across a field, is where happiness and contentment awaited. But if I wasn't content in the here and now, how could I expect the future to feel much different? "Forever is composed of nows," Emily Dickinson wisely wrote. If my nows felt unsettled, how could I expect the forever up ahead, woven of the same fabric, to feel any better?

Luke was on to something when he suggested in the heat of the moment that we question our engagement. But I didn't want to hear it. And so, instead of admitting that I'd heard a bird chirp—*Are you sure?*—I felt upset, betrayed even, by Luke's insistence on asking questions, and it made me even more determined to be positive. I was, after all, a big fan of gratitude, and so, instead of wrestling with the questions or dwelling in the depths, I floated on the surface, grateful for all of the things that felt right in our relationship. I listened to Luke's thoughts, squelched my own screams and tears, and then we kept climbing.

6. Sex Matters

What I remember best from the steamy August day of my wedding was the crowd. As weddings go, it was a moderate cast of a hundred and thirty, but it contained all the people I loved best in the world at that moment in time, gathered up in one place, to cheer on our love. I knew who was coming, I'd received all of their replies, but as I walked down the aisle of Pilgrim Church, arm-in-arm with my dad, on my way to Luke, passing through this beloved crowd nearly took my breath away, and I felt like part of something much bigger than the two of us.

Just before we said our vows, standing before a giant spray of white flowers that my mom and her friends had arranged in our kitchen, Jonathan asked us to turn around and face everyone. As Luke and I turned, shifting our gaze from each other to our guests, I felt suddenly self-conscious. *Look. At all of these people. Here for us. All dressed up and smiling in our direction.* Jonathan asked everyone to stand, and the crowd rose. "Marriage touches many lives," he began, "and each of you is an important part of that larger caring. Will you pledge your support to Amanda and Luke today?"

"WE WILL!" rang out in the sanctuary, a chorus of a hundred and thirty casting their votes in our direction, propelling us forward with their enthusiasm.

Luke and I turned back toward each other as the crowd sat down again. I passed my white bouquet to Emily beside me, in a blue dress she'd picked out from Anthropologie, and, holding hands, Luke and I made our promises. I practically shouted, I was so eager for everyone to hear me. The candles next to the flowers flickered. Outside it poured rain. Thunder cracked. "The gods have spoken!" Jonathan declared. Everyone laughed, clapped, and we were married.

✳ ✳ ✳

That night, after the party, a limousine dropped us at a hotel not far from the estate where our reception had been, and our wedding day became our wedding night. Now that we were married, people actually *expected* us to have sex; there was nothing to feel guilty about. I wondered if it might hurt a little, but I was ready, finally, just shy of twenty-seven, to have sex for the first time, and curious too—would I love it? But here was another thing that didn't feel anything like I'd expected. Though I'd imagined a bit of discomfort my first time, I'd never pictured so much pain that sex was pretty much impossible. My mind was finally saying "Yes!" but my body wasn't cooperating. I thought sex was supposed to come naturally and easily, but nothing about this sharp pain felt natural or easy, and certainly not pleasurable. Had I lived in an earlier century, or a less considerate culture, brute force might have had its way with me, but I had a kind and patient husband who didn't like to see me in pain, and so we joked that we'd had one-third sex, assuming that soon enough, with experience, I'd loosen up and we'd be able to go all the way.

We left on our honeymoon the next day. But even Paris, that city of love, couldn't make a woman out of me. We ditched one-third sex and resorted to more familiar, less painful practices, trying again every so often throughout the fall. But by now I was anxious every time, anticipating the pain, tensing up instead of relaxing, a cycle that I didn't know how to break, and it became apparent that nothing was changing.

In theory it felt as if I was missing out on something big, something I *should* be doing. But in reality, sex felt like just that—something I *should* be doing, not necessarily something I *wanted* to do. Which might sound completely lame, cold, and asexual, except for two truths: I didn't know what I was missing out on, and I didn't really want to do something that hurt *that* much. It might seem odd that, in the first few months of being married, we didn't try to deal with this surprise right away, to figure out what was going on and fix it. But honestly I didn't know what *to* do. My doctor said, "You just need to relax," and practically speaking, we weren't in a hurry to have children, so I figured that my "issue" would sort itself out in time. Luke didn't do anything to make me feel bad about my situation, but even so, I felt ashamed and inadequate that I couldn't do this most basic human thing. Teenagers did it! The elderly. Strangers who hardly knew each other. *What was my problem?* But when you're in the midst of a challenge, living alongside it every day, you get used to your reality, which has its practical points; if you spend all your energy focused on the frustrating parts of your relationship, you might forget to enjoy what's good. Assuming there is some good, that is.

And there was plenty that felt good being married to Luke. The first two years weren't blissful, but they were for the most part happy, as we crafted a life together, in a one-bedroom campus apartment. Luke was now a full-time minister, and I was a part-time minister as I finished up divinity school, and though our non-traditional schedules made it hard to have a "normal" social life as a couple, I didn't really notice that the sort of everyday socializing I loved—meals out with friends, dinner parties, weekends away—had pretty much disappeared from my life. I was too busy being married to Luke, wrapped up in the roles of wife, minister, and minister's wife.

Then, two years into being married, it was my turn to graduate. We bought a two-bedroom condo a few miles from campus; it took up the first floor of a small white colonial with an even smaller backyard and was an easy commute for both of us. Not that "easy commute" was a priority for me. This was a place where Luke and I differed in our approach. For me, vibrancy was more important than practicality, and I was drawn to Harvard Square in Cambridge, the small city that bordered our town, on the Charles River across from Boston. When I drove by a three-story brick house turned into condos, with a For Sale sign out front, just down the road from Harvard Square, where Luke and I had had our first kiss five years earlier, I fantasized about living in the tiny urban space. We could walk to dozens of restaurants and coffee shops, or meet up with Silas, who was now a sophomore at Harvard. In theory, Luke liked Cambridge too, but he didn't feel the same pull to live there and was content to stay in the suburbs, one town away from work.

Well, that makes sense, I thought to myself.

Even though it wasn't how I felt, what could I do about it? I saw much of the world in black and white—he wants this, I want that, so we have to pick either this or that—when in reality life is more nuanced. Sure, practically speaking, you have to make choices about where to live, but the conversation doesn't have to end there. Once you have a place to live, there is the matter of *how* you will turn your four walls into a *home* that speaks of who you are. While we talked about what sort of house we wanted to buy—wood floors and a fireplace in a pretty neighborhood— we stopped short of envisioning what sort of *home* we wanted to create, and this, I know now, is the detail that really matters in how well you live together. Will your home be like a retreat from the world? Or a gathering place for your nearest and dearest? Will you work on house projects together? Throw dinner parties? Host holidays? Plant a garden? Growing up, my parents did all of that, and I'd always assumed that, when I was married, my house would be a place where family and friends came and went, feeling at home in the cozy corner we'd created. But once Luke and I bought our first house together, I didn't think to have any conversations about how to create a home out of it. Not that you *have* to talk about such things, if you're on the same page, but we weren't. Instead of pausing to think about this though, I forged ahead in my black-and-white way, pouring myself into its perfection—painting, picking out furniture, arranging everything just so. I cooked bountiful meals for two in its lovely kitchen. And I was too busy perfecting to notice that we didn't invite anyone else over to enjoy the home we were creating.

✳   ✳   ✳

It's a New England phenomenon that church life slows down in the summer—families disappear on vacation, and even those in town play hooky so that attendance at Sunday services drops; committees and youth groups follow suit, breaking for the season so that, like a blanket over a birdcage, a hush descends upon the church from the summer solstice through Labor Day. I stepped into my first full-time job in the midst of this seasonal hush, as an associate minister, at a vibrant (though temporarily out-of-town) congregation in a woodsy suburb west of Boston. Often I was the only one in the historic meetinghouse; the middle-aged administrative assistant, Helen, a kindly gray-haired woman who brought her corgis to work, had reduced summer hours, and the senior minister, Simon, also kindly and middle-aged, lived just a short walk away in the church parsonage with his wife and stepdaughters and took advantage of the quiet to work from home.

Since my workday was an uninterrupted swath of solitude, and the office I'd inherited resembled a disorderly gym closet packed with supplies for the youth groups I'd be leading in September, I started off my career with a deep clean. Once I'd packed away the balls, bandannas, and board games, I had enough room for a couch, and Helen offered me a gently-used plaid sofa that her husband dropped off at the church one night. My own office, with a couch! I hung my diplomas, reminders of where I'd been, and a giant world map too, to remind me of all the places I had yet to see. And then, from a seat on my plaid couch, I got to work sorting and filing, but mostly tossing, years of musty paperwork that had been spilling out of my desk drawers. The upside to digging through detritus left by your predecessors is that you're bound to unearth details that bring insights into your new job, the sort they don't tell you in interviews.

So it was, on a slow July day, while sorting through piles, that I discovered the sex file.

What kind of a church is this? I wondered, staring at the manila folder, bursting with papers, the words *Sex Retreat* scrawled on the tab.

Gingerly I picked up the item, and, assuming it was a joke, but still hesitant to peer inside, I carried the manila folder down the hall to Simon's office and deposited it on his desk. Technically, since we were a Congregational church and this meant that the congregation governed itself, I had two hundred bosses (all of the church members), but in an everyday sort of way, Simon was my superior and like a boss. An intellectual with a dry wit and a big heart, he'd been at the church for five years when I arrived.

"Look at what the last minister left behind!" I announced, pointing to the folder on his desk, not sure if I wanted to be caught with such a risqué dossier just a few days into the job. I waited for Simon to look scandalized. Raise an eyebrow. Chuckle? He did none of that.

"Ahh, yes. That," he simply said, taking off his glasses and rubbing the bridge of his nose, as if he wasn't particularly excited about the contents of this folder either.

"Is it for real?" I asked, mild panic setting in. Sex was so not my thing. Two years into married life, Luke and I still hadn't consummated our relationship. But that was my personal life. I certainly hadn't expected sex to come up at work.

"It's very real," Simon continued. "But I can't tell you much, except that it happens every three years. And you're in charge. Oh, and it doesn't actually involve sex, but you probably already guessed that."

And then he closed the conversation with, "I suggest you ask the advisors for more details."

Oh. Great.

The advisors.

First, sex. Now those guys.

The advisors were my celebration and concern rolled into one, and I had yet to face them all at once; that meeting was on tap for later in July, though I hoped I might be "too busy" cleaning my office to attend. On the surface of it, the advisors were a blessing, likely to make my job a lot easier, a built-in support network of volunteers who would help me run the high school youth group, which had about thirty kids in it. Thirty might seem like small potatoes by some church standards, but for New England (home to some of the least religious states in the country), it was a big, successful youth group, and that it came with built-in advisors meant I wouldn't have to recruit kids or adults.

Better still, the advisors were young, in their twenties and thirties, and full of energy, which meant the high school kids loved them, *and* they were all alums of the youth group themselves; as kids they'd grown up in this town and cherished their own youth group experience enough to come back as adults, after college, and help out every Monday night. Which led to my concern: they were a tightly-knit group with a rock-solid memory of what things had been like "back in the day" when Bill, one of my predecessors, had started the group in the late eighties. Bill himself wasn't a minister, just a regular church member; he was also drawn to Native American spirituality, and though he'd since passed away, his legacy remained, the biggest piece of which was that youth group was Not Religious; even though it met in a church and was led by the minister, there was no mention of God or praying or any expectation of church attendance. While some of the kids came to church with their parents, others did not; and for the most part the advisors weren't churchgoers either.

I had been "warned" of this in my initial interview for associate minister, told in no uncertain terms that the youth group relished its identity as "spiritual but not religious" and was likely to resist anything to the contrary. Apparently another one of my predecessors—described by several churchgoers as "a young blonde who looked a lot like you!"—had tried to weave God-talk into youth group, and it had felt forced, stilted, and the advisors were wary of this happening again.

Now, I am not by nature a particularly devout person, which is probably why the church trusted me with their treasured group, but I *had* spent the past four years immersed in divinity school, learning how to lead a religious community, and the notion of a church-affiliated group that was intentionally Not Religious was hard for me to wrap my mind around. It seemed a curious mix: a Christian church that expected me to lead worship on Sunday morning yet hold back on anything religious on Monday night. I'd grown more comfortable with praying, for example, and thought of it as a good resource in life. But I knew it wasn't wise for a novice to make big changes early on, especially when the status quo seemed to be working, so I vowed to wait and see, to go with the flow for now, and try to tap into my spiritual-not-religious side.

✳ ✳ ✳

I met the advisors en masse for the first time later that summer, at a backyard barbecue a few miles from church. There were twelve of them, more guys than girls, loud and joke-y, and clearly very at home in each other's company. They were here for fun, and I was here for work, and already that made me feel out of place, but I'd been chosen by the church to lead their beloved youth group (a few of the advisors had been on the search committee too), and so as we crowded onto the back porch, I decided to start with the positive.

"Clearly you love this youth group, since you've all come

back to help out as adults, which is pretty unique. So tell me what you like best about it."

"I'll start," offered Jen, an outspoken accountant with long curly brown hair and glasses who'd been telling stories from a recent hiking trip in the Himalayas. "There are three things I love best about this group: our traditions, the sense of community, and the fact that no one's judged for who they are."

"My favorite part," said Dex, one of the veteran advisors at thirty, "is Closing Circle. At the end of each meeting, we light a candle, turn out the lights, and sit in a circle on the floor. Everyone, kids and advisors, has a chance to say whatever's on their mind. And like Jen said, you're never judged for what you say."

"That's my favorite part too," Katie chimed in. She'd just graduated from college and was young enough that some of the older advisors, like Dex, had been her youth group leaders.

"My parents got divorced when I was in high school," she added. "And it was pretty messy, but Closing Circle was the one place where I felt comfortable talking about it."

The sharing went on and on, and in spite of my initial unease in their company, I found myself touched by their heartfelt commitment to the group and their reverence for traditions like Closing Circle. They might be hesitant to pray or talk about God, but as one who preferred walking in the woods to more traditional spiritual practices, it would be pretty hypocritical if I judged them for their alternative approach.

As the formal part of the meeting wound down (well, as formal as anything with this lot could be), conversation shifted to an upcoming weekend getaway.

"Come to my lake house in New Hampshire," Dex offered as we walked toward the door. "We're going up next weekend. It's an advisor tradition!"

Dex and his older brother, Danny, also an advisor, lived down the street from the church in an old farmhouse that had belonged to their grandfather. They'd recently outfitted it with a homemade fieldstone bar, and I soon learned that it was where the advisors and their friends liked to have parties, but next weekend's trip was to their parents' place up north.

"There's a hot tub!" Jen said enticingly.

"And my brother's a great cook," Dex added.

Yet as welcoming as they tried to be, I felt like an outsider. Dex, Danny, Jen, and the others had grown up together in this close-knit town, had years of shared history, and helped out with youth group for fun, after their day jobs, whereas youth group for me *was* my day job, or rather, my night job. Divinity school had drilled it into my head that we weren't "supposed" to befriend our congregation, that we should maintain work-life boundaries, and while this was easy with most churchgoers (as they were either kids or my parents' age), now I'd be working with my peers, and I could tell they wanted me to be part of the gang. But not me. I was curious to see if I would fall under the spell of this beloved youth group, but I didn't plan to socialize with them outside of work. I was the minister, after all, a professional, and I couldn't picture myself huddled in a hot tub with this crew drinking beer late into the night, which is what they said they did in New Hampshire.

What's more, I was married, while all of them were single. In a few years they'd start getting married and ask me to officiate their weddings, but for now I was the only one who had someone to go home to. What would Luke think if I disappeared for the weekend with this gang instead of hanging out with him? I certainly couldn't imagine Luke coming along; I knew it would feel like "work" to him, and he had enough of his own work already. It would be easier to keep my distance. Besides, I treasured my downtime and didn't want to blur the line between work and play. I preferred to go to New Hampshire with Luke, where we'd read books on his mother's porch and eat the beautiful food she cooked us.

What I didn't know then was that the advisors also read books on the deck in New Hampshire, and picked blueberries, and cooked elaborate meals, and best of all made each other laugh for hours on end. All things I loved to do. But I was so set in my black-and-white way of thinking—minister/parishioner, work/social, married/single—that I didn't consider the possibility of middle ground, that it's okay (more than okay, it's normal!) to socialize with your peers. Every Monday night in the church parking lot, after the last kids got picked up and I had locked up the meetinghouse, one of the advisors inevitably asked if I wanted to come have a drink with everyone at the local Irish pub. It was a cozy spot, conveniently situated halfway between church and my house, and I drove right by it on the way home, but even so I always said, "No, thanks." I wished they'd stop asking, since I always felt somewhat lame and awkward for saying no, but after a long day it felt more relaxing to go home to the man I knew rather than to a tableful of people I didn't. Driving home, a few minutes behind the advisors, I'd see their familiar cars in the pub's parking lot, and even though I'd felt such a bond after that night's meeting, once again I felt set apart.

My life was neatly compartmentalized—work, husband, friends, family—and the only two parts that overlapped with any regularity were Luke and my family. Most of the time I felt guilty asking him to spend time with my friends or church, since it was clearly not relaxing for him. And instead of having a conversation about this, as usual I took the easy way out and continued to box up parts of my life and my emotions too. This was not a recipe for long-term happiness, but I didn't realize that at the time. I was too caught up in the supporting roles of minister and wife, and in what other people might think of me, to notice that I was neglecting myself.

Driving home that hot July night, seeking refuge behind my boundaries, I was just so relieved that my first meeting with the advisors was behind me. One day up ahead, in a change of scene I couldn't have imagined then, I would actually look forward to their company, but that was a few years away. That night, I was just glad to get home to Luke, who would listen to my account of the day over burritos on our blue couch, which sat on a wood floor (check), next to our fireplace (check), in a pretty neighborhood (check). It was just what I thought I wanted.

✳ ✳ ✳

It wasn't until early fall that I remembered to ask the advisors about the sex file I'd found back in July, and they suggested a meeting. As the twelve of us crowded into my office one Wednesday night, they looked about approvingly.

"Great improvement!" Dex said. "It used to look like a storage closet in here."

"Well, in the midst of improving, I found this!" I brandished the manila folder labeled Sex Retreat, and I blushed as I looked around the circle; even though I was getting more comfortable with the advisors, that certainly didn't mean we talked about sex.

"That must have been a surprise," Katie laughed good-naturedly.

"We told you this is a unique youth group!" added Dex.

"So what's it all about?" I looked around the circle expectantly.

"Should we start with the penis game?" Jen asked. The rest of the group chuckled, and then they got down to it, describing a two-day sex retreat which was really just a chance to talk openly about sex and issues related to it, for the teenagers to ask questions of adults who weren't their parents or teachers, but who cared about their safety and well-being. I imagined it might be a bit like talking to your cool Aunt Stephanie—an adult less awkward than your parent, but wiser than your peer, who never seems to judge *anyone*. Not that I had a cool Aunt Stephanie; maybe I'd be more of a blossoming sexual being if I had. One day, though, I imagined being a version of her to my future nieces and nephews. Heck, I'd be Aunt Stephanie to my own kids. That is, if I ever learned *how* to have sex in the first place, which felt like the great irony of the sex retreat—that I was leading conversations about something I couldn't even do myself.

Sinful. Immoral. Fornicator. Some of my least favorite religious-y words associated with sex would *not* be making an appearance at our retreat. Judge-y words weren't our style, but many other colorful terms *did* show up at the retreat that January, making their first appearances during the "penis game," as the advisors fondly called it from their own youth group days. We divided all thirty kids into three groups and gave them a few minutes to list as many synonyms for the male member as they could, and then we had them do the same with the words *vagina, breast*, and *sex*. Then we hung their lists, scrawled on big sheets of newsprint, on the walls of the lodge where we were staying. The common room looked like a giant sex thesaurus, but the penis game cut through the initial awkwardness of talking about sex and got conversation going, and soon even I was well on my way to warming up to this retreat, not to mention this "godless" youth group with its high-energy advisors, their honesty, and their constant laughter. Six months into my job, the youth group was growing on me—like a game of hide-and-seek, I was getting warmer, warmer . . .

That night when they ate my simple dinner—grilled cheese on thick slices of sourdough with tomato soup—and gave it high praise, I warmed up even more. Especially since they'd eaten the side dish too, sautéed zucchini, without complaint; the same zucchini that earlier in the day had been a prop in a condom demonstration, along with a bunch of cucumbers. When we'd finished with the hands-on demonstration of how to put on a condom, I'd thrown out the contraception, thoroughly scrubbed the vegetables, and chopped them up for dinner.

As soon as the platter hit the long table, a young voice piped up: "Are those the same zucchini that . . . ?"

"Yep!" I jumped in, smiling at everyone. "And I washed them really well. It's like recycling. Enjoy!"

The kids looked momentarily skeptical, the advisors laughed, and for just a moment I felt like cool Aunt Stephanie; the dual-purpose zucchini was just the sort of trick she'd pull. Before digging in, we each took a turn to say something we were grateful for; we might not pray *per se*, but we could still be thankful. And then, beneath banners of sex words, we ate zucchini that promoted safety, and I laughed and laughed at who knows what, and I was getting warmer, warmer . . .

✳ ✳ ✳

Perhaps it's not surprising that a few weeks after the sex retreat I finally felt inspired to figure out my own sex life. Two and a half years into being married, I still didn't know what was "wrong" with me, or how to fix it, but that January, after several false starts—doctors who didn't suggest anything beyond the initial advice I'd received "to relax"—my determination led to a gynecologist who specialized in vulvovaginal issues. Dr. Stewart diagnosed my condition as *vaginismus*, an involuntary tightening of the vaginal muscles that causes pain upon penetration, if not an inability to have sex at all. Once your muscles associate pain with sex, they anticipate more of the same, tighten further, and the cycle continues, as if there is a wall where an opening should be. In hindsight, this seems like such a common-sense diagnosis, one I could have discovered myself with a bit of research, but I'd felt alone and embarrassed, and the fact that several doctors hadn't offered any logical explanation had made me wonder if it was all psychological.

To know that my condition had a name, that I wasn't the only one, that it *wasn't* all in my head, as Luke had once wondered, was such a relief. For on that point my doctor was quite clear: the tightening happened involuntarily, often without one's awareness. Imagine clenching your muscles as if you're trying to keep from peeing; that was the sort of lockdown my pelvic floor muscles were in, not always but often, and now that it had been pointed out to me, I noticed The Clench everywhere: while reading on the couch, while driving, and even while standing in front of the congregation on Sunday morning.

I knew what was going on, but I didn't understand why. When I scanned the list of physical causes that could lead to vaginismus, like a painful childbirth or pelvic trauma, none applied, nor did some of the more obvious emotional ones: I'd never suffered a traumatic event like abuse, or had negative childhood experiences like "overly rigid parenting" or "unbalanced religious teaching" (i.e., sex is BAD), and so I just assumed that, as some of the literature said, there was no cause for my condition. *C'est la vie.* I was born with a tight twat.

But in addition to a diagnosis, Dr. Stewart offered me something even better: possibility. We could retrain my muscles, she said, to respond differently to the anticipation of sex. In other words, we'd teach them how to relax, my "wall" would come down, and I would be open for business. So to speak. This would happen, most notably, through weekly massage—soft-tissue massage by a physical therapist who specialized in helping women like me—followed by daily "practice" at home. And yes, the soft tissues the therapist massaged were the ones in my vagina, and yes, I was self-conscious to say the least the first time I showed up for my massage. (And no, in answer to a question my mom asked after the fact, it didn't turn me on; more often than not it hurt, at least in the beginning.) But Raquel was the perfect therapist for the task: a middle-aged Chilean Jew who talked to me about religion and her college-aged sons as she set to work desensitizing my nether regions.

Once a week I lay on her table, naked from the waist down, while she massaged the inside of my vagina and made meaningful small talk, and eventually, after a few months, I began to notice a measurable difference. Actually measurable, because after each massage, Raquel inserted a tiny probe while I contracted and released my muscles (think Kegels) and an attached monitor beeped faster or slower depending on how tight or relaxed my contractions were. She gave me a mini version of this biofeedback machine to practice with at home, as well as a graduated set of dilators—small hard plastic ones to start, the first one the width of a slender tampon, and then, when I could handle that without pain, moving on up to bigger versions.

If this approach sounds rather clinical, well, that's because it was, and my own approach wasn't far off. Sex was officially on my "to-do" list, and I would learn how to make it happen. I wish I could say I felt excited or turned on when I imagined the end result, but I think I just felt relieved and less freakish to see the end goal getting closer.

Where was my husband in all of this? Luke came to one of my appointments with Raquel, and for that I gave him great credit, but mostly it felt like my problem to fix. He was ready just as soon as I was. There were tiny steps forward that involved the two of us, like a visit to a local (feminist-friendly) sex shop my therapist Bonnie had recommended. We bought a movie and some fancy lubricant, but the experience was so outside my comfort zone that it seemed like more of a chore than an enticing prelude to intimacy, and later I felt sort of guilty when we watched the mild pornography.

I was dedicated to my practice, though—to weekly visits with Raquel and daily dilating and stretching on the bedroom floor—and in November, about six months after I started the massage therapy, Raquel suggested that I was ready to try having sex again, something I hadn't done in a few years. She was right, I was ready; it worked—not without a bit of discomfort, but it was certainly bearable—and I was so relieved I cried afterward, tucked beside Luke in bed. It felt more like a personal triumph than an intimate sharing with my husband; I think he was just relieved he hadn't hurt me. And while "certainly bearable" is hardly the highest of praise, I figured I would come to enjoy it eventually.

I'll never know for sure if my sex life could have begun differently. Maybe I *was* born with an inclination toward tightness, but looking back on it now I'm pretty sure there was more to it. No, I hadn't suffered any traumatic events, but your everyday thoughts and beliefs have a way of impacting your reality in tangible ways; just as water rushing over a rock, over time, alters the face of the stone, so, too, can tiny thoughts, repeated for years, alter our experience of the world. For years *sex* and *no* were intertwined in my mind, and instead of thinking about how fun it would be, I didn't let myself think about it at all. Maybe all of those years of telling myself *no sex*, of keeping it off-limits, on the top shelf in a box labeled marriage, had manifested in this very real physical condition. If I'd slept with Jake at sixteen, or that hot stranger on top of the mountain, or perhaps, more realistically, Dave, my college professor-turned-boyfriend, an experienced and gentle sort, would my muscles have been so tight? Which isn't to say that every woman who waits to have sex faces this issue. I have a friend who waited until her mid-thirties to sleep with a man and enjoyed great sex right from the start. What matters, I've learned, aren't the specifics of age, or whether you end up in a lasting relationship with your partner or not, but loving your body, all of it, and giving yourself permission to feel, because that way, the rest will follow.

What I do know for sure is this: I will tell my children that sex is beautiful. And fun. So yes, be thoughtful and safe about it, but *enjoy* yourself too. It's a gift from the gods (all of them!), and our bodies are made for pleasure.

* * *

A few months later, while out to dinner with my college roommates, I finally worked up the courage to tell them about the last year and my work with Raquel. Though I'd confided to them that sex was "difficult" at the start of my marriage, we hadn't talked about it in the three years since. Now, over pizza at one of my favorite restaurants in Harvard Square, I drank a big glass of red wine and all but ignored my meal, I was so caught up in my confession—as if this were a G-rated episode of *Sex and the City*. My friends couldn't believe I'd kept something like this to myself, and in retrospect I can't either. Kelley is the most down-to-earth, kind person I know, and Molly is a brilliant science writer with a penchant for research; chances are, if I'd shared this with them earlier, I would have felt less shame, and maybe even figured out my problem sooner.

Being out with my best friends and letting them see the real me felt like something from another life. I remembered the night at the end of senior year when I'd first hooked up with Dave; how I'd arrived home after midnight to candlelight and rose petals strewn in the hallway of our campus apartment, Kelley and Molly giggling in the next room, having waited up to hear all the details of my romantic escapade. They even took a picture of me walking in, dressed up in an old sweatshirt and jeans, my hair unwashed— it was the end of exam week—but I was so not caring *how* I looked because   Oh-My-God-I-just-hooked-up-with-Dr.-Burke!   The whole experience was the perfect example of going with the flow; normally I put a bit more thought into how I looked, but that night I couldn't be bothered, and look how well it had ended. My sweet, silly friends with their rose petals (where had they come up with those in the middle of the night?) and mood lighting couldn't wait to hear all the details. And I couldn't wait to tell.

Fast-forward to to this night nearly eight years later—in a new black top dotted with sequins and my hair freshly cut and styled—I had picked out the perfect places for us to eat and drink, but who was I trying to impress? My friends loved me no matter what I looked like and just wanted my happiness. And that night, in the company of those dear friends, reconnecting as I opened up about something *real*, it felt like a new beginning, but also like returning to myself.

7. Waking Up

"Which one of you is the minister?" our guide, Clint, asked.

I stepped forward from my spot in the circle, where I'd been standing between an advisor and a youth group kid.

"You look pretty young for a minister."

"I'm probably older than you think," I offered; in jeans, a sweatshirt, and a ponytail, there was nothing to set me apart from the rest of the group.

"Well, I'm just glad you're official. I'd like to serve Communion, but I'm not a pastor or anything. Would you help officiate? It's pretty non-traditional, I have juice and chips instead of wine and bread, but I figure God doesn't really care what we use."

This was a first for me; though I served Communion at church on Sunday, I wasn't used to flexing my religious muscles in front of the youth group. After two years in the job, I'd actually warmed up to the spiritual-not-religious culture of the group. Glancing at a few of the advisors, I got some encouraging smiles.

Well, when in Rome. Or rather, South Dakota.

I took my place next to Clint, a Lakota here on Pine Ridge Reservation. He handed me a bag of potato chips and looked at me expectantly.

"You're up, Pastor."

I fought the urge to say, "I prefer just Amanda, thanks." To me, *Pastor* sounded like an evangelical Bible thumper from down South. Not that there was much chance of mistaking me for that. I couldn't even remember the *exact* words for the Communion liturgy. No matter; they seemed too formal for this outdoor setting anyway—atop a small hill where Clint had just told us about the massacre that happened here at Wounded Knee, finally and gruesomely ending the decades-long war between the United States and the Plains Indians. Looking out at prairie grass swaying gently in the April breeze, it was hard to imagine such violence in this peaceful setting, but Clint's words had painted a vivid picture, and I was grateful that he'd suggested a ritual to mark the end of this meaningful moment. I wasn't surprised that our Indian guide was Christian—we had our overzealous forefathers to thank for that—but the liberal New Englander in me felt slightly uncomfortable that our ritual was more Christian than Native.

When in South Dakota! I reminded myself.

I looked around the circle, at the thirty teenagers and six advisors who were here with me on a weeklong service trip, and took a deep breath.

"History is full of broken bodies, and spilled blood, as we've just heard, and at times life can seem pretty dark. But the darkness never has the last word. Here, in this sacred, quiet place, let's thank God for the sun, and remember the gift that is life itself and the blessings it holds."

Then, one by one, the kids and advisors walked over to where I stood.

"The bread of life," I said to each one, as they took a chip from the bag.

Crunch.

"And this is the cup of blessing," I said, as they downed a swig of juice that Clint had poured in tiny plastic cups.

Ordinarily our kids were rambunctious and chatty, but now it was like a cloud of calm had enveloped us, as each one chewed a chip, lost in her or his own thoughts, quiet and pensive. That's what I love about rituals; how a song, a prayer, a grace has the power to bring us into the moment. Six years earlier, when I stood onstage singing "Amazing Grace" and felt right about being a minister, I couldn't have imagined this scene, feeding holy potato chips to a bunch of teenagers at Wounded Knee, but it was the sort of meaningful moment that made me grateful for my call.

"Excuse me . . ." I heard a young voice pipe up, and I noticed that one of the freshman boys had raised his hand. George was a mellow, good-hearted kid, though we were never quite sure if he was paying attention.

"Yes?" Clint asked. "Do you have a question?"

"It's not really a question, more of a statement," George explained.

"Let's hear it."

"I'm a descendent of General Custer, and I just want to say . . ." he paused, and I cringed, wondering where George was going with this. We'd all heard of Custer, one of the most notorious anti-Indian fighters on behalf of the U.S. government, and I wished George hadn't picked this moment to reveal his genealogy. While our youth group had many things going for it, diversity was not one; with only a few exceptions we were all shades of white, a reflection of the town where the church was too. And in this moment, guests on a reservation, witnesses to the retelling of a painful piece of U.S. history, our whiteness felt particularly obvious. But I reminded myself these were just kids, trying to process this experience in their own way.

Thankfully, George found his words: "I know it wasn't my fault, the awful stuff that happened here. But on behalf of my family I'd still like to say I'm sorry."

"Thank you," Clint said simply.

And the rest of us breathed a collective sigh of relief.

Apparently George had been listening after all. It wasn't much, one tiny truth, a simple "sorry," a mere footnote in a big, complicated story, but isn't that how life works? When we take the time to truly listen to someone else's story, no matter how messy or different from our own, it can tap into our soul, inspire us to share our own truth. In that way, tiny truth by tiny truth, each speaking the words that come from our heart, our world has the power to change.

The simple truth I remembered on the reservation, after Communion, after George's "I'm sorry," after picking up trash alongside the highway, after cooking dinner for forty people, was as unexpected as it was welcome: how good it feels to laugh.

The exact moment I laughed so hard I cried, I was playing a made-up game with the advisors after dinner. From the outside it looked pretty silly—at least that's what the kids seemed to think when they peeked in the kitchen to see what all the commotion was about. But let me tell you, that April, I was long overdue and so very ready for a good laugh that the ingredients weren't so important as the result: a belly-aching, pee-in-your-pants strand of laughter that felt like sun on the face after days of gray. I hadn't realized how much I missed the sound, the *feel* of letting go and laughing so hard it almost hurts.

It doesn't really matter *what* makes you laugh so hard you cry, only that you do, that at least some of the people in your circle are the sort who take the ordinary and turn it into the hilarious. I can count on one hand the number of very funny people I know—I'm always wishing I knew more—but the ones I know are like gold to me; a few hours in their company lifts me up and carries me outside myself, as if I'm looking down on life—and in those moments, everything seems like an easier, happier version of itself.

At the end of the week, on Saturday before our evening flight out of Denver, we stopped at the Coors Brewing factory. This wasn't the most traditional layover for a church youth group, but then again, we weren't that traditional. The advisors had suggested a brewery tour and, after a few days' moral dilemma (*Can I really take an underage church group to a brewery?*) I decided to look on it as an edifying encounter for the kids. Chances were that most of them would drink beer one day, so wasn't it a responsible thing to know how your drink traveled from field to can? What's more, our spiritual ancestors, the Pilgrims, had crossed the Atlantic quenching their thirst with beer (it survived the journey better than water). So yes, this would be an enlightening, spiritually relevant experience. Sort of. At least it would make the advisors happy, all of who had used up a week's vacation to chaperone this trip, and to whom I was personally indebted for helping me find my lost laugh.

After the tour, the advisors stayed inside for their free (small) sample while I waited outside the factory with thirty very well-behaved kids who joked and laughed and enjoyed the camaraderie that had developed over the week away. As I surveyed the scene from a nearby bench, I felt like a very contented mother hen, surrounded by her chicks, and when the advisors came back I broke into a big smile; my temporary "family" was truly complete.

We arrived home on a red-eye early that Sunday morning, and after just a few hours of sleep, I got up to go to church with Luke. It was a rare Sunday morning that neither of us had to work, so we walked to a church just a few blocks from our condo. Most towns in New England have at least one Congregational church that's probably been around for a couple hundred years, and this was our neighborhood "local." Although church was something Luke and I had shared in the beginning of our relationship, once we both became ministers, there was "his church" and "her church," and we rarely went together. When we did, it usually felt like such a treat to sit beside each other, but this morning as I sat beside Luke—handsome as always in a button-down and khakis—instead of feeling relief that my big work trip was over, that I was back home with my husband, I felt like something was missing. Where all of that energy and laughter had been, now things felt quiet and serious, and not just because we were in church. As we stood up to sing the first hymn, I closed my eyes for a moment, but a tear or two still found a way to escape. And I felt a long way from laughter.

✳　✳　✳

In May, a few weeks after South Dakota, the funniest advisor in the group, a brown-haired engineer named Colin, hosted a dinner party. In my senior year of college, dinner parties had been my great love, but that was the last time I'd had a nearby group of friends who I could sit around a table and laugh with. Now I had a chance to experience that again, and after our week out West, I knew the evening would be full of the fun and lightness I was craving in my everyday life. This time, instead of saying, "No, thanks," as I usually did when the advisors invited me out, I said, "Yes, please!"

Luke had been invited too.

"But you don't *have* to come," I said, when I told him about the invitation earlier in the week.

"Let me play it by ear and see how much work I have."

This was the answer I'd anticipated. I often felt nervous telling Luke about social invitations and anticipated his reluctance. I had the distinct impression that hanging out with my friends, or sometimes even my family, felt like "work" to him, not particularly enjoyable or relaxing, and I didn't want to saddle him with another source of stress.

Sometimes, though, I wished he'd just say, "Yes, please!" when I asked if he was free for dinner with so-and-so. Easy as pie. Not that I ever said this to him. By now I was a pro at keeping many (most) of my big feelings to myself, hugging them close to my chest like a running back headed for the end zone with her ball. I'd forgotten, if ever I'd known, how to let go of the load I was carrying and pass it to my teammate, so that he could understand something of my frustration. And now my comfort zone, of not talking about my feelings, of being the easygoing one, was starting to feel less comfortable.

But I didn't know where to begin, and I didn't want to hurt Luke's feelings. Or lose control of my emotions. So I stayed stuck in the role of the emotionally withdrawn, silent one.

Not Luke; he let his words fly. I was used to catching his passes, not without a bit of fumbling, but usually in the end, I positioned myself in such a way that his words didn't knock me over. But that Saturday afternoon, before Colin's party, I was completely blindsided by the fury behind his pass.

"Do you want to come tonight?" I asked.

"Where?"

"The dinner party my advisor friends are having. Remember? I told you about it earlier this week, and you said you might come, if you didn't have too much studying to do."

(Luke had left his job as a minister the year before and was back in school getting another master's.)

"I totally forgot. That's tonight?"

"It is, and I told my friends you might come, but you don't have to."

"But I thought we were going to hang out tonight. It's been a busy week, and I don't feel like we got to see much of each other."

"Well, I said I'd go."

"But it's Saturday night, and we haven't spent much time together recently, and you're choosing to hang out with your work friends instead of me?"

"You could come too."

"But I don't want to come; that feels like work to me." His voice was getting louder.

I stood there, unsure what else to say.

"Geez, Amanda. Sometimes you're *so* insensitive. I mean, I am miserable here. I'm in the midst of finals. I don't know what I'm going to do for a summer internship. I don't know what to do after graduation."

He was really screaming now.

"And you just breeze in here and say, 'I'm going out tonight. Without you.' As if you don't even care what I'm going through."

To which I *should* have replied:

"What the fuck? Your reaction to this party is completely over-the-top. It's just dinner! In fact, your reaction to life is completely over-the top. Lighten up! Come to dinner with me. Or don't. I don't give a shit, but this is the first dinner party I've been invited to in years, and I intend to go and have fun."

Alas, this was not a breakthrough moment for me, and what I actually said was something more like:

"I'm going because I said I would, and because I want to, but what if I leave by nine o'clock? That way we can still spend part of the night together."

"It's your call," Luke said, throwing his hands up in disgust. "Just do whatever you want, Amanda."

We didn't talk for the rest of the afternoon.

What I *wanted* was to back out of the room, out of the house, and not return at nine, or any time later that night. What I wanted was a husband who didn't scream at me as if I were a heartless idiot. It felt as if I'd been slapped with words, and part of me wanted to disappear into a deep sleep, and another part of me wanted to run away, but no part of me wanted to talk back to my husband.

That evening as I got dressed while Luke studied in the next room, I felt as if I were doing something wrong, as if I were a teenager sneaking out to a party. Putting on a new blue-and-white-checked button-down from J. Crew, jeans, and a pair of open-toed navy sandals, with a heel (this was really dressing up for me), I realized that it had been forever since I'd made an effort to look nice for friends, and it felt *good*, which made me feel even more wrong for going out. A few years ago I would have been content to stay home with Luke, wait until he was done studying, and then watch a movie and eat pizza. But now that I remembered how good it felt to laugh, and had friends who made it happen, I wanted more.

Halfway to the dinner, alone in the car, I called Emily. Even as I felt disloyal to Luke, I told her about the scene. I knew his outburst was out of character and not his finest moment. I also knew that he was trying to figure out his life as best he could, and that my approach didn't make things any easier for him. But I was scared and thrown, and I couldn't hold it in any longer.

"Manda, that's not right," she said. She knew that Luke wasn't as easygoing as our family—when she poked fun at him in a good-natured way, he didn't think it was funny, and I asked her to stop; and the previous Thanksgiving she'd felt unwelcome in our house because Luke was studying and said she was being too loud. But she had never seen this angry side to him.

Part of me was relieved that Emily was taking this story seriously. It meant my own feelings weren't an overreaction, but it also made me realize something had to change. This outburst hadn't been the first. A few months before, Luke had picked me up at the airport after a delayed flight and screamed on the drive home, angry that I'd taken him away from studying instead of offering to take a cab home. At the time I'd been so shocked by the intensity of his reaction that I'd assumed it was a one-off, and I hadn't told anyone.

Until now.

I peeked at myself in the mirror before getting out of the car. My eyes were less red now, and I applied a quick bit of eyeliner before walking up to the front door.

Colin answered my knock, a beer in hand.

"You came!" a chorus of voices cried out as I walked into the living room, and it felt so nice to be appreciated.

"You look so pretty," Jen said. "And I like your heels. Fancy!" I smiled on the outside, but inside I felt all torn up. What would my friends say if they knew the scene I'd left behind? Of course I wouldn't tell them—I *was* starting to think of them as friends, but I was still the minister, and they were still the advisors, and it felt like too great a confidence to share. Even so, it felt as if I had a secret life, not the sort that makes you blush happily as you remember what the two of you did last night, but the sort that feels somewhat shameful and embarrassing.

Was I really the sort of wife who just stood there and took it? Allowing her husband to scream at her, and then promising to come home early?

When the clock struck nine, and I stood up, I was met with, "Nooo! Don't leave yet. We haven't even eaten," from Jen.

"I have a husband waiting at home," I offered by way of explanation. Outside I tried to start my car, only to realize I'd left the headlights on, and the battery was dead. Waiting for Colin to give me a jumpstart, I called Luke, feeling as if I were making up an excuse for my lateness even though it was the truth.

As I finally drove home, I remembered a recent conversation in our kitchen, sitting on barstools pulled up to the counter, overlooking our tiny backyard through a big picture window. Luke was in an amazing Master's program at Harvard, but he worried about what he might do after he graduated in a year.

"I want a wife who hears that I'm worried, and can say something like, 'Let's pray together. I know that this is hard, but you're a wonderful man, and I have faith that God is with you. And it will work out. And I'm willing to go wherever God leads, whether it's Cleveland or Africa or DC.'"

Inwardly I cringed. Spontaneous prayer with my husband, or anyone else, was so not me. And we both knew it.

Still, I felt like a callous wife. What sort of a minister-wife was so self-conscious, so spiritual-but-not-religious, that she wouldn't offer to soothe her troubled husband with a prayer? Well, me, as it turns out; and I wouldn't have blamed Luke if he offered his own inward cringe at that. Were we really so far apart in what we wanted from each other? Because I did *not* want to sit there with uncomfortable feelings swirling about us, praying or not, and "just be" in this painful moment that seemed to weigh both of us down.

Maybe I should have prayed.

Though it might not have come out the way Luke wanted.

Oh my dear GOD! I'd shout.

I know that life has its hard moments, but here we are— young, healthy, with so much that's good in our lives. Please help my wonderful husband to lighten up and forget about the hard stuff for a while. L'chaim!

But sharing this with Luke would only have seemed insensitive and would have led to more conversation about how I didn't get it, how I just wanted things to be easy, but life *is* hard. So that afternoon in the kitchen I'd swallowed my words and just listened, and I felt myself fading away.

Which is pretty much the same thing I did when I got home from the dinner-less dinner party, to find Luke watching TV, and in a better mood. He apologized for his outburst, and even though I still felt unsettled inside, I chose not to talk about it. I'd faced enough emotion for one night, so I sat down next to him on the blue couch and ate some pizza and watched something until I got sleepy, and then I carried myself off to bed. It was a quiet end to a dramatic night, and as I fell asleep, I wished I'd stayed at the party.

✳ ✳ ✳

A few days later my mother-in-law called as I was pulling into the church parking lot. I hadn't talked to her recently, but Luke must have said something about the tension that was building.

"Amanda. My dear. I know that Luke is going through a tough time," she began.

This was a first. She'd never called to talk to me about her son. Though we saw one another with some frequency, we rarely talked on the phone, and never about Luke.

"He is," I agreed. "I had hoped things would feel easier when he left the church, but . . ." I left my sentence dangling.

"I know the transition from church back to school hasn't been easy for him. And I know that he's not sure what he wants to do after school. But I also know that you're such a great support for him. He's blessed to have you."

"Thanks," I said, glad for her encouragement.

"I'm sure it's not easy for you either, but please don't give up on him," she added.

"I'm trying not to," was all I could muster.

My mother-in-law was one of the blessings of my marriage. I remembered how happy she'd been the day we got engaged; she cried good tears, pulled a bottle of champagne out of the fridge, and made us a beautiful dinner in her lake house across the water from the mountaintop where I'd just said "Yes!" I looked up to her, admired her elegant style, her gracious way of entertaining, and how she had persevered after Luke's dad died, found new love, and remarried. Like a fairy godmother, she sparkled; she bought me pretty things that I couldn't afford for myself, took us to nice dinners, opened up her house to us, and really listened to Luke without judgment. Which wasn't always easy to do, as I was learning. But even my fairy godmother-in-law couldn't fix this, no matter how many supportive words she said.

"Don't give up on him," she'd said over the phone. Could she sense that a change was coming? Could she hear the tiredness in my voice? Could she guess that I was worn out by this version of reality? The one in which her son and I were acting out the most extreme sides of our personalities, Luke with his outbursts, and me with my silence, far from the best of us?

I wish someone could wave a wand and make life feel right again, I thought to myself as I crossed the parking lot, opened the door to the church, and stepped inside, grateful that I didn't have to think about my marriage for the next few hours. I might not have loved my job, but at times like this it provided a welcome distraction.

As it turned out, someone *could* make life feel right again.

Ever so slowly, like a chick pecking her way out of an egg, I would start to see how I was that someone. I didn't have a wand, but I had a heart, and a great joy for life buried beneath the layers of heaviness that had built up over the last few years, and I would uncover that delight again. I would reach out over and over to life, remembering lost loves (like laughing and dinner parties), and discovering new ones; reconnecting with old friends, making new ones too, and peck by peck by peck, I would, in essence, be born again, not in a religious sense—although I do believe Native American lady God was rooting for me—but in a holistic one. I would make my whole life feel right again, remember who I was, and save myself.

✳ ✳ ✳

As spring turned to summer and the pace of church life slowed down again, I called up Kelley, my best friend since college, the definition of grounded and wise, and also one of the kindest people I knew, because I needed her to kindly tell me the truth. We made a plan to meet in a Starbucks halfway between her house in New Hampshire and mine, and as soon as we sat down, I cut right to the chase.

"Do you think I'm different than I used to be?" I asked my friend of twelve years.

"Yes," she said, without a moment's hesitation, as if she'd been waiting for me to wake up and ask the question already. In her gentle but honest way, she continued without my asking.

"You used to be fun, spontaneous, adventurous," she recalled. "But now you're more serious and it's harder to talk to you. I know that people change as they grow up, but sometimes I wonder if this is *really* you, or just an approach you've taken because you're a minister, or because you're married to Luke.

"You used to say that Luke thought life was hard. But now it seems like you have that approach to life too; there's a lightness, a sense of joy, that's missing. And the worst is that now when I talk to you, sometimes it feels like I'm talking to a minister or therapist, not my best friend. As if you're evaluating what I'm saying, and weighing how you *should* respond, instead of just being there for me."

She paused.

"Like this winter . . ." she began.

I knew where she was going with this.

Earlier in the year Kelley had been going through some hard times, and she'd asked if she could drive down and talk to me about it.

I pictured the way that day should have gone—two old friends curled up on my blue couch, a fire crackling in the hearth beside us as we drank hot chocolate from mugs we used in college, and Kelley shared what was going on, how she was having trouble getting pregnant, and I asked a few thoughtful questions, but mostly I just listened, and sympathized, and gave her a big hug at the end. And then Luke and I took her out to dinner at the pub across the street.

But it didn't happen like that.

In reality we sat in armchairs across from each other instead of on the couch. The hearth was cold, and I just listened while Kelley talked, not sharing any thoughts or reactions of my own. At the time I couldn't find the right words, but instead of admitting that, I just said, "Hmm," and "That must be hard for you."

And then she left. No pub dinner across the street. No chummy hug from my husband. Luke poked his head in to say hello, then disappeared into the spare bedroom and closed the door to study. It wasn't that Kelley expected him to hang out with us, but something about the brief exchange and the closed door made her feel as if she were intruding upon our lives instead of being a part of them. It was the exact same language my sister had used after staying with us for Thanksgiving.

Our condo was pretty, and bright, and full of personal touches—my grandmother's dining table, the patchwork quilt I'd stitched after college, pictures from our travels. There were flowers on the rustic wooden coffee table, and everything was in place. "Like a house that might be featured in a magazine," Kelley had said during her visit, and though she was being generous, I accepted her praise; like Martha Stewart, if she was a minister on limited means, I had put lots of time and energy into making our house look just right.

But what does it matter how your house looks if your best friend and your sister don't feel welcome in it?

Sitting in Starbucks that spring day, I felt ashamed that I hadn't been there—I mean, really been there—when my friend needed me. I didn't like this more serious, less genuine version of me that she was describing. But I knew she was right.

"Remember our dinner parties in college?" Kelley smiled over at me, and I couldn't help but smile back.

"You made those parties happen, and those are some of my best memories."

"Mine too."

"You were so welcoming and loved having people over. It seems like you've lost that spark, and I miss that part of you. I miss the old you."

Like a researcher collecting data, I polled others in the next few weeks. Did they think I had changed too? Did they miss the old me?

"Yes," said Molly, our other college roommate.

"Yes," said Emily.

"Yes," said my mother too.

It wasn't a particularly large sample size, but the findings were unanimous. I had turned into a more serious (less enjoyable) version of myself. Which *would* have been okay if I was happy with whom I'd become. But I wasn't. When Kelley said she missed the old me, something within me started to stir—a piece of my spirit, perhaps? As if I were a bear waking up from her long winter's slumber. I didn't know exactly what this sensation meant for my life going forward, but I knew that it felt familiar, and right, and that I didn't want to fall asleep again.

✳   ✳   ✳

It's been my experience that when you're on the lookout for inspiration, clarity, or a way forward, a part of you that's ordinarily at rest perks up, as if the barista has slipped an extra shot in your latte and you're particularly awake to the world around you. Suddenly it seems like the lyrics in that song, or the snippet of that poem, or the line in that film were *meant* for you. When you're open to it, what you're looking for finds you. Sometimes in surprising places.

Like, perhaps, a bathroom.

Emily, now four years out of college, had recently bought a pretty little one-bedroom condo in Cambridge, just outside of

Harvard Square, and as I sat in her purple bathroom one June day, I noticed a book on the radiator across from me. I come from a long line of bathroom readers, so it wasn't surprising to find reading material in the water closet; what *was* surprising was that I'd never noticed this particular book before: *Jane Austen's Guide to Dating*. In the past few years I'd read my way through all of Jane's books, watched the film versions, and even dragged my parents and Luke to visit her country house on a trip to England.

How had I missed this little gem?

As soon as I opened the book, I discovered that Jane hadn't *actually* written the dating guide (oh, right) but its British author had used quotations from Jane's novels to inspire her common-sense handbook for the modern singleton looking for "the right one." Flipping to a section about finding your mate, a sentence jumped out at me: "Look for someone who brings out the best in you."

Huh, I thought to myself. *Does Luke bring out the best in me?*

I reached around the corner to the hall table for a pen, and then from my seat on the commode, I started to make my list, but I didn't get very far. Actually, I didn't get anywhere. With pen poised above paper, I thought and thought about what was "best" in me, but I couldn't come up with anything. Not one thing. Maybe I was having a particularly down day? Or year? I was so used to thinking about what I could do better—like communicate openly with Luke, or improve at sex, or learn to like my job more—that I hadn't spent any time thinking about what was *already* good in me. It felt rather lame that I'd turned into somebody who didn't think very highly of herself. What would Jane Austen have to say about that? She who dreamed up headstrong heroines who spoke their mind when it came to matters of the heart?

I didn't get very far on my list, but a seed had been planted in that water-closet session, and now I was determined to follow through with it; if I couldn't come up with a list by myself, I would recruit helpers. Though I felt a little shy about it, I emailed Kelley, Molly, Emily, Silas, and a few other close friends, and I asked them to basically say nice things about me. It might sound like a vain thing to do, but I assure you, it was just the opposite. My connection to Luke felt as if it was going down the drain, and I didn't know how to make it right. What I was starting to realize, however, was that I had to get myself to a stronger place before I could fix anything to do with our relationship. So with a little bit of gumption, and a whole lot of self-consciousness, I emailed my nearest and dearest to ask, *What do you think is "the best" in me?* And then I took a deep breath and hit send.

I'd always been better at giving than receiving. Advice, presents, compliments, you name it; I was happy to give it. But graciously receiving? Or asking for what I needed? This had never come easily to me, especially not in the last few years. The feeling of depletion had hit home earlier that spring when I had a breakthrough massage at a women's retreat in Asheville. (Well, not as much of a breakthrough massage as the ones that allowed me to have sex, but a very close second.) Halfway through my hour on the table, the therapist, Grace, began to massage my lower belly, just below the navel, the part of my body about which I'm most self-conscious; it's always been softer than I wish it would be, even when I'm at my thinnest, and pale too, sort of like a chunk of dough. I held my breath as Grace began to knead.

"It feels like you're holding on to something," she said.

I let her statement soak in.

Was I?

"It's okay to let go."

And just like that, something within me cracked open. I could almost hear it cry out. What was it? My heart? Soul? It was a part of me that I'd silenced over and over again, until I was a far cry from the fun, spontaneous best friend and big sister that I once was.

I started to weep, silent tears that seemed to come from nowhere, but I knew deep down that I'd been holding them back for a while now.

"I'm a minister," I said, as the tears ran down my cheeks and slipped along my neck. It seemed like a strange thing to say, but that's what came to mind.

"Well then, of course you're holding on to something," Grace said reassuringly. "You're holding on to lots of other people, and all of their problems. That's a lot to carry."

I nodded yes.

"Take a deep breath," Grace suggested.

I took a little one, too self-conscious to breathe loudly even though it was just the two of us.

"Here, follow me," she offered, sensing my hesitation, and she inhaled deeply, then blew it out.

And so I did the same, following her lead. In and out. In and out. Even as I did it I thought, *This is so not like me, to be sighing and weeping on a massage table. I'm the strong one, the balanced one. I don't lose control. I don't break down. I don't get emotional.*

Yet this was very much me. More me than I had been in a long time.

In the Hindu tradition, the seven energy points in the body are called *chakras* and the second, or sacral chakra, is rooted in the lower abdomen, just below the navel. It's believed that the sacral chakra is the center of feeling and sexuality, and when it's "open," you can express your feelings (without being *overly* emotional) and intimacy too, which leads to letting go, change, and transformation.

Now here I was, three months after that massage, letting go of the idea that I was self-sufficient and calling out for backup. Friends want to help you, if they know what you need, and this was no exception. Within a few days I had eight notes describing the best in me. My friends knew what this search was about, that I was wondering how to be true to myself in the context of my marriage, but no one referred to that in their note. They simply showered me with kind words, writing such nice things I was almost embarrassed to read them. But more than that, they described me, and that's who I was looking for.

And who was I?

Every one of my friends, and my siblings too, said I was thoughtful, and I liked to think that in the last few years I hadn't lost that. They also called me adventurous and spontaneous, and nearly everyone said I was fun-loving or something like it. Kelley's fondest memory of me was how, on a sunny fall Friday in college, she came out of class and I was waiting in my red Jetta with the windows down. "Hop in!" I told her. "We're going on a picnic!" My brother remembered how I used to dress up in crazy outfits and dance around. Molly called me brave. And my childhood friend Elizabeth finished up her note with:

As one of your oldest friends, I would love to see you find your strength, your laughter, your sense of self, and whatever path is going to make you happy . . .

I held tight to Elizabeth's words—*whatever path is going to make you happy*. There wasn't any *should* there, no judgment, or pointed advice, just a simple reminder to seek out my happiness. Buried in a job that focused on helping others, married to a man who believed that life is hard, I had begun to believe that the desire for personal happiness was a selfish goal. And wouldn't you know, happiness packed up to make a home elsewhere. Now I wanted happiness and her cousins—fun, laughter, confidence— back in my life, and my friends were reminding me what a happier me looked like. I held tight to the treasures they'd offered me. Like a shell you carry home from the beach to remind you of warm summer days in the midst of winter, their words helped me remember a warmer, more vibrant me: She who is thoughtful. Adventurous. Spontaneous. Fun-loving. Brave.

I printed out all eight emails, slipping them into my journal, which I'd begun to take everywhere. I tucked the journal into my brown suede bag, a gift from my fairy godmother-in-law, and I carried the bag, holding the journal, full of the notes, around with me for the next few months, as if to say, *The best of me is within my reach.*

8. Flying Solo

Driving home from a July day at the beach, Luke made it known that the time had come.

"I'm thirty-five. I'm ready to be a dad," he declared with a sureness that evaded me. "And you're thirty. Your biological clock is ticking," he warned me.

I listened hard, but I definitely didn't hear any ticktock toward parenthood, even if I *was* thirty.

All my life I'd known I wanted to be a mother. While some love-struck girls intertwined their first name with a boy's, I kept a running list of names for my babies, and I imagined the sorts of adventures we'd have together. But now that I had arrived—married four years to a man who wanted to have children with me—*nothing* inside me yearned for children. My husband's biological clock might have been ticking, but what I heard was more like the bell that rings right before a train whooshes by: *DING-DING-DING. Stop right now before you go any farther.*

Loud and clear, rumbling from the pit of my belly (or my uterus? my second chakra?), I heard such an absence of ticktock that the only word that came to mind was no.

"Do you love me?" Luke was asking from behind the wheel, trying to figure out why I was so quiet and didn't seem to share his excitement about starting a family together.

I didn't answer right away. *Was it really true? Did I not want children with Luke? But I already had their names picked out.*

"Don't you love me?" he asked again.

"Yes, I love you. Of course I do."

"Don't you want our marriage to work?"

Well, truthfully, I wasn't sure anymore, but Luke didn't pause for an answer. He was getting agitated now.

"You need to grow up," he demanded. "Stop making a huge deal out of every decision."

"But having kids *is* a big deal." I found my voice. "Especially if I don't feel ready. Being married to you feels hard for me, and I *don't imagine* kids will make it feel any easier."

It wasn't the first time I'd expressed such a sentiment, and Luke knew it.

"My God, Amanda! You always say that I make things hard. Well, maybe that's your cross to bear. Pick it up! Marriage *is* hard work."

Marriage was my cross to bear? Was he quoting Jesus to me? Bringing in the big guns because I sounded like a broken record? This marriage felt like a broken record—spinning around and around, on the same refrain: *Life is hard. Marriage is hard. Life is hard. Marriage is hard.*

"Do you think it was easy for Coretta Scott King? Being married to Martin Luther King?" Luke asked.

I wasn't sure why we were being compared to two civil rights pioneers, but I took a stab at it.

"Well, I'm sure it wasn't easy when he died, but I have no idea *what* their married life was like. Maybe it flowed quite naturally," I offered.

"Life is hard," Luke said. Again. "And you make it even harder by holding back and not sharing anything with me. *You are my wife*, but sometimes it feels like you don't even like me.

Like you'd rather spend time with everyone else. You're cold and selfish and you over-identify with your brother and sister. Grow up!"

I hated how Luke was talking down to me. I *wanted* to shout. Scream. Something. Anything! But I felt stuck in silence like thick mud. Tongue-tied. Nicer to say nothing than hurt Luke with my words. Easier to keep quiet than own up to the truth. But I knew I had to let down my guard, say something.

I took a deep breath and pictured myself kneeling in front of the candles at Saint John's, a chapel on the Charles River where I'd prayed for inspiration a week before. Alone in the dim stone sanctuary, I'd pictured a future without Luke—an image that had surprised me *and* comforted me by how right it felt. *Now what?* I'd thought, down on my knees. Out of the silence a few words bubbled up from within, like an offering from a deep spring I hadn't known flowed inside me:

Speak the truth in love.

This sounded vaguely familiar, like a line from Emily Dickinson, or a song. (Actually, it's from the Bible, though I didn't realize that at the time.) Was it divine inspiration that planted that line in my mind? Or my own inner wisdom? Is there even a difference? Maybe it's simply enough to know, to trust, that when you quiet down, the wisdom you need will rise to the surface.

When I went back to the chapel a few days later and knelt in front of the candles again, the words that emerged out of the hush said:

The truth will set you free.

And so these two bits of wisdom became my mantra:

Speak the truth in love. The truth will set you free.

I squirmed a bit in the passenger seat next to Luke. My palms were sweaty, and I heard my heart beat. I called myself a feminist. I preached heartfelt sermons in front of a hundred people without a flutter in my belly, but put me in an emotionally charged situation like this, and I became a giant *Shh*. I closed my eyes and the mantra came back:

Speak the truth in love. The truth will set you free.

Luke was still talking. Our car was overflowing with his words, and they kept coming, hitting me at a mile a minute, while I struggled to get a hold of my own thoughts, still tucked safely inside my head.

"If you can't figure out this kid thing, I'll be married to someone else, have three children, and you'll end up forty-one, single, miserable, and regretful."

What? It was the push I needed.

Speak the truth!

"Well, I *don't* think I'll be forty-one and single," I declared to Luke. "But even if I am, I will *not* be miserable and regretful. Miserable and regretful would be having children because you think you *should*, even if you don't feel it."

Right then I knew with a sureness that usually evades me that I could not have children with Luke and, even if I wasn't ready to say it aloud yet, that our marriage would end. Two roads diverged in a wood, and one was Luke and babies, and the other was leaving my marriage. If I took the latter path, I had no idea what my life would look like ten years from now when I was forty-one. Single? Maybe. But miserable and regretful? Not on your life.

I know this isn't the decision everyone would make in my seat. Some people choose to make a go of it, to have children even though they're not feeling "just right" in their relationship; maybe they hope things will improve, or they feel pressure to make it work, or they hear the ticktock that I didn't. But I was incapable of taking that particular path.

We didn't come to any major decisions on that car ride. Even Luke had a limit to how much hardness he could handle, and eventually, exhausted by emotion, we fell silent. But on the inside I felt sure, and I didn't doubt that a more joyful life waited up ahead. I guess that's the beauty of looking your truth in the eye, and choosing to follow where it leads, unexpected though it may be. It sets you free.

✳ ✳ ✳

None of my friends, their parents, or my parents' friends were divorced. The only divorcée in my family was my mom's cousin in Idaho, and we hardly ever saw her. (Not because she was divorced, but because she lived across the country.) I realize it's unusual in this day and age that I made it to thirty without knowing many broken marriages. It wasn't that my circle was anti-divorce; it's just that everyone I knew seemed to stay married, for better or worse. They were a traditional, practical batch of New Englanders who shoveled snow in winter and planted gardens in summer, and they knew that each season had its up and downs. Divorce was something *other* people did. Only now it appeared that I was the other.

Even though it was unexpected, my family rose to the occasion when I began to voice my discontent. My dad took Luke to lunch, for the first time, and suggested that if he helped out more around the house, our marriage might improve. It was wishful thinking, but I appreciated the effort. My mom mailed me the name of a divorce lawyer, "just in case."

Once I realized that I didn't want to have children with Luke, I wished I could simply walk away, but the idea of ending our marriage was such a surprising thought to both of us that it took some time to unravel. After the conversation in the car, we went through the motions of being married for another month, which ended with our fourth anniversary. It wasn't lost on me that we had dinner alongside Luke's family at the lake house, instead of just the two of us as usual. That night we had sex for the tenth and last time. I didn't mean to keep count, but ten is an awfully small number that's easy to remember. Once I learned how, I thought we'd do it often. But maybe that was naive of me. It didn't hurt, but it didn't feel great either, and I'm sure Luke could tell. Looking back, it's easy to think that we just weren't sexually compatible, but the truth is probably more complicated. Sex doesn't exist in a vacuum. In a relationship it's part of a bigger whole, a deeper connection, a sense of trust. Maybe that bigger whole had been crumbling for a while.

The next morning, driving home from the lake, I forced myself to broach a topic that had been on my mind: my friend Becky's wedding, which was just a week away.

"So you know our trip to California?" I asked Luke.

"The one we're going on next week?"

"Yes, well, I think," I hesitated, nervous to say what I had to say. "I think I should go alone."

"But we planned it months ago. I already have a plane ticket. After Becky's wedding, my friends are expecting us in Napa."

"I feel better going to Becky's wedding alone, and then, if you want to meet up after that, with your friends in Napa, we can do that."

"Are you disinviting me to Becky's wedding?"

"I guess so. Given how things are, I just can't imagine us spending all that time together."

"I can't believe you're doing this. It feels awful, Amanda."

I didn't know what to say.

"Well, I'm not going then," Luke continued. "But what will I tell my friends? That's just awkward. And when you come back, it doesn't feel right that you come back to our house. I need some boundaries too. I think that's only fair."

"Sure, that makes sense. I'll stay with my parents or Emily."

Which was just fine with me. Our condo didn't feel like home anymore.

✳ ✳ ✳

Flying alone to San Francisco, without Luke, felt odd—it had been seven years since I'd traveled by myself—but it also felt vaguely familiar, like meeting up with an old friend you haven't seen for ages, but in whose company you still feel at home. After the wedding, in place of the trip to see Luke's friends in Napa, I made plans to drive north and visit the Redwoods. An adventure on the open road, in a national park—it seemed like the perfect way to reacquaint myself with myself.

Just a few miles into my road trip, my economy-sized rental car started to shake. I slowed down. It still shook. I sped up. It still shook. I turned around, drove back to the rental dealership, and took a seat while the clerk made his way through a long line of customers.

"You again!" he said finally. "Thanks for waiting. What's the problem?"

"My car's shaking, whether I drive fast or slow, and I'm going to be alone on quiet roads, and just don't feel comfortable alone in a shaky car."

"Right," he said. "Let me see what I have for you."

"By any chance, is that blue car available?" I asked, looking over my shoulder into the parking lot beyond, where a sporty car sat basking in the sun.

"The blue convertible?" he asked.

"That one," I smiled back at him. "Only it must cost a lot more than the car I had."

"It does. But I could probably do something about that."

And he did.

Within ten minutes, I was driving north again—this time in an unshakable blue convertible with the top down. I drove roofless for the next four days. Even when the sun set and the temperature dropped and I had to put on a bunch of layers, tie the hood under my chin to keep it from flying off, and blast the heat, I drove with the top down. I wasn't flying, but it felt like I was as I wound my way up the California coast. *And if I'm flying solo / At least I'm flying free,* I thought to myself, remembering a favorite line from a song in *Wicked.* Luke would have suggested we put the top up hours ago (most people would have), but no matter how much sense it didn't make to "fly free," riding in a topless car when it was cold out, what *did* make the most sense in the world was listening to myself. Or as the song also said: *Too late to go back to sleep. / It's time to trust my instincts. / Close my eyes and leap.*

Six hours later, I pulled into a hostel in Redwood National Park—I'd never really warmed up to hostels, since I wasn't very good at meeting people on the fly, or listening to them snore, but they were affordable, and this one was pretty too: a dark green historic homestead, nestled into the side of a hill, just across the street from a rocky beach. Early the next morning I woke up ready to go and slipped out of bed and across the street to the Pacific. The shore was covered in mist, and I hoisted myself up onto a big rock, watching the early morning drama: birds swooping into the sea, waves dancing, fog lifting. Then I closed my eyes. Traveling alone can be quiet, and sometimes lonely, but beyond that, this trip also felt like a very long second date with myself. I knew the profile: thirty, minister, married (ish), but now I was getting reacquainted with the person beyond the facts; in the absence of expectations and compromise, how did I want to live this day? It was early, I hadn't eaten breakfast yet, and who knew when I'd find food, but I didn't care. On my own terms I had an easy, adventurous spirit. I wasn't indecisive at all, as Luke suggested. I knew just what I wanted to do.

I leapt down from the rock and walked across dark sand back to the car. Zipping up my sweatshirt, tying the hood under my chin, I took my place in the driver's seat, put the top down, and flew down the road to meet some trees.

✳ ✳ ✳

When he met the redwoods for the first time, the British poet laureate John Masefield likened the trees to "spirits" and the glens in which they grew to "haunts of the gods." I descended into the haunt of the gods on a narrow dirt road, deserted since it was still early, and though I felt a bit uneasy being by myself in a dim wood, it didn't seem like there was any real reason to be afraid. There was life all around me. The redwoods are the tallest living beings in the world. In city terms, they are thirty-seven stories high and grow quite quickly (for something so tall), and they live a long time too: five hundred years on average, though some are much older. Driving alongside these giants, getting out to touch their old skin, which felt surprisingly soft, I wondered at the poem Emily Dickinson might write if this orchard had been her dome. Inside the forest, light was subdued, not unlike being inside an old stone cathedral, and sunbeams streamed in through chinks in the branches as through stained glass. But this glen occupied a different realm of sacred than church; it was holy in a lush, green, wild way.

Anyone who has tipped her head back to gaze toward the top of a very tall tree, or peered into a grand canyon or across a wide sea to an invisible shore, knows this transcendent feeling. It's humbling and, I think, healthy to spend time in the company of things so much vaster and older than we'll ever be. Everyday concerns take a backseat to the moment right in front of us. There's nothing to do. Or say. Just look. With wonder. Take a step closer. The trees, canyon, and sea whisper their wisdom. Do you hear it? *Hush. Don't worry. This too shall pass. But we'll still be here.* And for just a moment you're part of their story.

After I emerged from the glen, I kept driving. According to my map, Crater Lake National Park was *only* four hours north, across the state line and into Oregon; though it wasn't part of my original plan, I couldn't pass up a chance to see the deepest lake in the country. In pictures it was an unreal cerulean blue, like the color a child paints the sea, only we adults know water's not *actually* that vibrant in real life. Except in this case, it is. Because the water in Crater Lake is so clear, it absorbs all the colors of the sun's rays except the blues, which bounce back, and that, along with the vast depth, give the water its unbelievable color. The bluest lake had been on my "to see" list since college, and last year I'd missed a chance when Luke and I were in Portland, but decided the park was too far a drive. (Well, not too far for me, but I wasn't traveling solo then.)

Late that afternoon, standing on a cliff looking into the deepest lake I'd ever seen, I realized that sometimes real life actually *is* as bright as it appears in pictures. I balanced my camera on a rock and set the timer to take a picture of myself in front of the deepest blue. The picture came out crooked, and I'm squatting to fit into the viewfinder, but there's nothing crooked or compressed about my big smile.

✳ ✳ ✳

Luke would love it here was my first thought the next afternoon as I unlocked the door to a spacious wood-paneled hotel room overlooking the sea. A fire was going, classical music was playing from somewhere, and a white robe was folded on top of a crisp white comforter. I felt slightly guilty for enjoying myself when I knew Luke was at home and upset. Well, I didn't know exactly what he was feeling; we hadn't talked in the week I'd been away, but upset was how I'd left him. Back home I had to deal with all of *that*. Luke's feelings. When to move out. And where to live. But sometimes, I've discovered, it's wisest to stop thinking about the things that upset you, especially when you can't do anything in the moment to fix them, and just enjoy where you are. It was a romantic setting here in Mendocino, and after driving eight hours down from Crater Lake, the robe and bed were calling to me like an enticing lover. So I slipped out of my clothes and sank under the comforter until dinnertime.

If I could offer three words of advice on dining out alone, they would be *Just do it*. There's something liberating about finding the courage to sit alone at a bar or table, with just a book or phone for company. Or, if you're really daring, no book or phone at all. But this was my first time eating solo in a restaurant in years, and I was just getting my courage back, so I brought a book. My dinner arrived, and I tried to keep my paperback open with my left hand while I ate with my right, but I soon gave up and put the book down. I took a sip of wine. A bite of greens that came from the garden out back. Without the distraction of my book, I felt a bit self-conscious. Was everyone looking at me? The only one sitting alone on this late summer evening. A surreptitious glance around the dining room revealed that no one seemed to care.

My eyes were drawn to a family of four sitting a few tables away, laughing and enjoying their meal together.

Someday I'd like to be part of a family like that, I thought.

The wish gladdened my heart; in recent months I'd become so focused on *not* having children that I was surprised to notice the desire was still there, peeking out from a corner of my heart. "No rush," it seemed to say. "Now isn't the time. But I'm waiting for you up ahead."

After dinner I wandered into the inn's boutique. While absentmindedly scrolling through a rack of cards, I found one that said:

I dwell in Possibility—
—Emily Dickinson

I'd never met this piece of poem before, but like a moth to light, it flew straight to my heart and stuck. That night I made a decision to dwell in Possibility.

Just before I flew home, I had one more stop. Back in San Francisco I met my second cousin for lunch. Our parents had grown up together in Ohio, but we'd only met a few times. Annie was in her mid-forties and arrived with a toddler in tow: a round cherubic babe with wild blond curls. Just a few years earlier, forty-one and single, Annie decided she wanted to be a mom, so she leapt alone—she had her eggs checked out (healthy) and selected a sperm donor (handsome), but when the first attempt at artificial insemination didn't take, her doctor suggested she wait six weeks before trying again. During the break, her friend invited her to a speed-dating event. And though she wasn't focused on meeting someone (she was focused on creating someone), Annie went to please her friend, and, of course, when she was least expecting it, she met her future husband.

After lunch I watched my cousin push her daughter on the swing, and even though I couldn't see the details of my future—like what my life might look like at forty-one—I dwelled in Possibility. I pictured a life as bright as the blue a child colors the sea. "But water isn't that bright in real life," the doubter might say. Only, it is. When it runs clear and deep, water is the brightest blue. And so too, I believe, is the human spirit; when we let ourselves be clearly, deeply our truest selves, we can reflect unimaginable brightness back to the world.

✳ ✳ ✳

Back home from California, I went down to the river to pray. I hadn't seen Luke in almost a month. Our recent phone conversation had been heavy and emotional, but at least we'd come to an agreement that it would be uncomfortable to go back to living together; one of us had to move out, and I was glad when he said he didn't have time to look for a new place. I'd already pictured myself living in Cambridge. Now I had a few more days of summer vacation before the church year and youth group started back up, and I needed to get my thoughts in order.

Sometimes prayer is all about listening, like when I went to the stone chapel and heard *Speak the truth in love.* But today I knew exactly what I wanted to say to God. I sat down on the bank of the Charles, just across from the stone chapel, with a pen and a blank piece of paper, and I remembered an exercise from the women's retreat in Asheville, the same one with the incredible massage. The task: to write a list of things for which you're "grateful in advance." Say you're looking for a new house; you might write: "I'm grateful for my cozy house—light streaming in the windows; plenty of room for my friends; a big kitchen with a long table." The thinking behind the exercise is that if you can identify what you want and imagine how good it will feel when it happens, your reality is more likely to follow your thoughts. Skeptics might say it sounds like wishful thinking. Which it is. But it works. Positive thinking, intentionally choosing to steer your thoughts in a certain direction, is a pretty powerful practice—I can attest to that now—but even when it was all hearsay, I was willing to give it a try. Six months earlier, on the retreat, I didn't have much to put on my "grateful in advance" list. I wasn't very practiced at dreaming, and I felt guilty asking for what I wanted. Today it was a different story. I was full of dreams, and learning how to ask for what I wanted.

I picked up my pen and stared at the blank page, picturing myself five years from now, when I'd be almost thirty-six, and I started writing:

Dear God!
Hear my prayer! Here it is!
Five years from now, I live in Cambridge in a
townhouse on Hilliard Street.

Hilliard was a three-minute walk from where I was sitting and home to a block of pretty brown townhouses I'd always admired. I didn't realize at the time that each cost upward of a million dollars. Details! I was dreaming up a big picture. As I kept writing, the words began to flow:

I live with a husband who loves life, and he loves his
job, and he loves me.

I didn't picture what he looked like, or what he did for work or fun; I just pictured the ease with which he greeted life, and me, and I felt calmer already. This was the sort of man with whom I could imagine having a family. And so I wrote:

> *We have a child, just one at this point, and we have*
> *our friends over to dinner. We both love company,*
> *and I don't get stressed out entertaining or keeping a*
> *perfect house.*

As if life could get any better than that! But it could, and I let myself take my dreams further:

> *My husband and I go to church together, but I don't*
> *work in a church anymore. I have another sort of job*
> *that feels like a better fit.*

I had no idea what that new job might be, but at least I'd allowed myself to admit I wanted one. Was I done? No, there was one more thing for which I was grateful in advance. Knowing that Luke yearned for connection and a family, I pictured a better life for him too:

> *Luke is happy, married to someone else, and they have*
> *a daughter.*

It surprised me how easy it was, to wish him happiness with someone else, whomever she might be. And with a daughter of their own. I'm not sure why I picked a girl; it's just what came to me.

I signed and dated my "grateful in advance" prayer-letter, sealed it in a legal-sized envelope, and wrote God's name on the front.

Now what?

It didn't seem right to hold on to this plea to the universe. I wanted to send my dreams out into the world. Get this party started. But I also wanted to know that one day in the future, I could read my prayers again. So I put the envelope with my letter to God in an envelope to Kelley with a short note of explanation:

This might seem funny, but these are my dreams,
written as a prayer, mailed to you for safekeeping.
One day I might like to see them again, but in the
meantime, thanks for keeping an eye on them. Here's
to dreams coming true.

And I mailed my prayers to New Hampshire.

Kelley isn't particularly religious, and her husband is an atheist. The first time he saw a letter to God in her sock drawer, he had no idea what to think. But she explained, and he understood, and I knew my prayers were safe next to Kelley's socks.

To ask for what you want, to believe you deserve happiness: this seems like common sense from where I stand now, but at thirty it was a new way of thinking. As a minister I'd been trained to ask, What does God want *from* me? I forgot to ask, What does God want *for* me? I was so tuned into what I *should* be doing that I forgot to tap into what I *wanted* to be doing. I like to think that on the riverbank that day, Native American lady God watched over me as I wrote my letter, and when I was done, She raised her fist in the air and said, "You go, girl!" In fact, I like to think She says this to all our dreams, when they're uttered from a place of personal truth and beauty. For God is love beyond anything we can picture, and love is always on our side.

✳   ✳   ✳

Up ahead, nearly a year in the future, when our condo sold and I had to move out in a final way, my whole family showed up, along with our friend Matt, one of the funniest people I know. They turned what could have been a downer into a party of sorts, lightening the load, and the mood, with their jokes. Afterward we went to brunch down the street, where we toasted "the end of an era," and I wish everyone could have such a band of merry movers in moments of transition.

But before Luke and I sold the condo, before the big move,

I made a smaller move. It happened on a quiet Labor Day, when Luke was up at the lake, my family was scattered and I was alone. For two years I'd poured energy into making our home look "perfect," but what makes a home is how it feels, and in spite of the prettiness, this one felt empty. I packed up some essentials—clothes, towels, sheets, pillows, a few books, and a single mattress that I'd borrowed from my parents—and I closed the door behind me.

Though it was a familiar twenty-minute drive back to Cambridge, that day it felt very unfamiliar; I had left my husband. It was right and sad at the same time: life is beautiful and life is hard wrapped up together, like bittersweet winding its way up a tree trunk.

As I glided to a stop at the first yellow light, I noticed a funny sound coming from the back of the Jetta. *Did I forget to pack something securely?* At the next light, I wondered what was wrong with my car. It wasn't until I slowed for a third time that I remembered: there were bells in my trunk. As I came to a stop, the funny sound turned into: *Ding! Dang! Dong!*

A gift from the advisors that spring, the Tibetan prayer bells had been collecting dust on a shelf in my condo, but something had compelled me to grab them at the last minute. I'm glad I did. Now that I knew what was making that sound, I imagined each ring as a prayer, buoying me up as I drove from here to there:

Ding! Kelley says: I'm proud of you, old friend.
Ding! Molly adds: You're brave.
Ding! My mom and dad reassure me: You're doing just fine.
Ding! Emily Dickinson reminds me: Dwell in Possibility.
Ding! Dang! Dong! Emily and Silas cheer from their own apartments in Cambridge: Welcome to the neighborhood!

In the Christian tradition, all of the believers who've passed on but whose presence you can still feel in holy moments are known as the *cloud of witnesses*. This was my version of that: invisible witnesses to an unconventional sacred moment, reminding me with each bell ring: *You are not alone.*

Driving away from your marriage is not a traditional holy event, and leaving your partner is not an enviable position to find yourself in. And though I was lucky enough that I *could* leave, that doesn't mean it was easy. If there was a wall with a crack in it, I could have written a lament and stuck it between the stones. For real this time. But holy is not about picture-perfect or uncommon greatness. It is the moment you decide to leap, whether you soar or fall. It is the moment you listen to the Yes or No in your heart and chose to follow. It is the quiet waiting for clarity to arrive. It is every little step that brings you closer to the person you were always meant to be.

A red Volkswagen filled with an invisible cloud of witnesses, a single mattress, and Tibetan prayer bells ringing: From the outside, it might not look like much. But from the inside? I chose to call it holy.

✳ ✳ ✳

Seven years earlier, I'd meant my move back home with my parents to be a stopgap fix until I figured out the next Big Thing. I ended up living with them for three years until I got married and moved in with Luke. Now, just a few September days before my thirty-first birthday, I was finally moving in with myself. It felt like unfamiliar ground; I was still married, after all, and yet I would be sleeping on a single mattress on the floor of a studio apartment by myself. I didn't know where this road led, but I had a room of my own, and I hoped that in leaving one home, I would create another that felt much more like me. For this possibility, I was grateful in advance.

That night, moved in and tired out, I knelt down and rang my bells one more time.

You are not alone, they sang brightly.

Then I curled up on my single mattress on the floor, beneath the rose of Sharon that bloomed outside my new bedroom window, and fell asleep.

Part Three: Doing-Over

From this hour I ordain myself loos'd of
limits and imaginary lines.
—Walt Whitman

9. Bittersweet

A few miles inside the northernmost entrance to Yellowstone National Park, down a half-mile walk on a well-worn trail, is a stretch of swift river where a hot spring mixes with cold river water. The result is a year-round hot tub where even in the midst of January, you can strip down to your swimsuit, tiptoe across a patch of snow, and lower yourself into the steam bath. Exhale, and your warm breath turns into puffs like baby clouds that rise up and disappear into the chill. It's hot, and it's cold, both at once, and sometimes this is how life feels too: contrasting sensations swirling about together. At least that's how it felt for me, in the midst of getting divorced: relief and sadness, too, freedom and loneliness, deep joy on the heels of hurt, as if I were sinking into a hot tub in the midst of a cold snap.

After I moved out in September my relationship with Luke reached an angry crescendo on his part. There were late-night phone calls full of: "How could you do this to me? You've ruined my life. Don't you care about me? About the vows we made? You're cold. Even my family thinks so. My sister wonders if you're a lesbian." And when I didn't answer the phone, there were chains of tearful voicemails. All of which dwindled down to next to nothing by Christmastime, a stalemate of sorts in which Luke seemed to accept the inevitability of our divorce without taking any proactive steps toward it. Divorce lawyers and dividing up our stuff would come in the New Year.

But even in the midst of the bitter, and then the stalemate, I felt the sweetness of life to a degree I never had before. Ordinary interactions took on beauty, as when the sun shines on an unremarkable green leaf and suddenly it turns golden. Sitting in my car one morning, I listened to a desperate voicemail from Luke, calling me ugly words no one ever had ever used to describe me before. *She sounds nothing like me,* I thought, but still the words stung and I wished I could un-hear them. I deleted the message and got out of the car, walking across a small parking lot and into Dunkin' Donuts, where the lady behind the counter smiled at me and said, "Hi there, sweetie."

Sweetie. It was just a word from a stranger, but it felt like a giant hug. A green leaf turned golden.

On a Saturday in November I stopped wearing my wedding band. I'd noticed that Luke wasn't wearing his when we had coffee earlier that week, and for some inexplicable reason I almost giggled when I noticed, relieved that he'd gone first. "Rings are an outward and visible sign of your commitment," I said when I married couples, and no ring was its own outward and visible sign too. I hadn't mentioned my separation to anyone at church, but they'd notice that my ring was gone. I slipped off the thick platinum band, with our initials engraved inside, and laid it to rest in the bottom of my red leather jewelry box, a hand-me-down from my grandmother Sally, who'd outlived her husband by a few years, but who'd worn her rings until the end. *Will I wear another ring one day?* I wondered as I shut the box and looked down at my naked ring finger, which seemed to scream *SINGLE.* Instead of giving in to self-consciousness, I grabbed my coat and walked down the block until I came to a modest salon, where I sat down in front of a Vietnamese woman about my age. She took my hands in hers and, before painting my nails, gave me the most exquisite hand massage. Another green leaf turned golden.

My fully equipped kitchen, of marble countertops and a picture window overlooking a sweet little backyard, had turned into
a cheap galley with a mini-fridge that I never filled once I realized
it's much less satisfying to cook for one. Instead I took up with
Zagat (the restaurant guide), which carried me into uncharted
corners of Boston, with friends or alone, where I'd devour someone else's cooking (Afghan, Ethiopian, Peruvian, Polish . . .); wash
it down with my new favorite cocktail, the cosmo (courtesy of
my sister and a belated introduction to *Sex and the City*); and
then run most of it off the next autumn morning, on a trail in the
woods, under a canopy of golden leaves.

Where life had felt black-and-white, now everything was
full color, the contrast between what I'd lost and what I'd gained
growing even brighter as November turned into December. Luke
and I had never put up a Christmas tree—because we spent the
holiday with our families, we didn't need one to pile presents
under—and though I missed the symbol of the season, I never
said so. When I was growing up, the tree was a well-established
tradition in my family; we'd chop it down at a local farm, Emily
and I lobbying for a thick one, my parents opting for the scrawny
variety. Back home we'd unwrap cherished ornaments in tissue
paper, as if they were the first presents of the season—a baby
mouse nestled in a walnut-shell cradle, a tiny wooden barn with
the holy family hiding inside, miniature stockings my grandmother had knit with golden coins in the toes. Like a bejeweled
skinny lady, our scrawny tree was weighed down with treasures,
but it sparkled nonetheless by the time our family friends showed
up for the annual caroling party, where we'd traipse around the
neighborhood singing Christmas carols and then come back for
supper and mulled wine.

"Don't you want something smaller?" my dad asked, survey-
ing the plump balsam fir I'd picked out of the field, now that I was
back to tree-cutting with the family. "Your apartment is . . . cozy."

But I was already underneath the tree with an orange-handled
bow saw. After years of going without, I was going all the way. When

Silas helped carry my conquest into my apartment, we discovered it *was* a bit large for the "cozy" space, but I didn't care how squished it was; I was just so glad for everything it stood for: family, tradition, living in the moment, and getting into the spirit of things. I had a box of ornaments that I'd been collecting over the years, but now that I finally had my own tree, I decided to forgo jewels for simplicity. I wrapped the branches in sparkly white lights, then stood on a chair to add just one decoration to the top. She looked like a gingerbread angel, the details of her face and gown painted in white icing, but she was sturdier than that, made from clay, a Christmas gift a few years back from Luke's stepfather, and I'd been touched by the present because he was Jewish and the fact that he'd picked out something for our tree seemed particularly sweet. Not that we'd ever hung her. This was the clay angel's premiere. She looked as if she were flying, and in her arms she clutched a star.

I stepped down from the chair, turned off the overhead light, and plugged in the tree lights, standing back (well, as far back as I could stand in my snug room) to survey simplicity: evergreen, lights, angel. It was a bit of forest magic in my bedroom, and I promised myself that wherever I lived, whether my home was big or small, whether I spent the twenty-fifth of December there or not, I would always have a Christmas tree. I slept beside it that night, since I lived in one room, and from my bed I smelled balsam and watched the lights twinkle. It felt magical, as if I were a kid again, and I made myself a second promise: that even when I moved into a bigger house with an actual living room, I would always sleep next to my tree its first night at home.

And I have.

✳   ✳   ✳

I often wondered that season, *How can something so right for me feel so wrong for someone else?* My first Christmas without my husband had felt like a breath of fresh air, easy and free compared to negotiating the holidays together, but it was clear when we talked on the phone—we hadn't actually seen each other since that coffee in November—that Luke was in a lot of pain. He believed I'd ruined his life. He shouted this at me. But if making his life feel right again meant us being together, I couldn't do it; I couldn't save his life. I had to take care of my own. And if that sounds selfish, well, maybe that's because it was. Being selfish isn't *always* the right answer, but sometimes it is. You are, after all, the only person who wakes up to your reality every single day, and the life you wake up to will be a lot more pleasant if you choose yourself at least some, if not most, of the time.

I can still picture Luke and me parked in front of a diner a few months before we got engaged. We'd just eaten fried eggs, sunny-side up, and English muffins, but I felt like I wanted to throw it all up. Luke was half shouting, "If you don't want to get engaged, we should just break up now. I love you, but I don't want to wait around for you to make up your mind," and I was leaking tears and clenching all of my muscles, scouring my mind for the right way to respond. I hated to see the man I loved upset like this and know I was the cause—or at least, it seemed I was the cause. I wanted to be his savior, not his tormentor. But it's never our job to save someone else; we can only ever save ourselves. Looking back on it, I thought I was being generous, steady, and strong by not responding emotionally. Maybe. But I was also afraid of conflict and the hurt feelings that might result if I dared speak from the heart, if I said something like, "Maybe you should break up with me, because I can't rush my feelings."

Here's the thing I know now: feelings always move on. Yes, breakups feel bad for a time, but they're a perfectly natural part of life—the fate of most of your relationships, actually—and assuming you're somewhat well-adjusted, your feelings will eventually move on, and you will too. Don't bury your feelings inside where doubts and fears can take root and grow into something ugly. Toss your words into the light; take responsibility for what you feel and how you react, knowing that you have the strength to handle whatever follows.

Once I left my marriage, I wondered if I would feel lonely being single again and regret my decision to leave, but I didn't look back. Not once. The sureness surprised me, but it shouldn't have; that's what happens when you listen to your truth and follow. Still, as if to test my resolve for any chinks in this armor of assuredness, I curled up on my parents' couch one winter night after Christmas, when the rest of my family was out, and watched our wedding video from that steamy August day four and a half years earlier—the great crowd; my loud "I do!"; the crack of thunder. Would hearing my vows from that big day, full of promise, produce a pint-sized portion of lonely regret? I watched and waited, and waited, to feel something. But all it felt like was that I was watching someone else get married.

I remembered the bird on my shoulder, in the moments after I got engaged, chirping, "Are you sure?" But this time I didn't hear any bird. She had flown away.

✳ ✳ ✳

When a relationship ends, you suddenly have a lot more time to yourself, with no one to consult about how you spend it. I can see how this might feel intimidating, a quiet house and empty evenings where another person used to be, but I relished the gift of time that came with being single. It seemed alive with choices and possibility, and, while sometimes I enjoyed a quiet night at home—watching a movie on my laptop, trying not to spill red wine on my white bedding—for my new hobby, I picked socializing. The first time I went to the pub with the advisors, after avoiding their Monday-night ritual for two years, I felt like I was dressed in neon, my presence was such an anomaly. The bartenders greeted the twelve of them by name as they trailed in, headed for their usual table in the back, and all ordered a pint of something. I think it was the first time I'd had a drink with the advisors, but no one seemed to notice. I looked down at my empty ring finger, took a deep breath, and told them I was getting divorced. I wasn't used to sharing confidences with these people, all but one of whom were still single, but a change in life circumstance meant pushing through some of my rigid boundaries too.

After a surprised silence, Jen spoke first: "None of us really knew Luke. He seemed like a nice guy, the few times we met him, but we are *totally* on your side. Whatever you need, let us know. And besides," she added, "maybe his loss is our gain, and you'll come out with us more often."

Everyone else nodded in agreement, and then there was a pause and I took a big gulp of cider. "Hey, can someone pass the popcorn?" Dex asked, and just like that, the conversation moved on. I'd survived my first somewhat-public revelation and, true to Jen's prediction, rarely missed a Monday night after that, not least because I'd developed a bit of crush on Colin, the same brown-haired engineer who'd had the dinner party last spring. He was funny and engaging, and we lingered in the parking lot long after everyone else had left, chatting in the cold dark before slipping into our cars and driving home. This ritual happened often enough that, by the time Colin invited me to dinner, I was excited, but not too surprised.

He showed up early that Saturday night and sat perched on the edge of my new loveseat as I finished getting ready. Behind the bathroom door, while steadying my hand as I put on eyeliner, I felt that good jittery that accompanies a first date with someone you already know you like. Beyond that, my first first date in seven years felt like a gift after months of hate mail from Luke. I thought back to the last time we'd talked, on a cold wintry weekend when he was shouting at me over the phone, and I'd slipped on a patch of ice, landed on my back on the cold wet ground with my phone out of reach, and looked up at the sky through pines. *This is my life now?* I'd thought. Yes, all of this was my life: the bitter and, in comparison, the very sweet.

"So where are we going?" I asked Colin, the two of us bundled up on the sidewalk, walking toward the train. Neither of us was smooth enough to hold hands, or even link arms yet, but it felt decadent that it was just us and that we had a night to ourselves.

"We're going to a little Persian place in Beacon Hill, since I know you like to try new food, but we have plenty of time, so I thought we'd go someplace for a drink first."

Boston isn't the most romantic city, but if I had to pick a quaint and cozy corner of it in which to have my first first date in seven years, it would be Beacon Hill—a historic hilly neighborhood of narrow streets and brick townhouses with gas lamps twinkling over all of it. As we rode the train across the river from Cambridge, Colin took my hand. Half of me felt ridiculous for being this excited to hold a hand on the subway, and the other half loved that something so little felt so big. Strolling hand in hand after dinner—the word *stroll* comes from the German word *strolch*, meaning *vagabond*, one who wanders, and it certainly felt like I was wandering through a scene from someone else's beautiful life—we paused on a corner. Snowflakes sprinkled down, illuminated by the gaslight above us, clinging to our wool coats, and when we kissed it felt like we were characters in a snow globe, suspended in a perfect moment.

And then some kids walked by and laughed. *Maybe we should get a room,* I heard a voice in my head suggest, even as I marveled that this was really Amanda kissing her not-husband on a street corner. We rode the train back to Cambridge and, since Colin had parked on my street, he walked me home, still holding on to my hand, and when we arrived beneath my window, it seemed the most natural thing to invite him in. I'm fully aware that most of my peers had been doing things like this quite naturally for a decade, but it was the first time I'd ever lived in my own apartment, let alone invited a man to spend the night. There was no internal debate. No judgment. I just made the suggestion that we not kiss and tell the rest of the advisors (he agreed), and the rest just flowed.

Not in a million years did I picture myself doing something like this—sleeping with someone who was not my husband, while I was still technically married, and enjoying it. But then, I never pictured divorce either, and here I was. One by one, *shoulds* and *shouldn'ts* were falling away, like leaves on an autumn tree, and yet I didn't fall with them; I was still standing, stronger and surer than I'd felt in years. Discarding worn-out ideas about life and how I *should* be living meant I could grow into something new; I'd be made of the same essence, but I'd be a fresher version of myself, like a tree dressed in her springtime green. The most amazing thing was how organic this transformation felt; once I let go of how I thought I should be, life in all of its simple glory unfolded quite naturally.

Colin and I went on a handful of dates after his sleepover, and then we drifted back to being just friends. I never told him what a milestone this had been for me—that he was my first besides Luke; that I was so relieved everything worked; and better still, that it didn't hurt. For all he knew, I was an ordinary woman who enjoyed sex; and for the first time in my life, that's what I felt like too.

✳ ✳ ✳

Partway around Walden Pond in Concord, a mound of stones marks the spot where Thoreau's cabin stood, along with a wooden sign quoting a line from *Walden*, the book he wrote when he lived there: *I went to the woods because I wished to live deliberately, to front only the essential facts of life, and see if I could not learn what it had to teach, and not, when I came to die, discover that I had not lived.* To live, and to do so deliberately, sometimes comes easily— you feel like your best self, and life flows one inspired moment after another. But when you're in a funk and can't pull yourself out, then what? I went to the woods, on a rainy spring afternoon, when I felt more low than high, more gray than sunny, because I needed a sign that lighter days were on their way. A spiral of negative thoughts was dragging me down: I'd failed at my marriage; Luke couldn't stand me anymore; I wanted this process to be over *yesterday*, but our court date, to get divorced, was still months away. I tried talking myself out of this funk. I mean, who was I to feel so down when other people were *really* suffering? Children were hungry, women were abused, grandparents were sick. What was one failed relationship and its emotional aftermath in the face of all that? But comparing yourself to someone else is never a particularly useful strategy; it might make you feel guilty, but it rarely makes you feel *better*. So here I was, in a bright yellow raincoat, walking and crying my way around Thoreau's pond in Concord. A few years before, while walking around a different pond, I'd passed a girl on a bench talking on her phone, tears streaming down her face. It felt like such an intimate thing to witness a stranger's moment of grief, and I wanted to reach out, hand her a tissue, or give her a hug, but instead I just walked by with a silent prayer that she'd feel better soon. Today I felt like her: passing other walkers, even on this drizzly day, I imagined they were looking at me, wondering why I was crying, but I was too self-conscious to make eye contact.

It might seem like common sense for a minister to pray for God's help, but I wasn't in the habit of petitioning God for myself. Saying thank you, yes, but asking for things? My "grateful in advance" prayer-letter, sitting in Kelley's sock drawer, had been an anomaly. God and I had a cordial relationship, like with an esteemed professor who's much older, wiser, and a bit intimidating; I said, "Thank you!" often and, "Please help me," occasionally, but the rest of the time I just tried to figure out the assignment by myself, assuming God had bigger problems to attend to. Humility, though, can be its own brand of hubris: Who was I *not* to ask for help? To judge for myself what was worthy of God's consideration? That rainy afternoon, I felt so low that I let go of judgment and asked for something: *God, please send me a sign that everything is going to be okay.*

Out of the woods, and back in the car heading toward Cambridge, I was out of tears, but still dragging, on my way to dinner with my eighty-nine-year-old grandmother, Jinny, the Blonde

Bomber who'd provided shelter on my drive home from Duke. She'd just moved from her house in New York to an assisted-living apartment in Cambridge and was still chatty and cheerful in spite of this big life change. Even so, I suspected that a night in her company couldn't lift this mood. I sighed and stopped for a red light, absentmindedly staring at the pedestrians crossing in front of my car. But wait—I recognized that guy in a red jacket. I rolled down my window in spite of the rain.

"Jesse!" I hollered.

The tall figure, with a ski cap pulled tight over his head, looked up and then gave a grin of recognition.

"Hey there!" he shouted, lifting a hand in greeting and walking over to the car. Jesse was a friend of Emily's. We'd met for the first time at a party back in December, where he'd professed his love for the outdoors and suggested we go running together come springtime. I hadn't really thought of him since then, but I was glad he remembered who I was.

"It's springtime!" I announced.

"It's raining!" he announced back.

"Well, when it stops raining, can we go for that run?"

"You bet," he smiled.

I wanted to set a date right then, but I could already tell Jesse was a live-in-the-moment sort of guy who didn't plan much in advance. I was pretty sure, though, that if he said, "You bet!" he meant it. The light changed to green. Jesse reached over and gave my arm a gentle squeeze. I looked down at his big hand resting on the sleeve of my yellow raincoat, and with that very simple gesture, I felt a little bit less alone.

"See ya!" he smiled, his bright blue eyes crinkling at the corners, and he walked away.

Ingrained in my head was the belief that it was selfish to ask for what I wanted, that I should just be grateful for what I had, but now I see that's a stale way of thinking; if we don't knock, maybe the door never opens; if we don't ask, maybe we may never receive. I'd brushed by this wisdom in church—Jesus said: "Ask, and you shall receive. . . . Knock, and the door shall be opened for you"—without really applying it to my own life. Now, as I watched my tall, lanky sign from God finish crossing the street, I felt lighter already. Picturing a sunnier day and a run with a new friend, I let a familiar prayer float above me: *Thank you!*

✳   ✳   ✳

Spring turned into summer, and on a mild late-June morning, I woke up early, dressed quickly in a navy blazer, cream linen pants, and heels, and drove to the courthouse. I'd practiced this drive the day before, knew exactly where to park and where to enter, and though I'm almost always running late, that morning I was first in line when the door was unlocked. I hadn't seen Luke since November, but today we were set to meet again. Our lawyers had filed for a no-fault divorce, and because we'd reached a written agreement about dividing up our things, it was also uncontested; all that was left to mark the end of us was to stand in front of a judge this morning. If all went as planned at the hearing, she'd grant our divorce and file her judgment, and ninety days after that, the dissolution of our marriage would be official.

I was sitting by myself on a wooden bench in a spacious hall outside the courtroom when Luke arrived with his parents. In spite of all the time that had passed since we'd been in the same place at the same time, or maybe because of it, we didn't greet one another that morning. Which felt weird, but also easier. I hadn't seen my in-laws in even longer, since the previous summer, and I was surprised that they'd come too. It hadn't occurred to me to bring anyone with me today except for my lawyer, Dan, a gregarious ex-Navy officer who wore a leather jacket and made me feel like everything was no big deal (in a good way) and who, unfortunately this morning, was late. My mother-in-law, always a gracious hostess, offered a tiny glimpse of that and came over to give the brief greeting her son couldn't: "*Hello,*" "*You look well,*" "*I'm surprised your family didn't come.*" I didn't admit that my family didn't even know I was here today; worried that Luke might back out at the last minute and that the whole process would drag on endlessly, I hadn't told anyone this was The Day, and though it was a (mostly) irrational fear, not telling my family and friends felt like assurance that everything would go smoothly.

After an hour's wait, on the heels of Dan's breathless arrival, the six of us—two lawyers, two parents, and one almost-no-more-a-couple—were called into the courtroom. Taking a seat a few rows away from Luke, I tried to distract myself by listening to the cases being heard before ours. When the judge called our names, we approached the bench with our lawyers. Our eyes met once, and there was—I think—the faint trace of a smile between us, but I couldn't be sure. The judge asked a few basic questions; it took less than a minute. We were done.

Outside the courtroom, I wondered what to do. A hug seemed too familiar. But a handshake seemed too "It's been nice doing business with you," and it hadn't, really, not in the past year anyway. Since I couldn't think of anything to say that might make this feel easier or nicer, I didn't say anything. Besides, Luke was talking with his parents and lawyer, and I didn't notice any obvious movement in our direction. Now we were, finally, beyond words.

If you share children or lots of friends with your ex, for better or worse, you'll see him again; or if your parting is cordial, perhaps you'll want to grab coffee and chat somewhere up ahead. But that was the last time I saw Luke.

Standing on the front steps after it was all over, Dan gave me a big hug, turned to go, and then turned back around. "Next time," he said, "sign a prenup, just in case," and then he bounded down the steps, on to his next client, and I was standing alone with my first piece of advice as a divorcée. "Next time" seemed a long way off, but the assumption that I could begin again with someone else felt like a gulp of fresh air after the heaviness in the courthouse. Today, though, I had more immediate things to plan. Like who to tell first? On a whim I pulled out my phone.

"Deric! It's Amanda. Look out your office window."

"Um, okay, but why?"

"Can you see me?" I asked, waving up at the building in front of me.

"What are you doing down there?"

"I just got divorced, and I think I need a hug."

"Oh, wow. I didn't realize that was today."

"Well, I didn't actually tell anyone. You're the first."

"Hang on a sec. I'll be right down."

Standing on the corner, waiting for Deric, an old friend from high school in the midst of his own divorce, I felt a trio of worn-out, relieved, and a little bit giddy, like the *I made it!* after an exhausting hike. Where divorce had once sounded like someone else's reality, now it was mine, and I was grateful it had finally, officially, arrived.

"Congratulations!" Deric said, emerging on the sidewalk, and, even though he wasn't much taller than me, he wrapped me up in a giant hug. We'd lost touch for a few years while I was married, even though we lived nearby and our parents were friends from church, but one of the blessings of my solo existence was waking up old friendships. I'd worried that friends might be annoyed with me for losing touch over the years, but it turns out true friendships can weather a season or two of silence, like perennials that winter-over to bloom again in summer. I leaned into my old friend as we stood together in the sunlight, on the corner, beside the courthouse that had just given me the freedom to begin again.

10. Letting Go

It seemed that life had offered me a do-over, a second chance to try again at happiness, and I took this gift and ran with it. Or rather, ran with *him*, for to aid me in the quest to follow my heart, Mother Nature offered me one of her champions: a very tall, very fit man with a huge appetite for running or any other adventure under the sun. Or in the rain. Or on the snow. It really didn't matter, so long as it was out of doors. Jesse's level of physical activity was so legendary that when Anne, a mutual friend, learned we were dating, she proclaimed, "That's great! He's so nice." And then after a moment's thought, she added, "If you can keep up with him, you're going to be *so hot!*" I was pretty sure I'd never be as "hot" as Jesse (he was built like an aspen; I was more of a shrub), but since he was drawn to the outdoors like a fish to water, his enthusiasm was inescapable, and I was becoming a fit shrub.

After he'd crossed the street in front of my car, my rainy-day sign from the universe that lighter days were on their way, Jesse and I had gone on that springtime run together, and then another and another. We'd been running together a few times when he emailed me at work one afternoon. "Tonight!" was the subject line, which was followed by an invitation to go camping that night, which was a Wednesday, and we both had to work the next morning, but I loved that Jesse was so spontaneous. Like an extreme version of me, his in-the-momentness was refreshing after the last few years and their lack of adventure, and now the pendulum was swinging in the opposite direction. Would I go camping tonight? Was there even a question?

After work I stopped at my favorite bakery for our picnic supper: a quart of carrot soup, parsley sprinkled on top, and a hunk of rustic bread. Jesse had an old truck parked in the driveway of the house he shared with three roommates, but it didn't work (he biked to work and everywhere else), so I picked him up that evening, and we drove an hour to his friend's empty beach house on a bluff overlooking the Atlantic. The house was boarded up for the season, but we set up our tent in the backyard as close to the edge of the short cliff as we dared, and then we each draped one of my patchwork quilts around our shoulders and huddled on the edge, dipping crusty bread in lukewarm carrot soup as we listened to the waves break. The only thing missing was a bottle of wine, but Jesse didn't drink, and I was practically drunk on fresh air and freedom.

It was dark by nine o'clock, and when we settled into the tent, in separate sleeping bags and patchwork quilts, our conversation slowed down, but I could tell that neither of us was asleep yet.

"Let's play a game," I suggested, coming up with something on the spot. "I'll sing the first word of a song, and you come up with the second word. Like I'd say, 'A . . .'"

"B," sang Jesse.

And we sang the alphabet, volleying each letter back and forth like a tennis ball, and I liked that he didn't mind singing in a tent. Actually, Jesse's passion after the great outdoors was music: he was a songwriter, played guitar, and had even recorded an album. Most of his songs were deep and meandering, and I could only listen to a few before coming up for air and sunshine, but he had a beautiful voice, and tonight our singing was carefree.

"This . . ." Jesse sang. I thought for a moment.

"Land?"

"Is . . ."

"Your . . ."

"Land."

I started another one:

"The . . ."

"Hills!"

"Are."

"Alive."

"With."

"The."

"Sound."

"Of."

"Music!" I finished up. And so on. Until eventually, our spontaneous lullabies fell silent, and we said goodnight.

The next morning we got up with the sun, ran a few miles on the beach, and still made it home in time for work. It had been our first sleepover, and nothing had happened in the tent besides the singing and sleeping, but that I was in a tent at the beach, on a random Wednesday night, *that* felt like a big deal. For practical reasons, most people I knew wouldn't go for such a last-minute adventure on a weeknight, but I liked that Jesse was always looking for ways to turn the ordinary into an adventure. Time in his company meant action, not contemplation. He couldn't be more opposite from Luke when it came to talking about our relationship, or rather, not talking about it. We just did stuff together, and had easy conversation along the way, and before long our adventures were a regular part of life, and, even though we never had a conversation about the state of us, we were definitely dating. It was the best sort of "rebound" relationship, not in the sense of short-term or shallow, but in how easily it unfolded and how healing it felt, like gentle rain after oppressive heat. Now, years later, I still find evidence of the gentle rain: just the other day, I opened my copy of *Eat, Pray, Love*, the same dog-eared one I'd carried alongside my *Zagat* guide back when I was first flying solo. A scrap of brown paper fell out of the pages. In Jesse's writing it said: *You are beautiful* ☺.

The first time we slept together it felt as easy as the rest of our relationship, but there was even more. No matter how he slept, Jesse reached an arm toward me, as if to say, *Here I am.* It was just an arm, I know, but compared to all of the nights I'd spent curled up on my own side of the bed, trying not to disturb Luke, who was a light sleeper and needed his space, that arm was comfort, kindness, and ease all rolled up in one long, tan appendage. I'd always thought that sharing a bed with someone night after night was such an intimate act—he's next to you when everyone else in your world is behind their own closed door—except that when I was married, it often felt lonelier than sleeping alone; at least when you're by yourself there's no expectation of connection. But this, *this* was how I'd always pictured it might feel: contented rest in each other's company.

In August, after four months of running, and dating, even though we didn't call it that, Jesse was ready to pop the question.

"So . . ." he began, putting down his veggie burger and taking a sip of milkshake.

My stomach dropped, as it always did when things appeared to be turning serious; it was a leftover reaction, like an involuntary flinch, after years of big emotional conversations with Luke, but so far all my conversations with Jesse had been pretty lighthearted.

"I was wondering," he continued, and I could tell this was going to be big—at least, big for Jesse. He often had significant windups to nice but pretty ordinary sentiments. Like, "I really have to tell you something" might be followed by a pregnant pause, and then: "I'm having fun with you."

I waited expectantly. Jesse cleared his throat, looked up, and asked, "Would you like to come to Italy with me?"

Jesse was the most frugal person I knew. Even though he had a well-paying job as a computer programmer, at thirty-eight he still lived with three roommates, slept on a mattress on the floor in an attic under the eaves, and cooked all his meals from scratch with vegetables that he biked into Boston to buy cheaply at an outdoor market on Saturdays. Twice a year, though, adventure trumped frugality, and Jesse bought a plane ticket to Europe and cycled or hiked his way through some beautiful stretch of mountainous trail. This year he planned to walk a route through the Dolomites, or Italian Alps. And, much to my surprise, it appeared he wanted me to come too.

"But it's only a month away!" I reminded him. "Do you think I could actually do it? I mean, I love running in the woods, but this is much more rugged: ten days in 'real' mountains, carrying a pack. I'm not like you. You ride your bike a hundred miles a day. In the mountains! And ski down those backcountry trails in Idaho."

"Well, this doesn't involve a bike or skis," he reminded me. "And yes, I think you could do it. Remember our epic run on Cape Cod earlier this summer? That was seventeen miles. On sand. In the heat. And you didn't stop once. And as for the backpack, I'll help you pack light. We'll stay at *refugios* along the trail, and they'll serve us dinner and breakfast, so we won't need to carry much food or a tent."

I had to admit, I liked the *idea* of camping and campfires, but the reality of rustic inns and homemade Italian food was even more appealing.

"You're *sure* I wouldn't slow you down?"

"You know I don't care about that. It's so beautiful out there we'll want to take it slowly. Besides, you're tougher than you think."

Then he looked down at the table and cocked his head to the side, an endearing combination of bashful and uncomfortable, which is how he got when he had something emotional to say.

"I don't want to sound cheesy," he began, "but I think you're amazing. When we're on a trail, you're focused, and you're fun, and you have a graceful spirit too. It's made for some great adventures so far. You know I wouldn't invite just anyone on a trip with me. But I think we'd have a wonderful time."

I knew it was a big deal for Jesse to say all of that, and I was honored that he thought I was up to the challenge.

"You don't have to tell me now, though. You can think about it."

Right away I felt a hint of Yes! in my belly. Though I might not trust Jesse to pick out a bottle of wine (since he didn't drink) or a suit (since he didn't dress up), he was in his element when it came to the great outdoors, and I knew that I could trust him to lead me into the mountains and back out again in one piece. Still, I gave myself a few days to think about the trip. I'd only been divorced for a few months, and this would be my first time traveling with a man since Luke. Was it too soon? Did I really *want* to hike for ten days, or did I just think it sounded cool and rugged? As I pondered these questions, I was glad that my parents were away on vacation, otherwise I might have been tempted to tell them, and I was pretty sure what my mom might advise. A few weeks earlier, my mother had taken me to lunch. It was one of her periodic attempts to discuss, and influence, the state of my love life. Like in college when she'd taken me to lunch "to talk about something" and confessed over seafood sandwiches that she worried I was becoming "too much of a feminist" and that men might not like me for it. Or the time she and my dad sat me down at the kitchen table, before I got engaged, and suggested that Luke talked everything to death, and I might prefer to be with someone "easier." (Okay, maybe there they had a point.)

This summer she'd begun with: "Nothing against Jesse. He's nice, but I think you should be dating *more* people, not just one. Have you considered online dating?"

"Umm, not really, because I'm already dating someone I like."

"But you have a second chance to find someone who is a better fit for you than Luke was. Now that you're single, you should *use* this chance to meet more people."

"But I'm not really single. I'm dating Jesse."

"Well, *I know*, but you can date multiple people at once. You don't have to get so serious with just one."

"But Jesse and I aren't so serious. That's what I like about it. It's not like we're planning to get married."

"You don't want to get married again?"

"Yes, I do, but not yet. We're just having fun for now."

"But can't you have fun with multiple people at once?"

"Of course! I have lots of friends that I hang out with too."

"I don't mean your friends; I mean other guys."

At which point I finally said what all conversations that include my mom and relationships should begin with: "Mom! Please, let's talk about something else."

There was no convincing her. I *wanted* my mom to get it, to be excited for where I was in life; instead it was like she had her own agenda for me: date, remarry, children in quick succession. I wanted all of that too, but not right away. Even when she wasn't sitting across from me, my mother's voice was the one most often in my head; she wanted the best for me, I knew that, but she thought in black-and-white terms while I was getting comfortable in the gray areas, and often her well-meaning advice felt more judging than generous, not taking into account how different my life was from hers at thirty-one. A line from Jane Austen's *Sense and Sensibility* was often in my head that summer: "I wish, as well as everybody else, to be perfectly happy; but, like everybody else, it must be in my own way." Right here and now, spending time with this kind outdoorsman made me feel happy, but more than that, it made me feel strong and adventurous—and wasn't I trying to be a stronger me?

Opposite my mom, Emily suggested I spend more time alone, that I use this time freshly unmarried to get to know the real me again, before jumping into the next big relationship and losing myself just as I was finding her. She had a point; different relationships bring out different sides of you, and with Jesse I was an extreme version of Adventurous Me. On my own I wouldn't camp on Wednesday. Or hike the Alps. For now, though, after a few years of feeling stuck, I was enjoying this amped-up version of life. I was pretty sure Jesse and I didn't have a future together, but frankly I didn't care; it was the first time I'd ever dated a man and not pictured us being married. And that felt freeing. The one time I'd asked if he imagined having children, Jesse chuckled and replied, "I'm an old man."

"You're only thirty-eight," I pointed out.

"Well, I'm not sure I'd be a good dad," he amended.

I disagreed with that—he was kind, patient, fun—but I dropped the subject. I knew that Jesse had had a troubled upbringing, which he occasionally, cryptically, alluded to, and that he was in sporadic touch with his family, but he liked talking about the past as little as he liked talking about the future. He was a man in the moment, and that summer I decided to be a woman in the moment too. One run in the woods, one curled-up night at a time, I felt as if I were relaxing into the arms of this unfamiliar feeling: of being cared for. Why not see how it felt with a pack on my back?

And so, a few days after his heartfelt invitation, sitting in my office, I sent Jesse a one-word email:

Yes!

Jesse was over the moon, and he sent me an intimidating packing list and links to detailed trail maps that I couldn't decipher, but that didn't matter—he understood it all. I was pretty excited too, but I kept the news to myself for a few days, savoring this new sensation, holding it close like a treasure, this knowledge that I was doing something that felt "big" to me, with no one's blessing but my own.

When I met Kelley at my cousins' farm a few days later, I couldn't hold on to my news any longer.

"Guess what?" I asked her as we picked raspberries in the field.

"Knowing you, I'll never guess."

"Jesse invited me to go hiking in the Alps, and I said yes!"

"When?"

"In a couple of weeks, early September."

"That's so soon!"

"I know, but it's all working out. I didn't take much vacation this summer, so I have a few weeks left. And I'll miss the first youth group meeting, but the advisors can run it without me."

"That sounds amazing. What did your parents say?"

"They're away. I haven't told anyone but you."

"Well, I'm proud of you," Kelley said.

"Proud of me?"

"For doing what feels right to *you*. Not worrying what anyone else will say. That's a big step."

That's the beauty of a friend: she can support you without the baggage that family may carry into such conversations. By the time my parents came home from vacation, I'd already bought my plane ticket, and even if they weren't excited by my choice of companion, I knew they'd look at our pictures afterward and be proud of me too. And that could be enough.

✳ ✳ ✳

It seemed ambitious to me: we'd land in Innsbruck, Austria, catch a train into northern Italy and then a bus to the trailhead, and begin our hike to the first *refugio* by early afternoon, straight off the trans-Atlantic plane then train and bus. Like a puppy, Jesse was eager to get going. But when we missed our bus and it threw off our timing, I was secretly relieved to trade a hurried start for a huge pile of pasta—this was Italy, after all—and a good night's sleep at an inn at the base of the mountain before setting off for ten days. In spite of Jesse's reassurance, I was nervous about the hike; deep down I guessed I would *probably* be fine, that my body and spirit were up to the challenge, but I wouldn't know for sure until the journey was over. Which is oftentimes how life works, isn't it? Armed with our best guess, we set out.

For all his spontaneity, Jesse was a very thorough planner, and the pack I carried was refreshingly light thanks to his packing advice: just two hiking outfits, a fleece, a raincoat, pants, and toiletries, all for ten days of hiking plus a rest stop in Venice. Even my deodorant was mini-sized, though Jesse had done one better, ditching the container altogether and bringing only a small chunk of deodorant that he kept in a plastic bag. (Not that it helped much. According to Emily, we didn't smell like deodorant when she picked us up at the airport two weeks later.)

Thanks to a good night's sleep and my light pack, as Jesse had predicted, I was up to the challenge that first day, and the next four days too, as I huffed and puffed up mountain trails and across grassy valleys dotted with cows wearing bells and big rocks that we leaned against for picnic lunches, like characters in a painting.

And then, five days into our ten-day trek, I got stuck.

The way up this steep stretch of trail was carpeted in tiny rocks like gravel, which shifted underfoot, so that with each tentative step forward I felt as if I might slip backward. Sliding downhill has never been my thing. Unlike Jesse, who'd ski every day if he could, my skiing career had ended the same season it began, at age ten. The tiniest hint that I'm slipping down an incline, forward or backward, sends the contents of my stomach heaving, like when an airplane dips or an elevator drops quickly. The way up kept getting steeper, until I began to fear that with the next step, or the one just after that, I would slip backward and tumble down, rolling, rolling, gathering momentum like a human avalanche until finally landing, bruised and battered, bits of gravel enmeshed in my being, at the base of the trail. The end of me.

I didn't want to fall backward, but I was too scared to move forward and scramble up the chunk of rock that was staring me down.

From behind, Jesse tried to push me.

Heave ho!

He didn't actually say it, but he might as well have. No matter how hard he pushed, I wouldn't budge. Not that I was physically incapable of moving, or too heavy, but my mind had taken over and wouldn't let me go. I didn't want to lose control.

"Hand me your backpack," Jesse instructed.

"It's okay. I can carry my own pack."

"I know you can, but I'm offering to help."

"You don't have to do that. I'm strong," I sniffled—yes, sniffled, because I was crying and my nose was running.

"Amanda, I *know* you're strong. Just hand me your pack."

Gingerly I let go, one hand at a time, as Jesse eased the pack off my shoulders and put it on his chest. Then he climbed around me, navigating the steps that seemed so impossible to me with, if not ease, then at least with more strength than I could muster. And now he was above me, offering more encouraging words. But I was really crying by now, and frozen in place. I couldn't turn around and back down the steep trail. The detour would take us miles and hours out of the way, and besides, I had as little desire to hike back *down* the steep, gravelly incline as I did to hike up it. I could feel that my palms were super-sweaty and that my nose was still dripping, only I couldn't wipe it with my sweaty hands because I was clinging to the rock for dear life. If I'd been able to feel anything other than fear, it would have been that I was being totally lame. I like to think that a stronger, braver version of me could have done it—grabbed hold of the rock above and pulled myself up. But this real-time version of me was so completely stuck she couldn't even wipe her nose.

I had no *idea* what to do next.

But Jesse did. Looking down from above, he offered the magic words:

"Let go."

"No!"

"Let go," he said again, "and grab on to my hand. I'll pull you up."

"But I'm heavy," I warned him.

"I'm strong," he countered.

"But I'm scared."

"I've got you. You just have to let go and grab on to my hand."

"But I can't."

"Yes, you can," he urged me gently.

Every fiber in my being told me not to let go, that clinging to this rock was what was keeping me upright. And that was true. But it was also what was keeping me stuck, unable to move ahead.

I let go of the rock.

And grabbed on to the hand above me.

Jesse pulled me up to the higher ground, where he was already standing.

"I can take my bag back," I said through tears. It was a bit premature, as I was still shaking, and Jesse could have shouldered the added weight a bit longer. But I was unaccustomed to feeling so out of my element and was grasping to take back a bit of control.

"Are you sure?"

"Yes, please. And I think I need a few minutes to myself, before we start walking again."

"Of course. Whatever you need," Jesse offered, and he wandered off while I stood where I was, looking down at the path I'd just traveled, and beyond that at the big picture view, of rocky hills and blue sky. Eventually my breathing slowed down, and I stopped crying. *Here I am.*

The remaining hike to the top was steep, but not as steep as it had been. When we finally crested the peak only to head straight down the back side, I was officially out of pride and scooched myself down the mountainside on my bum. The butt of my bright orange shorts was dirty brown when we finished, but I didn't care anymore what the "stronger, braver" version of me would do because this *was* me, getting down the mountain the best way she knew how.

A few hours later, done hiking for the day, in an off-season ski motel somewhere in northern Italy, I unfolded my tired body in a bath of hot water. Jesse had gone to the only shop in town in search of something to celebrate my big climb. I heard a key in the door.

"Look what I found!" he hollered, and came into the bathroom with a bag of corn chips and two glass bottles of Coke. It seemed like a feast to me.

"Are you hungry?" Jesse asked.

"Yes, please."

He put a chip in my mouth.

"Aren't *you* tired?" I asked. "You did the same thing I did and helped take care of me, too."

"Don't worry about me," he smiled. "I couldn't be happier."

"Well, thank you. For the help. And the trip. I feel very lucky to be here. With you." (Which, for me, was a lot to admit.)

"My pleasure. You were brave out there."

Brave? I thought to myself. *Come on. Plenty of women would have scrambled up that mountainside like he did. They wouldn't have sniffled and cried and needed a hand up.*

But maybe, I was learning, bravery is when you do something that requires courage for *you*. No matter what it is. No matter how easily it might come to anyone else. I remembered what my cousin Barbara had said, about placing my hand in God's. Maybe eight years later I was finally getting what that meant: to let go and trust that other hands are there to catch you. Or as the naturalist John Burroughs wrote: "Leap and the net will appear." Or knock and the door will open, or ask and you will receive. There are a thousand ways to talk about risk, and just as many ways to face it bravely.

Jesse wandered back into the bedroom and lay down to rest. It was reassuring to see him tired for once. Alone in the bathroom, I stretched out in the tub, let go of my thoughts, and sank my brave body deeper under the warm water.

✳ ✳ ✳

Back from the mountains, starting my fourth fall at the church, I was feeling antsy for a change—but what?

I looked across the desk at my colleague Clark, a blustery sixty-something-year-old with wispy white hair and a somewhat affected accent, and tried to feel something akin to respect.

"So, Ah-mah-nda, how are you doing here at the church? People seem to love you, but how are *you* feeling? How can I help?" he asked from behind his mammoth desk, leaning back in his chair, his hands clasped behind his head.

Clark was the complete opposite of his predecessor, Simon, the first senior minister I'd worked with, the scholarly, conscientious forty-something-year-old who'd told me about the sex retreat and had since moved on to a church in Connecticut. I missed Simon's earnest, serious way. Clark was all hot air and scattered energy. He'd just left a thirty-year position at another church, and he probably should have retired instead of taking this job, as he was always coming up with excuses for not coming in to work: he was moving; furniture was being delivered; his car died. No one called him on it because he arrived with a good reputation, but even I thought he was slacking off, and I was far from a workaholic.

My attention wandered back to Clark, who had turned the conversation to himself. "Not a day goes by that I don't wonder, *What if I had become an attorney instead?*"

It seemed a woeful thing to admit, in the golden years of your career, that you'd always wanted to be something else.

"Don't get me wrong," he continued. "This is good work, but I used to think about becoming a lawyer, and instead I followed in my father's footsteps and became a minister like him."

I thought back to a Tuesday night a few months earlier. After a long church council meeting that ended on a positive note, I'd overheard Clark say to Sue, head of the council, "Let's go back to my office and celebrate with a glass of Scotch. I have a very fine bottle."

There was nothing technically wrong with this, nothing secretive or scandalous going on; after all, I had drinks with the advisors after youth group. But something about a beer in a bar surrounded by good energy felt different from a whiskey in the office, and I saw myself, thirty years from now, bitter and resentful, slugging cosmos in the church after dark, and wondering, like Clark, *What if . . . ?* and I knew that the church and I deserved better than that.

I imagine most jobs are tough if you're not feeling the love, but being a minister is particularly hard to fake your way through; the prayers, sermons, and even casual conversations require a presence and spirit that I didn't feel. Eight years earlier, in search of the next Big Thing, I'd settled upon minister for reasons that were solid, but what was missing was passion for the work itself and the greater mission of the church; though I'd always felt at home in the church, I didn't want to "sell" it to anyone else. Being a minister was starting to feel like a yoke upon my shoulders, and every Sunday that I put on my black robe it felt like I was dressing up for a role that wasn't really me.

But what *did* I want to do next? What was my equivalent of Clark's attorney? It was the same question that had baffled me right after college, but at least now I was getting closer to admitting that I had to try something. Or else. Or else end up like Clark. Drinking in my office. With no one to blame but myself. So that fall, when my old friend Deric, the one who'd hugged me outside the courthouse, told me that he'd lost his job, I was as excited as you can be for someone in an unexpected predicament; Deric was arguably the deepest and smartest of my friends, and I knew he'd be wrapped in discernment about what came next. Perhaps I could benefit from his soul-searching.

We met for breakfast on a Wednesday just because we could—what at treat! It was nice to have a friend who, at least temporarily, could match my unconventional schedule. Rounding the corner toward my favorite bakery, I saw Deric at a table in the front window and waved. He grinned back, looking faintly like Tom Cruise, as usual, but in wool and corduroy. As I pulled open the door, the cozy smell of baking bread wove its way around me. I inhaled and felt my shoulders relax. To the right was an open workspace where bakers in white caps and aprons worked their magic on dough at a long counterlong counter. Straight ahead were the results: baguettes, boules, and other baked goods such as their chocolate brioche, quite possibly my favorite edible invention. Deric stood up to give me a hug. Our parents went to Pilgrim

Church together, and I was pretty sure his father wished Deric and I were dating—good looks, brains, *and* recently divorced, it would have been convenient if there were any sparks, but there weren't. I was grateful that our paths were converging, though; friends don't have to be in the same boat to get what you're going through, but it's a comforting kind of companionship when they are.

After a few pleasantries, coffee, and thick egg sandwiches oozing melted cheddar, avocado, and tomato, I dove in:

"Okay, so I know I need to make a change, but I have no idea what to be instead of a minister. I'm thirty-two, but this indecision makes me feel like I'm back in college."

"I have a great way for us to think about what comes next," Deric launched right in. "I think it'll make sense to you, too."

"As long as it's easier to digest than string theory."

"String theory?" he looked at me quizzically.

"Remember when you came to visit me in Budapest, the year after college? It was February, and cold, and we took a long walk then stopped at that dark smoky café where old men were drinking espresso at the bar, and we sat at a table in the corner."

"Oh, wow. You have a good memory; that was a long time ago. When you were teaching in Hungary, and I had that consulting position in Munich."

"Ten years ago. And somehow you got on the subject of string theory."

"Why was I talking about that?"

"No idea. But I probably kept asking questions, which kept you going."

"You do ask lots of questions."

"And you like to talk."

"Well, I promise this is easier than string theory."

I took a sip of my latte and waited.

"To figure out the job for you, picture three circles intersecting, like a Venn diagram. The three circles are your skills, the needs of the marketplace, and your passion. When these three intersect in a job, that's it: the right work for you."

"That's actually pretty simple!" I tried on this model. "I have the skills to be a minister. In fact, the only negative feedback I've ever received was about my hair."

"Someone actually commented on your hair?"

"Well, not in a rude way, but after church one Sunday, this older man said a stray strand of hair hung over my face when I preached, and it could be distracting. He suggested I pull it back with a bobby pin. Or maybe that was his wife's idea. Anyway, I did, and that was that. So I guess I've got the skills. And the bobby pins."

Deric chuckled. I kept going.

"And there's certainly a need for young ministers like me too. Our denomination is shrinking, and maybe young energy can help."

"But that doesn't make sense. Isn't our denomination pretty progressive, which would be appealing to people like us?"

"Yes, if you actually want to go to church. But how many of your friends are religious? New England is one of the least religious parts of the country. Or maybe our denomination is shrinking because we don't make people feel guilty for skipping church. In *any* case, there's a lack of ministers like me. So that makes two out of three: skills and need."

"But as for passion . . ." Deric began.

"*That's* where I get tripped up. I'm good at what I do, and there's a need. Shouldn't that be enough? Is it selfish or indulgent to search for what makes me happy? I mean, there are plenty of people who have less-rewarding jobs than I do, and they have no way out. And others who have no job at all, and would be so grateful to have a well-paying, somewhat-flexible position like mine."

"Do you seriously think that everyone who's jobless wants to be a minister?"

"Well, no, probably not. Working on Sunday mornings and officiating funerals isn't the most exciting work. But who am I to leave a job that looks perfectly fine, just because it drains me and doesn't *feel* right?"

"Who are you *not* to? Amanda, you worry so much about what people on the outside think. What do you feel on the inside? You know your happiness matters. Isn't that why you got divorced? Because it didn't feel right anymore? And now, aren't you happier?"

"Well, yes, but I didn't have to find a new husband right away. If I leave the church, I'll have to find a new career. Right away."

(Looking back on this now, I realize it wasn't *exactly* true. While I *did* have to work, I didn't have to jump into a new "career." I could have found temporary work to bridge the gap.)

"Let's start with what you're passionate about, what you love," Deric suggested. "I mean, what kind of work would you *like* to do?"

"I don't know. That's always been the problem."

"Well, okay then, let's take 'work' out of the equation. What do you like to do?"

"I like to host dinner parties."

"Okay, that's a start."

"And I like to cook. Eat. Read. And . . ."

Another conversation with Deric came back to me, also from that weekend in Budapest. Before the café and string theory, we'd walked through an obscure park, where we found a statue of a hooded figure labeled "Statue of Anonymous." The figure was holding a pen, and, according to my guidebook, anyone who touched Anonymous's pen would become a better writer.

"You like to write, don't you?" Deric asked me, ten years ago.

"The only thing I write these days are emails, but, yes, I've always loved to write."

"Well, then, touch the pen, and I'll take a picture."

I reached out a gloved hand and touched my pointer finger to the tip of the pen, looked at Deric, and grinned. He snapped a picture.

"Amanda?" Deric brought me back to the present. "You like to cook, eat, read, and?"

"Write. I like to write. The only thing I write these days are sermons, usually last-minute, but it's one part of my job that I actually enjoy."

"That's right. I remember that you like to write. My mom still talks about how you swiped the English award from me freshman year. Keep going!" he urged.

And so we kept on like this for a few more minutes, talking about my favorite things. As we focused on what I loved, my energy shifted, and by the end of our conversation, frustration had given way to inspiration. I didn't let myself worry about how my favorite things would lead to paid work. That was putting the cart before the horse. If I wanted work that felt more authentic, I'd have to invest time and heart in this journey. Right now, to start, it was simply my task to dream.

As I kept talking about what I loved doing, an unexpected thought showed up, like a surprise (but welcome) guest at a party: *This is how God wants me to feel.*

Deric didn't go to church anymore, but he had a spiritual side, so I felt comfortable asking him about my unexpected guest.

"Do you think God wants us to love our work?"

"Of course! It's even possible to be a minister and love it," he added. "Look at Jonathan. He still loves being a minister after all these years."

"But I've always assumed that God would be disappointed in me if I left the ministry. I mean, what could be more pleasing to God than me leading an institution that's all about God? Even if I don't love it."

"Maybe you have to let go," Deric offered, "not just of being a minister, but of the mistaken idea that God, or the world, thinks you *should* be doing something. The fact that you don't feel any energy or excitement for your job probably means it's not the place for you. Remember that song we sang as kids: 'This little light of mine, I'm gonna let it shine.' Not, 'This little light of mine, I'm gonna squelch it for the greater good.'"

Deric had a point. Where had this traditional idea about sacrifice come from? Was I just using God as a catchall for my deeper insecurities about making a change? Was I feeling guilty because I'd already experienced so much good in my life? Was I valuing others' approval over my own joy? Yes to all of the above. Yes, *and* it's never too late to change how you think.

When I was a girl, I dreamed of being a lawyer who wore bright blue suits, lived in a big brick house, and had a husband named Michael with whom I had four daughters named after plants: Pansy, Daisy, Fern, and Rose. My eleven-year-old self *knew* how to dream in full color. Back before I felt guilty for what I had or felt wedded to the *shoulds*, I'd flung my dreams out into the world. I'd even announce them to my kid sister as we fell asleep side by side in our grandparents' guestroom. Within minutes Emily would be breathing deeply, but no matter, I'd keep describing my dream house, wardrobe, and children named for plants. I loved picturing my future, the possibilities of which seemed to mirror the last two lines of a Shel Silverstein poem my dad read to me growing up:

> *Anything can happen, child,*
> *ANYTHING can be.*

I've had only that one very real experience of God, when She appeared as a large Native American lady, sitting in a circle of other women next to a fire. She called me to Her, and as I went and knelt in front of Her, that's when She held my head in Her lap and said, "You are beautiful and greatly loved, just as you are." It happened the year after college, when I was living in the Hungarian countryside, lonely and in want of a hug, only everyone I knew and loved best was halfway around the world. The lonely was so overwhelming one gray November morning, that I stopped along a deserted stretch of dirt road where I'd been walking, and fell down to my knees. I'd never prayed on my knees before. Not that I was praying, exactly. I didn't know what I was doing down there, but I must have been especially open in that instant because it was there that God found me. The complete love I felt in that moment, in my vision, surpassed anything I'd ever felt in real life. It was as if I were floating in a warm, wide lake of unconditional acceptance.

After breakfast with Deric, I asked myself: *Now, how could a God who held me like that want anything other than my happiness?* I pictured that God now, and to Her blessing I added an additional line:

> *You are beautiful and greatly loved, just as you are.*
> *Anything can happen, child, ANYTHING can be.*

11. On the Way

A bell jingled overhead as I pushed open the glass door and wiped my wellies on the welcome mat. In my rubber rain boots, I felt rugged—like I was a rider, just back from an invigorating gallop or mucking out the stalls, en route to a pint in the pub—instead of what I really was: a malcontent minister on her lunch break meeting another minister for tikka masala.

I shook off my hood and looked around the near-empty restaurant for my friend; it wasn't hard to spot Julie at a table tucked in the corner. Julie was my friend from divinity school, and was the only person that Luke and I still shared. She'd been one of his youth-group advisors, along with her husband, and though they were older than we were, with grown kids from earlier marriages, the four of us had had an easy friendship. For a few years, we'd been intertwined in the significant events of each other's lives—Julie had read at our wedding; we'd celebrated a few New Years together; she'd even been the first to say, "It sounds like you're not in love with Luke anymore."

When Luke left the church to go back to school, Julie had been hired as his replacement; she'd been in that associate minister position for three years now, a job similar to mine in the next town over. But in spite of our proximity, we hadn't seen each other in months, and Julie jumped up, wrapping me in an embrace that lasted a good ten seconds longer than the average hug, as was her earth-mother style. The first time she'd hugged me like that I felt awkward, but now I'd learned to lean into it. Eventually she pulled away and held me at arm's length.

"You look beautiful!" she gushed. She was like my mom, always saying nice things about how I looked, even when it was a stretch and I was in flat, damp hair, a raincoat, and rubber boots.

We sat down and caught up on little things. Julie's hair, for one. We shared a stylist, but she was much more adventurous than I was, always changing up her look, which today was short and brown, but last time had been a bit longer with an auburn tinge. She had a discreet nose ring too that I'd never seen before, and I admired how, at fifty-something, she was not stuck in place but courting change. We ordered food and talked about our youth groups, and I wondered if she'd bring up Luke or if, nonchalantly, I'd have to inquire if she had any news of his life. Luke hadn't been in touch since the day we got divorced, nearly a year before, and even though it was easier that way—what we had had broken, and there was nothing connecting us now—I couldn't help but wonder how he was, what he was up to. Last time I'd seen Julie, she'd mentioned his new job, and that he'd moved to Cambridge, which explained why I'd seen his car on my way to work, parked by the Charles River. Although, come to think of it, I hadn't seen his car in a while now.

I took a first sip of mango lassi, sweet and creamy, as Julie began, "Did you know," and then she paused slightly, as if what she was about to say might carry weight.

I looked up from my sip. *Did I know what?*

"Did you know that Luke got married?"

I can count on one hand the number of times I've been speechless. This was one.

"You didn't know."

I shook my head no.

"I'm sorry if this is hard for you to hear."

"No, no, it's okay," I said as I found my voice. "I'm glad you told me. I'm just surprised. How do you know?"

"Well, I was there, actually. I married them."

"You officiated?"

"I did. It was a few weeks ago, at his mom's house at the lake. And I get it if that feels a little weird for you, that I was there, and that I officiated."

Julie was the most forthright communicator I knew and was also incredibly empathetic. If there was anyone I could be myself in front of, it was her. Still, it was a unique situation—to learn that your friend had just officiated your ex-husband's wedding, and you didn't even know he was getting married.

"I get it. It's weird," Julie repeated. "But I want you to know you can ask me anything. I'm your friend too."

Which was the upside of having your friend officiate your ex-husband's wedding: that you have access to the sort of intimate details you wouldn't otherwise, and after the initial shock had subsided, I was just plain curious. How did they meet? Who was she? And most importantly, what did she look like? (Well, not *most importantly*, but that's the kind of detail you can't help but wonder about your replacement.) Before I could form my first question, though, Julie said, "There's one more thing I should tell you: His wife is pregnant. They're expecting a baby in November."

November? I did a quick calculation. That was only five months away, and they'd just gotten married a few weeks ago. Apparently I wasn't the only one who'd decided not to wait until marriage the second time around.

If you're going to be decked with surprising news, it's nice when the messenger arrives fully prepared to indulge every one of your curiosities, and Julie was. They'd met online a few months after our divorce, she was a few years older than I was, and she thought she might have missed meeting Mr. Right—until she met Luke. And yes, the baby had been a surprise, but a happy one. Julie's husband had been the best man at their wedding, where everyone ate lobster at the lake house under a tent, and Luke, Julie said, was "beaming." That much I saw with my own eyes; though I wasn't on Facebook yet, a friend was, and a few days later we found a link to the wedding pictures. Even though I felt *slightly* guilty for looking, like I was "spying" on Luke and his new life, I did it anyway. I hadn't seen Luke or his mom in the year since our court date, and the rest of his family in two years, but they all looked the same, only instead of me in the pictures beside Luke there was a pregnant lady who looked vaguely like me. (That's what Julie had said when I asked what she looked like.) At home I had our wedding album tucked away in my trunk—a traditional black leather book with thick pages and our initials intertwined on the cover; inside it was filled with photos we'd selected together, sitting side by side on our photographer's couch a few weeks after our wedding. When we'd divided our things, our album had become my album, and even though our marriage was over, I still liked to look at it occasionally and remember a beautiful day. It was odd to think that now Luke had a new beautiful day to remember, as if our wedding, like the photos, had become just mine.

As lunch wound down, I'd asked Julie almost all the questions I wanted to, and now, there was only one left: "Will she make a better wife for Luke than I did?"

As I'd guessed she would, Julie said: "Yes. She's stronger than you are. Not that you aren't strong," she smiled over at me, "but she's strong in a different way. She's not intimidated by Luke's approach to life and his way of communicating, not hesitant to share her thoughts, not afraid to talk things out with him."

"I get it," I said.

And I really did. With Luke, most of the time I never *really* said what was on my mind. Instead of speaking my truth, I followed his, accommodating even when it didn't feel right, albeit with limited success, until, eventually, I felt like a less-strong, less-joyful version of myself—like a shell that used to be home to some colorful creature and that now sat empty on the beach.

By now I was crying, not because I was sad, but because it

felt like a great weight had been lifted. Selfishly, I felt something akin to relief. Luke had been pretty adamant that I'd ruined his life. And even though I hadn't wanted to believe that it was in my power to ruin his life—and had envisioned a happy future for him without me in it—I realized that his hurt was a burden I'd been carrying. Now I could let that go.

"Okay, one *very* last question," I wondered aloud. "Are they having a boy or girl?"

"They're having a girl," Julie answered.

I guess a girl isn't *that* surprising; there's a near-fifty-fifty chance after all. But still, I thought back to my letter to God, the one I'd written on the bank of the Charles River nearly two years before, now living in Kelley's sock drawer.

I told Julie about the letter and what I'd written about Luke.

"Well, thank God for answered prayers," she smiled. "And yours will be answered too, one way or another. You've come so far, you're a strong woman in your own way, full of wisdom and so much love to share."

We stood up, and she gave me another lengthy hug.

"You're okay?" she asked.

"I'm okay," I smiled back at her. And it was the truth.

It was still raining when I stepped outside, and I pulled up my hood and made sure to step in all the puddles with my tall boots just because I could. Water splashed up from the ground, and rain poured down from above, and I was still crying, but not sorrowful tears—I was just overwhelmed with emotion, with life and how it unfolds. Thoughts of remarriage and babies seemed so far away. I imagined I'd want those things one day, but right now, at thirty-two, coming up on the one-year anniversary of my divorce, I was still getting used to my newfound independence and figuring out how to be my own strong self again. I wouldn't be ready to plan a life with someone else until I was surer of who I was. But Luke, he really was ready to move ahead with those dreams—to be a husband again, and a father for the first time. He'd found the chance to begin again.

I thought of Luke's new wife and how my Mr. Wrong had become her Mr. Right, how the same things that frustrate one person can work so well for another. Except for the fact that I'd let Luke go, I had nothing to do with their coming together or their future; our initials were no longer intertwined. Luke and his wife certainly didn't need my blessing. But I offered it even so. By myself, walking through puddles, I took a deep breath and pictured the handsome man who'd been my husband and his new strong wife, and I wished for a couple I'd probably never meet a happy marriage, full of connection.

I like to think that when, if ever, Luke and his bride imagined me, they imagined me being happy for them, but that's not mine to know. What I do know is that hurling my good wishes into the universe certainly made me feel lighter and freer as I walked on. That wet June day, I didn't know whom I would marry, or even what I would do next, but I knew that I was on the way toward those things.

* * *

"The journey of a thousand miles begins with a single step," the sage Lao Tzu said. One foot in front of the other, or one positive thought before another, over and again, will eventually get you where you want to go. I tried to remind myself of these wise words with each step I took, but—*Dear God!*—a step is much easier when a foot isn't covered in blisters.

I took another stinging step and noticed a crumpled tissue alongside the trail. A few paces later, there was an abandoned water bottle.

"Who throws trash on a holy walk?" I asked Jesse. "It's gross. There wasn't any trash when we hiked in the Dolomites."

"Well, that's probably because there weren't any people either," he replied matter-of-factly. "But two hundred thousand hikers come through here every year."

As if on cue, footsteps approached from behind, and I pushed to the side of the dirt trail to make way for another hiker to pass.

"*Buen camino!*" offered a tall lean man who walked alone and looked somewhere north of seventy. Like many other hikers on this Spanish trail, he carried a walking stick, and a scallop shell dangled from his backpack. The shell swayed from side to side as he walked briskly by.

"*Buen camino!*" we replied in Spanish, a greeting that stood for Hello-goodbye-have-a-good-journey! Most trails don't have their own salutation, but the Camino de Santiago, or Way of Saint James, is no ordinary trek: it's a thousand-year-old pilgrimage route through northern Spain, where walkers are referred to as pilgrims—whether or not they're actually religious—and where, after five hundred miles, the path ends in a cathedral on the coast, in Santiago de Compostela. The cathedral holds the remains of the apostle James, one of Jesus's twelve disciples and a missionary to Spain, who was later beheaded in Jerusalem. Legend has it that as his remains were sailing back to Spain, a rough storm tossed the precious cargo from the boat, and eventually James washed up onshore covered in scallop shells. The cathedral was built near the site and, in the early days, pilgrims walked on trails from throughout Europe to visit the relic. Now most travelers began their journey in southern France, crossed the Pyrenees, and followed waymarks (yellow scallop shells on a blue background) to the cathedral on the coast. Most hikers also wore a scallop shell around their neck, or swinging from their backpack, but this sort of symbolic jewelry wasn't my style (I'd never felt the urge to wear a cross either), so Jesse and I followed the shells, but didn't wear any.

I watched our fellow pilgrim and his scallop shell breeze by. Jesse had slowed his pace to match mine and tried to lighten the mood with silly jokes, but I was a wimp when it came to pain, and Jesse's lightheartedness simply annoyed me.

"How are your feet?" he asked.

"Ugh." I looked down at the brown hiking shoes that had served me so well a year ago in the Dolomites, but now felt like size 7½ traitors. It was only the first of ten days, and I didn't relish the thought of nine more days in shoes like this.

"Why don't you change into your flip-flops?" he suggested.

"I can't hike in flip-flops."

"Why not?"

"That's lame. Who hikes in flip-flops?"

"People who have blisters."

"That reminds me of some Japanese tourists I saw once, hiking up Mt. Monadnock in New Hampshire, wearing white Keds."

"Did they have blisters?"

"I don't know. The point is that they were hiking in Keds. On a mountain. And I thought that was stupid. I don't want to look like an inexperienced hiker."

"Come on now," Jesse countered, and I knew by now this was his way of saying, "Chill out." If I were Jesse, I would have rolled my eyes at me, but he was too nice. Instead he said, "I know you're frustrated, but the blisters aren't your fault. It's hot out, and your feet are probably just sweating and that's causing friction. Let's stop. I'll put moleskin on the worst ones, and then you can put on your flip-flops. We're only two kilometers from town, and we can give your feet a nice soak when we get to the hotel."

I sat down on the dirt next to a wrapper from someone else's energy bar. I picked up the crinkly silver paper and put it in my pack. After the trip, comparing notes with my friend Cristina who'd hiked the Camino earlier that summer, I asked her what she thought of all the trash. "What trash?" she wondered. I couldn't believe she hadn't noticed it, and she couldn't believe I had. It's true that there was more litter than on your average woodland walk, because of its popularity, but I was letting the litter and the blisters get the best of me, too busy focusing on the negative to notice all the beautifully trash-less bits of trail.

Jesse knelt in front of me, took off his pack, and unearthed a small roll of fabric and some scissors as I pulled off my shoe. It reminded me of the first run we'd taken together, in the woods, when an uncomfortable toe cramp kept returning and Jesse had knelt in front of me just like this to massage my foot. Back then, before we'd known each other well, I'd been embarrassed by the toe cramp, worried that I was slowing us down, that he'd think I wasn't fit or tough. Not that Jesse cared. "Come on now," he'd urged gently that afternoon in the woods, using the same expression he did on the Camino. "A massage will help, I promise." In the light of day, in the middle of exercising, my bare foot in a man's hand seemed so intimate that I kept on my ankle sock as I stretched out my leg, my foot coming to rest in the palm of his hand. The sensation of strong hands on your often-overlooked feet is a singular balm, like when the stylist massages your soapy head before a cut. I wish I could say I closed my eyes and sank into the moment like I do at the salon. Instead I felt awkward, acutely aware of the uncommon position in which my new friend and I found ourselves: Jesse on his knees touching my foot.

How many easy moments do we turn into complicated ones? How often do we allow our thoughts and insecurities to distract us from the present? Rather than letting go and sinking into the beauty kneeling right before us? Now, a year and half later, and partway around the world, I was doing it again: stubbornly clinging to my thoughts and judgments, turning a rich possibility into a frustrating reality because it wasn't unfolding as I had pictured. Jesse took my foot in his hand again. This time, I didn't hesitate to peel off my sock. As he dressed my blisters in moleskin, I tried to muster some feeling of gratitude for this man and this sacred old trail. Yet instead of feeling incredibly blessed, on two weeks' vacation in rural Spain with a kind companion, I just felt annoyed. The blisters, the trash . . . even the landscape was browner than I'd expected, and all of it mirrored how dried up I felt inside. How had I ended up here?

✳ ✳ ✳

Two months earlier, in midsummer, Jesse had planted the seed for this trip. Though originally, it wasn't meant to take place in Spain. He was planning his annual September trek through a European mountain range, and he asked if I wanted to join him on a walk through Provence in southern France. After a year-plus, ours still didn't have the marks of a "traditional" relationship. We didn't talk about the future, plan beyond our next adventure, or share many friends, and although the low-key ease of things had been a major attractor in the beginning, I was starting to feel like we were outgrowing our connection. I still indulged the occasional fantasy that we'd move to the plot of land Jesse owned out in Idaho, where he'd build a cozy cabin, cook pizza every night, and teach me how to ski. But I didn't *really* believe that lifestyle would suit me. When it came to outdoor adventures, we were on the same page, but when it came to a lot of other things I enjoyed— like dressing up in something other than Patagonia, driving a car, lingering over the paper on a lazy morning—we couldn't have been more different. Besides the outdoors, and playing his guitar, what were his dreams about? He didn't say, but I was pretty sure they didn't involve anything typical like marriage or family.

Or wearing a suit.

That summer Jesse had been invited to my friend Laura's wedding. Laura was my willowy gospel singer friend from divinity school, who still hadn't settled upon a career; since her denomination, Christian Science, didn't ordain ministers, it was always a little unclear what she planned to do with her divinity degree. But she *had* settled upon a husband, and she'd asked me to be a bridesmaid. Jesse met me at the chapel, where I was waiting before the ceremony with the rest of the wedding party. It wasn't your typical chapel, a contemporary cylinder of copper and glass on the campus of the Harvard Business School and, as it turns out, my date wasn't your typical wedding guest.

"Hey there!" I heard from behind, and I turned around. Jesse was beaming, like a kid who'd dressed himself for the first time.

"How do I look?" he asked eagerly.

Inwardly I cringed. His tie wasn't knotted properly. He was wearing a casual button-down and even more casual Carhartt pants, a fabric belt, and Birkenstocks with socks. When he'd asked about the dress code ahead of time, I'd suggested a suit. When he'd said he didn't have one, I'd asked if he had a tie. "Yep!" Jesse had grinned. We'd left it at that, but I was secretly hoping he'd offer to buy himself a suit. I mean, wasn't it "normal" to have at least one suit in your closet by age thirty-nine? But it wasn't Jesse's "normal," and looking back on it, if it was that important to me, I should have *asked* him to get a suit. But as usual, I didn't say what was on my mind, feeling guilty for my "shallowness." *It shouldn't matter what he wears,* I scolded myself for being superficial. Well, sure, in the scheme of world peace, it doesn't matter what you wear to a wedding, but it always matters that you're authentic; that instead of swallowing words and presenting a less-genuine version of yourself, you own who you are, never mind how others may respond. Besides, I have a sneaking suspicion that if Jesse had known I cared so much, he would have bought a suit. Or at least a proper dress shirt and khakis. After all, how many pieces of Patagonia, sporty shoes, and general miscellany had I bought for our outdoor adventures? I now had an entire bureau drawer devoted to outdoorsy-ness. "It looks like Eastern Mountain Sports in here!" Emily had said when she opened it looking for something to borrow. "What *is* all this stuff?" she asked, holding up a small gray sack.

"That's a raincoat for my backpack."

"Oh. Right. And this?" she asked, holding up something that resembled a stiff black sleeve with Velcro up the side.

"That's a gaiter. It goes over your boot and up your leg, for hiking in winter. And those," I nodded at the black spandex with a built-in butt that Emily had found hiding in the back of the drawer, "are bike shorts. But I've only worn those once. And my butt *still* hurt."

I had an outdoor drawer, but Jesse didn't have a fancy drawer, and I'd missed my chance to suggest he start one; the day of the wedding was too late for *that* conversation. So when Jesse stood outside the chapel and asked eagerly, "How do I look?" I said the only thing I could say, "You look great!" But I didn't really mean it, and I felt embarrassed by my boyfriend's outfit, and like a jerk for being embarrassed. After the ceremony Jesse changed into Carhartt shorts, rode his bike to the nearby reception on the Charles River instead of driving with me, and was offended when the guard at the boathouse didn't recognize he was a wedding guest. Sometimes it felt like we were reading from two different how-to manuals on life. Maybe it was time to move on. But then Jesse asked if I wanted to go on another hiking trip, and I remembered how great I'd felt after last September's trek through the Dolomites. Even if our relationship was winding down, maybe I could enjoy one last trip.

A few days after I said yes, Jesse lifted a big picture book onto the dinner table and faced it toward me.

"Check it out!" he beamed. "I found it in the library—it's pictures of Provence, so you can see what I'm thinking of and how beautiful it is there."

Over Thai food, we peered at pictures of French food piled on café tables in that effortlessly elegant way I admired—wedges of cheese, baguettes, fruit tarts, bottles of wine. "Look! There's even a museum devoted to bakeries. You'd love that," Jesse pointed out. I'd been to France, but not to the south, with its fields of lavender, sunflowers, and villages built of stone, filled with bread.

"C'est beau! Oui?" Jesse spoke a bit of French and was keen to practice with the locals. I flipped through the pictures. *Mais oui.* It *was* beautiful. So I said the only logical thing: "How about hiking the Camino instead?"

Which, of course, wasn't very logical at all.

"The Camino in Spain?" Jesse seemed surprised. "But I thought you loved baguettes and flowers?"

"I do, but I . . ."

"And I thought you *didn't* want to hike the Camino because it's a pilgrimage route and has 'religious' connotations that feel too close to your work?"

"I didn't, but I've been thinking about it, and I'm sort of intrigued by the fact that people have been walking this same path for a thousand years. I mean, there has to be *something* special about it, right? Maybe it will give me the inspiration I need to figure out what's next. Plus, my friend Cristina just hiked the whole route, all five hundred miles, and she loved it. Even though we'd only do part of that, I'm sure we'll still get a lot out of it."

"So let me get this straight. You weren't interested in hiking the Camino, but now you are? You'd actually prefer the pilgrimage route to a walk through the French countryside?"

"I think so."

"And you're not just saying this because you know *I've* always wanted to hike the Camino, are you? Because I think this Provence trip would be amazing too."

"I'm sure it would. But no, I'm not just saying it to please you. I think the Camino will be a good challenge."

Jesse didn't need any convincing. As long as we were outside every day, he was a happy camper. He set to work planning the logistics of our trip to Spain while I ordered travelogues and read about other people's experiences on El Camino, hoping that ten days on this ancient walking route would infuse my life with a sense of rightness that had been missing. I didn't feel a connection to God or the divine in my work anymore. Going to church on Sunday felt like a job. Well, technically speaking, it *was* my job. But there wasn't any joy to it; I was just going through the motions. The one time I *didn't* dread visiting a parishioner in the hospital was the night I got a call after two margaritas. Luckily the hospital wasn't far from the Mexican restaurant where I'd been drinking with my friend Elizabeth, and the tequila softened the edge of being called into work on a Thursday night. But tequila wasn't a long-term solution to a bad career fit. Maybe the Camino was the magic answer and would open me up to what came next. Maybe I'd return home a more energetic version of myself. Like my friend Cristina who, between careers and recently divorced, had returned from her hike in Spain bubbling with energy and tales of new friends she'd met on the trail (one of whom she married five years later). The fact that I didn't feel any connection to the apostle James, relics, Spain, or the idea of a pilgrimage, and was second-guessing my relationship with my boyfriend, *probably* should have figured into the equation, but it didn't.

In addition to my search for meaning, another small possibility waved at me—that this walk would change things, that despite all the evidence to the contrary, I'd feel *something* divine and would be called back to being a minister. It was my last-ditch attempt to wring some life from my call. Not unlike the night I'd watched my wedding video before Luke and I got divorced, just to be certain I wasn't making a mistake.

Now I was testing myself again. Instead of giving in to the part of me that loved sunflowers, baguettes, and men in seersucker suits—yes, that's what I *really* wished Jesse had worn to the wedding—I chose the pilgrim's path that ended up in a cathedral. A church! The exact sort of structure I was trying to escape. Sometimes you're just so wrapped up in what you think you should do, you forget to ask yourself what you really *want* to do.

By day three, Jesse left me in a café reading the paper. My blisters had gotten worse, and we'd decided I'd take a taxi to that night's destination while Jesse walked alone. As disappointed as I was in my feet, a small part of me was delighted that blisters gave me the excuse to linger over a coffee and the *International Herald Tribune*. Ah, but a larger part of me felt guilty that Jesse had to hike alone, lame for missing a day on the trail. Rather than giving into delight, I let guilty-lame win and didn't relax into the moment.

After two days of taking it easy in taxis, my feet toughened up, and I got back to walking every day, but the trip didn't get any better. Pilgrimages may be spiritual, but they aren't magical. They don't take what's there and make it disappear; the things that annoyed and frustrated me at home had followed me to Spain. I carried this baggage like a second backpack on my chest, blocking my heart. You needn't go someplace "holy" to be inspired. I'd known that all along, but I'd temporarily forgotten my own wisdom. The one time I'd truly felt God had been on that walk in my sleepy Hungarian village. The most peaceful place I knew was my cousin's small farm. Neither of those were your typical sacred spot. Even hiking in the Dolomites, on a plain old trail, had felt more sacred than this ancient pilgrimage.

Maybe Jesse was onto something when he'd suggested the south of France. A few years later, he took that walk in Provence, through the Luberon Mountains, alongside lavender fields and into the bakery museum in Bonnieux. When he got back he showed me his pictures, after we ate one of his homemade pizzas and drank red wine—the same man who hadn't touched a glass of wine in Italy now drank half a bottle in my living room, and I was so surprised I could have kissed him. Almost. His pictures looked as beautiful as promised. Maybe one day I'll walk through Provence myself. But I know now it doesn't really matter *where* you go, only that going there feels good and right to you, regardless of how it sounds to the outside world. Because no one really cares where you spend your vacation. Or whether you walk all day, or plant your butt in a café and read. What would make *your* heart sing? That is the question to ask.

Ten days after it began, our pilgrimage ended on the coast, down a steep hill, through an archway into the city of Santiago de Compostela, and up the steps of the Cathedral of St. James. I filed past James's tomb, squished in a long line of other pilgrims and tourists, but I didn't feel much of anything as I looked at the elaborate gold coffin behind glass. And when the bells chimed shortly after that, for the eleven o'clock Pilgrim's Mass, standing-room only, I was more aware of body odor (my own included) than anything particularly holy.

I felt as if I should arrive home in a T-shirt that said: *I hiked the Camino and all I got were six lousy blisters and one ex-boyfriend.*

A month after we got back from Spain, Jesse could sense that I was pulling away and initiated The Conversation, since I was too chicken to bring it up.

"I can tell you're not happy. What's going on?" he asked, sitting beside me on my bed, as I got teary and confessed that my heart wasn't in our relationship anymore.

Jesse wasn't surprised by my admission, but I was surprised by his.

"I've loved having you as my girlfriend," he admitted. "You've taught me how to use my heart again. And even though it hurts now, it was worth it. I wouldn't trade a minute of our time together."

It was the first time he'd actually called me his girlfriend.

"Thank you for letting me love you," he went on.

It was the first time he'd said he loved me.

"No one has made me feel this like," he finished up, as if a year and a half of *not* saying what he'd held in his heart was pouring out all at once.

And I realized this: I was incredibly grateful for all the heavy conversations we never had—it had been such a relief to meet a man who didn't need to delve deeply into emotional depths like Luke. But the flip side of never talking about your feelings is that you miss out on the beautiful bits. Yes, some things are better left unsaid, but others are better said. Knowing this didn't change anything, but I was touched and wished it had come earlier. Wished that I had "dared" to ask him to wear a suit to Laura's wedding, because I'm pretty sure he would have done it for me. In fact, I sensed that, if Jesse had his way, there would be no end in sight to our hikes, which made me appreciate his kind words even more. To show such grace when someone is breaking up with you is a pretty rare gift, and I was very grateful.

Jesse got up from my bed.

"I don't think I should stay over tonight," he suggested. And even though it would have felt nice to curl up next to him one last time, I knew it would only make things harder in the morning.

"No, it's probably easier that way," I agreed.

I crawled under the covers, still dressed. Instead of getting in beside me, Jesse tucked me in, kissed my cheek, and, without looking back, gently pulled my apartment door shut. A moment later I heard the downstairs door bang behind him. And he was gone.

✳ ✳ ✳

Crushes have a way of brightening up life. Especially when they're reciprocated. Now you actually have incentive to eat less. Exercise! Toss some of the ratty underpants that make you feel the opposite of alluring and treat yourself to a new pair, or ten, because someone might actually see them. And as for your annoying job? *My job? What job? Who cares about that, I'm in love!* But when the initial excitement of lust fades, whether into a lasting connection or not, and you're still stuck in a frustrating job, wearing pretty underpants, but no closer to figuring out your heart's calling, maybe it's time to invite the search for nine-to-five love onto center stage. After Jesse and I broke-up, I promised myself I wouldn't date again until I'd figured out my work life.

12. Dance!

Sunlight was streaming in the window of my favorite bakery as I sat with an unopened book on the table. Emily had promised it was a must-read, but this was one of those paperbacks I felt slightly embarrassed to be caught with. In flowery script the title streamed out of the blossom of a calla lily—*This Time I Dance!*—and purple italics promised it was a book "for every person who has yearned to find their true work in the world."

Why do so many self-help books insist on cheesy covers? I wondered. Just because I was feeling a little desperate didn't mean I'd lost all semblance of taste. It didn't mean I wanted my reading material to announce to the world, "Look at me! I need help." Not that anyone was paying attention; the other patrons were too engrossed in their own conversations, or the *New York Times*, to notice my flashy cover. At least this one didn't have a life-size photo of the author on the front.

Emily had me warned me that it might take a few pages to warm up to *Dance!* "I know you'll think it's cheesy in places, but it's very helpful, I promise. Just overlook the stuff that makes you want to roll your eyes."

I opened to the dedication, and saw that the author had dedicated the book to her former self, the part of her that sailed ahead in stormy seas.

Did it count as an eye roll if I did it with my eyes closed? *Okay, don't judge,* I reminded myself. *You are stuck. You need inspiration. Be open.* After all, Emily *and* her college friend Denise, a whimsical social worker in Austin, had both recommended this book. Denise was funny and quirky, but decidedly not cheesy. I trusted her recommendation too.

Okay, back to it, I urged myself, but not before glancing at the clock. It was already ten o'clock, and I felt I needed to get to work by twelve. While I didn't have a set time I had to show up (frequent night meetings and weekend obligations meant I had some leeway in the morning), I felt guilty showing up past noon. Ideally, I *wanted* to wake up with the sun, with a spring in my step and a can-do spirit, but that was never what happened. I'd always thought of myself as an early morning person, but these days I was sleeping until eight or nine. Ordinary things felt like work, even after a good night's sleep. Making my bed? S-u-c-h a chore. Taking a shower? Ugh. As for standing in front of my closet and figuring out what to wear? *My pajamas. No, Amanda. Okay, fine, I'll wear what I wore yesterday.* I didn't want to wake up dreading the day that awaited me, but my job had come to feel like a weight upon my shoulders, a heaviness pulling me down. No matter how lucky I told myself I *should* feel—to be gainfully employed, to have some flexibility in my schedule—I couldn't trick myself into liking my career. The seeds of discontent had sprouted and truly blossomed, in the form of lethargy, and I couldn't ignore them.

So when I finally emerged outside, in the same clothes as the day before (except underpants—those were usually fresh), it was no surprise that even though I *meant* to drive straight to work I made a stop first. For if Heaven had a smell, it would be baking bread. And once I got behind the wheel, it felt as if something deep within—a primal urge for comfort, maybe, or a taste of

Heaven—took hold, and, like a hound to scent, I followed it half a mile up the road, knowing that this sweet, comforting smell, and the warm bakery that held it, were the push that I needed to propel me into another day. It wasn't just about the caffeine or the carbohydrates, although both were lovely. The whole place felt like comfort incarnate: familiar, cozy, and warm. Like sinking into a favorite armchair. Only edible. The bakery's owner, Pierre, wasn't French, but he looked like he could be: a slender, prematurely gray-haired man who decorated his bakery in the style of Provençal countryside. There weren't actually any armchairs, just one long farmhouse table with benches on either side and few café tables with sturdy ladder-back chairs, where Deric and I had sat to talk about finding work we loved last fall and where, nearly every morning, I stopped for a latte and chocolate brioche. It felt decadent to come so often; neither the coffee nor the food was cheap, but beyond that it felt like a decadence of time. For a whole hour I had nothing on my agenda but to eat, drink, and read. I didn't wake up with the sun, or even with a spring in my step, but this ritual was my chance to start the day on a better foot.

I once met the owner of another coffee shop, a successful roastery tucked in the woods on an island in Puget Sound. Its quirky location belied its success: their biggest account was Starbucks's competitor in China, and when I'd asked the owner Gary how he drank his coffee, his answer surprised me:

"Sitting down," he said, as he opened the valve on a roasting tank and hot beans came tumbling out. He elaborated, "I have an espresso and croissant every morning, as you can tell," he chuckled and rubbed his round belly. "But most importantly I sit down while I do it, even if it's only for ten minutes. Take the time to enjoy your coffee, and your croissant, or whatever it is you need, and *then* get on with your day. You'll have a better day for it."

Gary's reminder that little rituals matter was one I hung on to. Especially when some of the big things in life seem too, well, big to solve in a day, it's the simple pleasures that can help you shift from feeling overwhelmed to content: A cup of coffee. A pot of tea. Flowers from the garden. Birds at the feeder. A good book before bed.

So this morning, as usual, I took a sip of latte from a seat on the bench at the bakery. The table was part of what I loved about this place: a rough-hewn slab of wood, probably an old piece of barn, that stretched almost the entire length of the eating space and that could fit eight people on either side. I dreamed of having one like it in my own house someday, filled with familiar faces, but for now I enjoyed the long table in the company of strangers. Two effortlessly stylish mothers—at least they looked that way to me, as I wore the same dark jeans and navy sweater as the day before—sat with toddlers in elaborate strollers, which took up most of the walking space, and talked about nursery schools. A clump of bookish scientists trailed in discussing something I didn't understand. String theory, perhaps? With some effort an older gentleman swung his legs over the bench and sat down beside me, nodding pleasantly before unfolding his *Times*, careful not to hit the jar of flowers on the table. The flowers came from a cheese shop and gourmet market around the corner, which sold tastefully understated arrangements for which people in the neighborhood were willing to pay prettily. I was more likely to pilfer a daffodil from the patch in front of my apartment or, at the urging of my friend Lelia, an armful of lilacs from the nearby cemetery; you could easily snap a branch undetected, she'd suggested, and really, who would miss them? But I always had a bouquet of something at home; it might seem like a frivolous detail, daffodils on your desk or lilacs in the living room, but such a simple thing can change the whole feel of a space, and in so doing, the energy of the people in it.

Besides the flowers, the long table, and breakfast, there was just one more piece to this morning ritual: a book. Reading has always been an escape for me, a chance to hide out in someone else's story, real or imagined, but this morning I was reading to help me create a life I didn't *want* to escape, and *Dance!* was here to help. This was my first foray into a new landscape, self-help,

and *Dance!* was about creating work you love. So I dipped a bite
of brioche into my latte and got back to the task at hand. Flipping past the dedication and on to the introduction, "Follow Your
Love Instead of Your Fear," I lost the urge to roll my eyes and kept
reading. And reading. And yes, in some places the language was
a little cheesy, but it was also practical, and it made me feel more
positive. "Every rosebud starts in the mud," one chapter began,
and I pictured myself a tiny bud, poking through a layer of muck,
blossoming into a more joyful version of myself.

I wish I could say that as I read my way through *Dance!*,
energy flowed immediately into my life. That I shot up from the
mud toward the light of my *true* calling. But I didn't. I kept reading, though, because at least I felt better with those words in front
of me. They gave me a sense of possibility. Like the plow that
turns over the soil, preparing the ground for seeds to be planted,
reading *Dance!* stirred up my thoughts, helped me break down
old assumptions (it's selfish to ask for your own happiness; work
has to feel like "work"), and encouraged new ideas: Pay attention
to your dreams. Listen to your heart. You, too, can follow where
it leads.

✳ ✳ ✳

My friend Matt turned forty in February and was throwing himself a party at his favorite Italian restaurant. Emily and Silas came
over first—both were temporarily home from abroad; Emily had
moved to London, and Silas was living in Oslo—and the three of
us were heading out together. Just as soon as I figured out what to
wear. Since Jesse and I had broken up, I'd stopped running, and
most of my jeans and tops felt a bit snug these days. I settled on
some well-worn jeans and ripped the price tag off a pink turtleneck I'd bought to wear on casual days off, *not* to parties, but it
was the only thing that seemed even remotely stylish and somewhat comfortable.

The three of us walked into the restaurant, where the tables had been pushed aside and the cozy space was overflowing with Matt's friends, most of whom were connected to the local music scene. Matt wasn't a musician himself, but the gregarious, irreverent man with dark curly hair ran the music club where Emily had worked before moving to London—and where Bob Dylan and Joan Baez had played back in the day. "It's the MacKenzies!" Matt bellowed, and he came over to give each of us a warm hug. Hugging Matt was like hugging a teddy bear; he was one of those people whose embraces are more generous than average, longer and tighter in a way that makes you feel special. Over his shoulder I spotted Jesse with his back to me, deep in conversation. We'd seen each other a few times since our breakup, but in spite of our kindhearted separation, our interactions since then had felt a bit stilted, and I knew a chat with him wouldn't perk me up.

"Go get yourselves a drink!" Matt suggested, and he moved on. Emily and Silas floated away too, caught up in conversation with other friends. I scanned the room for someone else I knew and, in the absence of anyone to talk to, busied myself with a getting a drink. It was one of those nights when I didn't feel good on the inside *or* on the outside, and while I knew the answer wasn't red wine, for tonight it softened the edge of unhappy. I took a generous gulp.

"Hey there."

I looked up at a tall man with a headful of thick silver hair.

"I'm Mitch," he said in a voice like a lazy river, deep and mellow, a sound you could relax into. Though I recognized him from Matt's club, we'd never actually met.

"I'm Amanda."

"Very nice to meet you, Amanda." With his gray hair, deep voice, and easy confidence, Mitch seemed like a real *man*. He probably had a generous patch of hair on his chest, and picked girls up for dinner in his car, not on his bike. I guessed he was in his mid-forties, but he dressed like he was younger—casually stylish in a dark hoodie that zipped up the front, slim jeans, and Converse.

"And what do you do, Amanda?" Mitch asked.

His question killed my buzz.

In social settings I dreaded the ubiquitous "What do you do?" I didn't enjoy talking about my work, but more than that I was embarrassed to be doing something that felt so far from who I was. People harbor stereotypes about ministers, most of which didn't fit me—which is probably true for many professions, and which is why stereotypes are annoying, to say the least—but they have an origin, and I couldn't fault people for thinking I was pious or serious; I mean, I *was* a minister, after all, just *not* a particularly pious or serious one, and that usually surprised people. A year earlier, at a birthday party for my advisor friend Jen, I ran into her brother and his friends, just out of college and only loosely connected to the church, but connected enough to know who I was. Later in the night one of the boys whispered to Jen, "Do you see that? Amanda's drinking. And dancing!" I was shocked that they were shocked. There are sects of Christianity that discourage drinking and dancing. In fact, you can probably find a church that prohibits just about anything: Caffeine. Playing cards. Jewelry. Halloween. Celebrating your birthday. But my church was far from that.

Jesse used to say that out West, when someone asked, "What do you do?" that meant what do you do for fun. Though he worked as a computer programmer, when asked, "What do you do?" Jesse usually said, "I'm a musician." Or, "I ride my bike." The first few times I heard him say this, I thought he was cheating. Here in Boston, "What do you do?" means what do you do for money, not fun. Jesse knew that, but he was a mountain man stuck in an East Coast city, and I admired his willingness to hold fast to his version of the truth.

That night, tired of the same old response, I decided to take a page out of Jesse's book. Heck, I was already at a party in a pink turtleneck. How much dumber could I look?

"I'm a minister," I admitted to Mitch, "but I don't like to tell people." Okay, so it wasn't totally a Jesse response, but I was getting closer.

"What would you *like* to say?" Mitch asked.

"I work in a bakery!" I blurted out. *A bakery? Where had that come from?*

Mitch called his friend Avery over.

"Meet Amanda," he said. "Ask her what she does."

"Hey, Amanda. What do you do?" Avery asked, being a good sport.

"I work in a bakery!" I practically sang my reply. And even though it wasn't true, and neither Mitch nor Avery seemed particularly impressed or interested in my "career" as a baker, I felt a surge of excitement and pride when I imagined working at the bakery, with its smell like Heaven, long table, and jars of flowers. Doesn't my bread smell like coming home? Doesn't it taste like comfort? Don't you feel so *r-e-l-a-x-e-d* here in this pretty place, where time creeps by and your only task is to wrap your hand around a warm cup and drink slowly? I pictured myself in a white apron instead of a black robe, and suddenly I felt more like me.

Had I been in another setting, like my therapist's office, and not a party partway through another glass of red wine, it wouldn't have taken much digging to uncover that it wasn't *really* about the baking. I'm actually more of a cook than a baker. It was about working someplace that felt like a right fit, that felt inspiring, beautiful, welcoming. Which, ironically, was part of what being a minister was all about too—preaching uplifting messages in a pretty sanctuary that was open to all. Only there was a lot of additional luggage that went with it.

I remembered back to a recent Sunday morning before the service, when a choir member poked her head in my office to tell me that her grown daughter was coming to visit from Texas. I didn't know this choir lady well, and I certainly didn't know her daughter, and all I really wanted to shout was, "I DON'T CARE! *Why* are you telling me this?" Of course I knew why: it was my job to care. Instead I smiled and nodded appropriately and murmured, "That's nice." But really, I wanted to close the door in her face. Hide out in my office. Skip church altogether to stare dumbly at my computer screen. I know that doesn't sound very nice, but that's how I understood I was so ready to be done: I envisioned doing unfriendly things to perfectly pleasant people. I imagined bypassing the choir lady and running down the hall, out of the building, and into my car where I'd speed home to hibernate under a pile of quilts, emerging at midday to eat chocolate brioche and read Jane Austen at the bakery. Or maybe self-help. I really was starting to warm up to the genre.

Is it any wonder then that I'd get a little jolt from pretending to work in a bakery? Because for just a minute or two I got a taste of what it might feel like to love what you do. To feel proud of the imprint you're leaving, no matter how tiny, on your corner of the world. And it didn't take a suggestion from someone else, or a wild idea, or a big fancy job, to bring it about. The opposite, really. Imagination. Letting go. Not thinking too hard. Not caring what anyone else thought. Deep down I knew that it didn't really matter how other people responded to my job title, what mattered was how I felt about it.

I'd been having such trouble *figuring out* the next Big Thing, when maybe what I needed was to simply imagine myself into something. Why not exchange a Big Thing for a small thing, something good enough for now? The author of *Dance!* described something similar, what she called "drop-out" work in the sense that it didn't define your life like a full-blown career might; rather, a drop-out job covered expenses and still left time and energy to dream about what else came next. Then, when it was time to move on, you could drop-out easily enough, no strings attached. I hadn't considered temporary work. It seemed like a step down. Or back. But maybe I didn't have to figure out *everything* at once. Maybe I could step away from the church and into the arms of something good enough for now. Try it out and see. Kind of like dating, but jobs, not men.

Eventually the silver-haired man drifted away, and I was drawn into another conversation, but Mitch had left an impression. I briefly contemplated asking Matt for Mitch's email. It would be easy enough to find a pretext for getting in touch and to see if he responded. At the end of the night, though, when I noticed his arm around a younger, thinner, blonder girl—a musician of some renown—I told myself to forget it. He'd never go for a minister/pretend-baker in a pink turtleneck. Besides, wasn't I taking time off from dating?

✳ ✳ ✳

"When's it happening?" my therapist Bonnie asked, from her seat in an armchair across from me. I'd been seeing Bonnie for seven years, but she didn't usually ask such direct questions, and I was caught off guard.

"When's what happening?" I asked back.

"When are you leaving the church? Let's start with that, and then we'll know how much time you have to plan for what's next."

For a few years now I'd been telling my wise hippie therapist Bonnie that I wasn't exactly happy being a minister. Sometimes I wondered if she wanted to shout, "All right already! Leave the goddamn church!" She was a Unitarian who read tarot cards and sent me *Happy Solstice!* cards every December. I liked her casual, earthy approach, and having a place to talk openly about whatever. It wasn't lost on me that, though she was the same age as my mother, they were total opposites. At sixty Bonnie was divorced from a man, child-free, and partnered with a woman. She wore blue nail polish on her toes, Birkenstocks in all seasons, and flowing purple garments, and she'd been trained as a sex therapist, which had been pretty handy when I was going through my "sexual awakening." I think she'd been as shocked as Luke when, early on in our sessions, we arrived at the topic of my fantasy life and I admitted to not having one. By now Bonnie had seen me through all the big changes in my adult life, and my professional earth-mother was about to see me through one more.

She sat across from me expectantly, pen above paper, waiting for my "when" so she could write up a timeline on her yellow legal pad and send me home with a copy, no doubt, to keep me from chickening out. I knew she was going to hold me to it.

"I'll leave right now!" I announced in answer to her lingering *When?*

She smiled but didn't write anything down.

"Umm, okay, well, the church year is like the school year, which means our programs end in June, so that's a natural time for me to leave."

"June," she said, writing something down on her pad. "Early June? Mid-June?"

"End of June," I suggested. "That gives me time to leave things in an organized place for my successor." My successor. Someone was going to replace me. I couldn't believe I was actually having this conversation. Sure, it was taking place within the safe confines of my therapist's office, which was very different from telling the church, or my parents. But even so, something about this felt real. I felt practically giddy with anticipation, and something else too—a sense of control over my life. I was actually going to do it. I was actually going to leave being a minister. *YES!* There's something powerful about imagining things to yourself, but to bring a thought out of the dark and into the light, to say it aloud to someone else, to hear yourself making a plan, is another sort of inspiring altogether.

"It's the end of February now," Bonnie said, "so that gives us four months to get a plan in place. How much notice would you like to give the church?"

I thought ahead. Mid-April was the annual service trip with the youth group and advisors. This year we were going to volunteer in Tucson with immigrants and a water-conservation program; everyone was excited about the week, and I didn't want my news to overshadow any of that.

"End of April," I decided. "After the Tucson trip."

"Okay, so now you have two months to get used to the idea that you're actually going to leave the church before you officially tell anyone. You can do it." Bonnie smiled over at me and handed me the yellow sheet on which she'd been taking notes. And just like that, I had a timeline. Bonnie had been my marriage counselor and sex therapist, and now she was my career coach too.

✳   ✳   ✳

I had four months to figure out what came next, and I was getting comfortable with the idea that it wouldn't be the next Big Thing. Searching for that, I'd come up empty-handed. Maybe it was time to rephrase the question. To exchange *what* for *where*: where did I like to spend time? The bakery was high on my list, but practically speaking, my hideout that smelled like Heaven was just that, a hideout, and I'd lose the bakery as a place of escape and peacefulness if I applied for a job there. But there *was* a bustling cheese shop around the corner from the bakery, just a ten-minute walk from my apartment. I'd been inside only a few times, but it was a high-energy gourmand's paradise doubling as a neighborhood grocery store (if you weren't too concerned about how much your groceries cost). Three adjoining rooms overflowed with everything from local salad greens to craft chocolate to wine, but the epicenter was the legendary cheese counter. I didn't have the experience to work behind that counter, but I wondered if they might be hiring for cashier or something like it.

I rallied my courage one March morning—asking for a job made me feel vulnerable, but my new life had to begin someday—and stepped inside the cheese shop. On the right was a wooden counter, and behind it were baskets of bread and a man with a beard and brown ponytail. He didn't look too intimidating.

"Hey! Can I help you?"

"Hey. Good morning. So I'm actually interested in a job. Is there someone I should talk to?"

"You'll want to see the manager about that. Just head over to the cheese counter and ask for Zack."

Zack, the owner's son, was a tall, striking twenty-something-year-old whose expertise and brusque manner didn't ease my nerves, but he told me to email him my resume and we'd set up a meeting with his dad. A week later I was sitting in the basement, the only part of the store big enough to fit two chairs, with Zack's father. Ed was a former Olympian and had coached at the college level before opening the shop. He had an intensity befitting a driven athlete, which could manifest in charm or anger; rumor had it he threw things when he got really angry, and while I never saw him do that, I certainly heard him yell. But I didn't know any of that yet. I just knew that I desperately wanted to work in his shop.

"I see you're a minister," Ed observed, looking over my resume. "There's a minister who lives near my summer place in Westport. His name is Don. Do you know him? He's a great guy, loves one of our champagnes; I usually bring him a few bottles."

That was the extent of our conversation about my being a minister, which was just fine by me. I was being interviewed to ring up groceries, stock shelves, and sweep; it didn't really matter if I could chair a meeting, or stand at a graveside and say something meaningful. Ed said they had space for me as a part-time cashier, with shifts stocking produce and staffing the bakery counter. The only part of the store where I wouldn't be working was the cheese counter, but that was also fine by me, as it seemed pretty intense on that side of the shop. The best part was that I could start at the cheese shop while I was still at the church. I'd work Fridays and Saturdays, the equivalent of my weekend as a minister, as well as the early shift on Monday before youth group. This way I could see how the cheese shop felt before actually leaving church, giving myself an out just in case.

As I emerged from the basement, past displays of produce and flowers, and waved goodbye to the friendly man with a ponytail behind the register, I felt my eyes well up. I held it together until I rounded the corner and shut myself in my car. And then I felt such an immense sense of relief that I cried behind my sunglasses, out of gratitude for the chance to try something new. I didn't care that I'd be working seven days a week. That I'd be the lowest on the totem pole. That I didn't know where this might lead, if anywhere. I was just so ready for a change of scene, so grateful that I'd finally given myself permission to just go for it, without needing all the answers. Up ahead wasn't the point; I knew that now. A plan for right now was the only thing I had to figure out.

A week after my basement interview, Right Now began. I woke up at six thirty on a Friday morning; dressed in a fitted sweatshirt, jeans, and my gray patent leather clogs, which, along with a white apron, would become my unofficial uniform; and walked ten minutes to my first shift at the cheese shop, where I learned, among other things, how to use a cash register and how to judge a baguette. The store sold bread from three local bakeries, in addition to baking their own, and all of it looked the same, but it wasn't; and though none of the baguettes came from France, they *did* receive a weekly shipment of other breads from a famous bakery in Paris. Compared to my circle of friends, I knew a thing or two about food, but in the company of these professionals, I felt like a culinary bumpkin. A few were friendly and generous with their knowledge, but most were too busy doing their jobs to pay attention to a novice like me. Yet even with the indifference, and a paycheck so much smaller than I was accustomed to that I cried in the basement the first time I opened one, I was glad to be there. Without traveling more than a few blocks from my apartment, I was introduced to a whole new world of food. I met the kaffir lime and the Meyer lemon; I ate oranges the color of blood, muscat grapes so sweet they tasted like candy, and tiny spoonfuls of honey sweetened from lavender eaten by bees who flew in Provence.

And lo, the cheese. The cheese counter stretched the length of the third room—a glass case filled with rounds and blocks and wedges of mostly New England and European varieties—and on top of the cheese case was the "cheese wall," more piles of cheese that were taken down and refrigerated every other day. (That hard cheeses like cheddar and parmesan could be stored at room temperature for a couple of days was news to me.) Sticking out of each chunk of cheese was a tag with its name and provenance, something like: *Adrahan / Made by Mary Burns near Kanturk, County Cork, Ireland.* This was followed by a colorful description of the sort you'd usually see attached to wine: *A washed-rind cow's milk cheese with a pungent, farmhouse aroma. Creamy and nutty in flavor, with a lingering saline finish; a great pairing with a strong ale.* I was pretty sure that *lingering saline finish* was a fancy way to say "salty aftertaste," but here at the shop, cheese was an art form, worthy of colorful prose. And it worked: I could picture myself in County Cork, on Mary Burns's farm, gazing at green pastures full of brown-eyed cows, eating nutty cheese, washing it down with a pint of Kilkenny. A walk through this neighborhood shop made you feel like you'd traveled across the world, and that was part of its appeal. For a small fortune, though a lot less than it would cost to travel to Ireland, you could buy everything you might need for a gorgeous dinner party. My work wasn't as gorgeous as the food; at the end of a shift I'd sweep the floor, collect the trash, and carry it out to the back alley, banging the door loudly to make sure the rats scattered first. But it *was* something different. And it was good enough for now.

✳ ✳ ✳

A second place came to mind as I pictured where I liked to be. Alongside the cheese shop, it could be the perfect bridge to carry me out of being a minister and into whatever came next. On another brisk March morning, I drove out to the country, down a tree-lined drive, and into the parking lot of Nancy's Airfield Cafe, pulling up beside my cousin's blue truck. Inside the restaurant the hostess waved me toward the back room, where picture windows overlooked a landing strip and my cousin Dwight and his wife Barbara were waiting for me.

"Hey, kid! Good to see you." Barbara stood and gave me a

hug. She was nearly six feet tall and thin as a rail but still strong for seventy-eight, and with naturally brown hair without a hint of gray in it, people were often surprised when I told them how old she was.

"Hello," said Dwight, nodding, and he stood to wrap one arm around me in a gruff embrace. He was eight years younger than Barbara, bald with a bushy gray beard, and a man of very few words but a very gentle spirit. Even though Barbara and Dwight were family—Dwight was my mom's first cousin, and he and Barbara had been married nearly forty years—I felt nervous about this conversation. I'd never asked them for anything before.

"We're so glad you called us. What a treat to have lunch together," Barbara began as we settled ourselves at a table overlooking the runway. I looked over at Dwight, who nodded, and I smiled back at him.

"Have you started planting in the greenhouse yet?" I asked, the only sure way to get Dwight talking. It worked, and I bided my time. An hour later, plates cleaned, greenhouse and family gossip covered, I finally worked up the courage to ask what was on my mind.

"Well, there's a reason I called you for lunch. I mean, aside from seeing you," I explained. "I've decided to leave the church in June, and I'm not sure what comes next, but for now I want to be someplace that feels right with my heart. And if you'll have me, I wondered if I might work on the farm this summer."

Barbara clapped her hands like a child. "The Lord has answered our prayers!"

"Your prayers?" I hadn't been expecting the Lord to figure in our conversation.

"I've been so worried about this season and how short-staffed we'd be, but this makes all the difference!" she beamed.

I looked over at Dwight, who nodded again.

"I was so nervous to ask you. I mean, you're sure?"

"Oh, we'd love it. What an honor. But isn't the church sad you're leaving?" Barbara asked. Dwight wasn't religious, but Barbara was my most churchy relative besides cousin Bob, the minister. I wasn't surprised that she was concerned about my church's reaction.

"I haven't told them yet. I want to figure out my plan first, but I'll tell them in April, and I'm sure they'll be fine. It's just not in my heart anymore."

"You mean you're quitting cold turkey? That's it?"

"I don't know how I'll feel in the future, but for now, yes, I need a break."

"Nancy, come over here," Barbara called over to the chef, for whom the restaurant was named. "This is Amanda. She's our cousin, and she's going to work at our farm this summer. Isn't that neat?"

I had to agree too. It was pretty neat.

Driving home that afternoon, a winding pastoral ride that would soon become my forty-minute commute, I felt a sense of rightness I hadn't felt in a long time. Come July, I'd get to spend half my working days (the ones when I wasn't at the cheese shop) and, best of all, my Sundays, not in a sanctuary, but outside in a field. The farm felt like my outside home, and with its birds for a choir and trees for a dome—reminding me of Dickinson's poem about keeping Sabbath in the orchard—I had a guess that, that summer, I would feel like I was right where I was meant to be. At least for now.

This, then, was my plan for the "nows" that came as of July first: I would work Monday through Wednesday at the cheese shop around the corner from my apartment in the city, pushing buttons on a cash register, selling baguettes, and stocking produce; and the other four days of the week I'd commute to the country, where I'd plant produce and flowers, and pick them in time to sell at the farm stand on the property, where I'd push buttons on a cash register too. It was all several steps down from preaching sermons and officiating weddings; instead of being up in a pulpit, I'd be down on my knees pulling weeds, or behind a counter counting change, manual labor instead of a white-collar profession with a title. But for now, this was exactly what I wanted, and I could already tell: this time I would . . . eye roll, if you like . . . *Dance!*

13. Beginning Again

I didn't need a master's degree or even a high school diploma to do this work; my colleagues were fourteen-year-old boys, and dirt was embedded under my nails and in the cracked skin of my fingers. I wore old tank tops, cargo shorts, and boots; I carried a knife in my pocket; and I loved everything about it. Especially the weeding.

"Hey, kid! We're closing!" my cousin Barbara called out to me in the herb garden one July evening. The fact that she still called me "kid" made me feel younger than thirty-three and carefree, like I was nobody's pastor, and that felt like such a relief.

"What time is it?" I yelled back.

"After six!"

Already? I'd been so into pulling weeds that I hadn't noticed the sun getting lower in the sky. It was mindless work—down on my knees, yanking tenacious green shoots out of the dirt and tossing them into the wheelbarrow beside me. I could think about whatever I wanted, or better yet, nothing at all, just focusing on the task at hand in a meditative sort of way. It was so *satisfying* too; in just a few minutes—or a few hours, depending on the size of the overgrown patch—I'd wrought a noticeable transformation with my hands alone—bright green parsley plants popped out of the dirt in tidy rows, waving in the breeze. Pick me! Pick me! they seemed to say, and before heading back to the stand, I obliged, cutting a bunch of stems down low to create a parsley bouquet. This was one of the perks of my new job—an endless supply of fresh herbs, flowers, and vegetables all summer long. Looking at the spot where I'd cut the parsley, you couldn't even tell I'd taken any, which was something else I loved about the farm: the abundance of everything. Even on the busiest days, we never ran out of flowers to cut, or lettuce to pick. It just kept coming. I smiled down at my bright green bouquet, like a proud parent. I'd put it in a glass milk bottle next to my kitchen sink: a taste of country back home in the city.

Standing up, I brushed dirt off my knees and peeled off my pink-and-white gardening gloves. Even with the gloves on, I still got dirt on my hands, but I liked them: a parting gift, along with the knife in my pocket, from a couple at the church. I looked over at Barbara and Dwight, who were stacking boxes of vegetables in a wheeled cart, which I'd take down to the cooler in the barn for the night. I closed my eyes for just a moment. *Now I finally get it. This is what it feels like to love your work. As if you are right where you are meant to be.*

I'd watched musicians lost in their song, preachers on fire, teachers passionate about their subject, but I'd never experienced it firsthand before: to love what you're doing so much you're caught up in the moment. Now here I was, actually getting paid to do something that I loved. Even though I was making less than I'd made before, my gratitude for the money was infinitely greater; along with my job at the cheese shop and some savings that I'd managed to squirrel away, it was enough for now.

For now. Those two words had become my mantra. They were the words that I reminded myself of whenever I started to worry about the future or what came next. This was the right job, for now. I had enough money, for now. It was okay that I wasn't dating, for now. *For now* scrolled through my mind, reminding me to let go and enjoy the here and now; I was exactly where I was meant to be.

I knew this for sure one Sunday morning on a short walk to the kale to fill my bucket for the farm stand. True to its name, it didn't take long to get anywhere on "small farm," which was how Dwight liked to write it, no capitals. When I'd asked if this was the official spelling for the farm, Barbara had said, "Oh, that's just Dwight. He likes it that way. I think it looks stupid." And then, with a wave of her hand, she added, "But whatever. He's the farmer." By which she meant *he'll do it his way, I'll do it mine,* an arrangement that, after forty-three years of marriage, seemed to be working pretty well for them. At twenty-four acres, only five of which were planted (the rest were marsh and woodland), the property was small, however you spelled it, compared to the average farm.

Walking past a clump of wild blackberry bushes, I reached for one of the deep purple berries. It was soft to the touch, still warm from the sun, and I popped it in my mouth. Back in my office days I used to keep peppermint patties in my desk drawer for a midafternoon pick-me-up, but those had nothing on these. This was another perk of the job: snacking on sun-warmed berries and sungold tomatoes that seemed to drip off the vine. In the heart of the season you could stand in one place and pick a whole pint in under thirty seconds. For lunch I'd gotten into the habit of picking a handful, along with a small head of lettuce, and making them into a salad with whatever else was on hand: raw corn straight off the cob, a cucumber, a radish, and a generous pour of homemade dressing over the top to finish it. I wasn't usually a salad-for-lunch sort of person, preferring something a bit more substantial, but my favorite bakery and its gorgeous sandwiches, were forty minutes away. Besides, this was free and easy, and best of all I felt good eating food straight from the field.

I picked another berry for the road and continued down the dirt path, passing perfectly straight lines of red and green lettuce I'd pick for lunch and a row of orange zucchini blossoms that would soon offer up green and yellow fruit. I stopped when I reached the kale. My ears perked up. *What is that sound?* A ringing. It was familiar, but even so, it took a moment to place the noise because it was so out of context. Or rather, *I* was out of context.

Church bells!

It had been more than a month since my last Sunday in church, my longest church-less stretch in thirty-three years of life, except for college, but I didn't miss it. Not that I was anti-church; it was just that for now, I was enjoying my newfound freedom on Sunday. I still believed in God, or what I preferred to call the divine—an energy bigger and more loving than we can imagine, that connects all of life. I just didn't believe that you have to go to church to access that energy. Rather, you can tap into it anytime, anyplace, if you're open to it. Hiking up a hillside. Listening to music. Surrounded by friends. Alone in a field. Like right now. What a sweet relief it was to be just me, with only kale for a congregation, a chorus of birds and bees and bells in the background.

✳ ✳ ✳

My last day as a minister, I'd been so eager to mark the moment that I stayed awake to watch the clock change from 11:59 to 12:00 a.m. When I was a kid, and staying up until midnight was an annual treat reserved for New Year's Eve, we'd welcome January by opening the front door, banging pots and pans with wooden spoons and shouting, "Hap-py New Year!" to the neighborhood. If I hadn't been so tired that night, I would have banged a pot and shouted. Instead I just whispered, "Hap-py New Day!" and fell asleep.

My cousins had left my starting date up to me, and while I could have taken off a few days between the church and the farm, I was so ready to be out with the old, in with the new, that I started July 1, the day after staying up to watch the clock turn. To be excited to go to work was a totally new feeling for me. Even the cheese shop with its overwhelming array of worldly goods didn't make me feel like this. I pulled into the modest gravel parking lot at noon, parking beside Dwight's blue pickup, and wondered if I *should* have taken a day off, since I'd slept in and was late. Luckily, I would learn that my cousins were quite forgiving when it came to details like running late; the whole farm had a casual, easy-going feel to it, and Barbara's cheerful greeting erased any guilt about my late arrival.

"Good to see you, kid." She hugged me. "You're just in time for lunch." And she picked up a metal mallet, warned me, "Look out!" and hit a rusty cylinder that hung from the roof of the farm stand.

The sharp clang of metal on metal, also known as the lunch bell, reached out to the farthest field, and a few minutes later, four sweaty boys, along with my cousin Dwight, walked up the dirt road from the field.

"Look at you! You're filthy!" Barbara said to Dwight, gesturing to his soaking green T-shirt and arms covered in dirt.

"Well, what do you expect?" asked the farmer, chuckling as everyone took a seat around a picnic table set up under a white tent behind the farm stand. The boys started to unpack their lunches but paused before digging in. Barbara had them well trained.

"Amanda, would you like to say the grace?" she asked. Dwight and the kids looked over to me. Grace before lunch was Barbara's idea; either she said it, or she asked one of the boys or a guest to do the honors (there were often visitors at the lunch table). Generally speaking, I liked grace. As a minister, I'd often been asked to say the blessing before a church supper or a wedding meal, and at family dinners we still held hands around the table and said thanks before eating; usually one of us inserted something mildly irreverent into the short prayer, but we were serious in our gratefulness, if not our style. Today, though, my first day on the farm, it was the start of something new. As a minister, I'd never said no to leading a prayer, but I didn't have to be a "professional" religious person anymore. I could simply listen to a prayer, not lead it, blending in with the crowd—well, as much as a thirty-three-year-old can blend in with teenage boys and two older farmers. Still, what a relief to be one of this little group, not standing apart or above, but sitting beside. It felt as if that yoke had been lifted from my shoulders. As if I could take a deep breath, sit up a little straighter, and feel more like myself.

Everyone was staring expectantly at me. Next time I'd do it, but for today I asked Barbara, "Would you mind saying it in my place?" hoping she'd understand. And she did.

"Dear Lord," she began, bowing her head and closing her eyes, but instead of closing my eyes as usual, I gazed out at the green before me; it had taken me a while to get here, and, like a tall glass of water after a hot summer hike, I didn't want to miss a drop. Dwight, I noticed, kept his eyes open too.

"Finally, God," Barbara was finishing up her short prayer, "we thank you for bringing Amanda to our small farm. Amen."

I pulled my eyes away from the view and smiled over at my cousins. "Thank you," I offered, grateful for this chance to begin again. Wherever it led, I was glad to be here for now; I was just twelve hours away from being a minister, and already I felt more free and easy than I had in months.

*　*　*

Saying goodbye to the church had been a lot less dramatic than saying goodbye to my marriage, but it raised a similar question. If leaving felt so right, were we ever a true match to begin with? Or had I been so *insistent* on figuring things out that I'd imagined a call where there hadn't been one? I decided to ask Jonathan, the minister at Pilgrim Church who'd planted the seed of ministry when I was searching for the next Big Thing nearly ten years before. He'd moved out to Oregon, but we kept in touch, and that summer when he was back for a visit, we met for lunch at the bakery.

"So, how are things?" Jonathan smiled across the table as he took off his Stetson hat. Even though I hadn't seen him in a few years, he always looked the same, brown hair, glasses, youthful even at fifty-something, his mustache exchanged for a goatee.

"Well, my big news is that I've just left the church. Nothing bad happened. I just fell out of love with being a minister. If I ever *was* in love."

He smiled back at me, sensing I had more to say.

"Do you think I was really called to be a minister?" I asked. "Or did I just make it up because I wanted a job? I mean, I *thought* it felt right back then, back when I went to divinity school. It made sense with the bigger picture of my life, with Luke being a minister, and my parents being into church too. But now," I confessed, "it's the leaving that feels so right."

Jonathan offered me one of his easy smiles. He was the same relaxed, thoughtful mentor I remembered from my growing-up years.

"Oh, I think you *were* called," he assured me.

"But how could you *tell*?" I wondered aloud.

"I could just see it in you. Every time you got up front to speak, you had a gift with words, and a connection with people, and I could feel the energy shift in the sanctuary. People responded to you. There was a genuine connection. And now, even though you still have those gifts in you, you're just called to something else. That's life."

Jonathan wasn't a Buddhist, but he could have been for the truth he was reminding me of—that everything around us is always and forever shifting, that change is inevitable, and suffering comes when we cling on to that which was/is. It's when we let go, accepting the inevitability of change, that suffering gives way to peace.

"I know you'll find what you're looking for," he added, smiling kindly at me across the table.

From the man who had laid his hand on my head at my ordination and proclaimed me a minister of God, his understanding now was another gift—a less-public, less-formal blessing to follow my heart. Sitting in this space that still smelled like Heaven, across from my mentor, I accepted this gift of understanding and let go of one call to listen for another. This wasn't how I thought my life would go down. In my twenties I'd assumed the choices I'd made would last for good, but now I understood that to live is to learn and grow, and thus to change. Growing doesn't always necessitate *major* life change, but for me it had. Maybe that's because what I had to learn was how to listen to my inner voice, to find the courage to follow where it led, even if that looked different from what I imagined. If I'd been listening all along, would I have become a minister? Would I have married Luke? Well, you can always look back, indulge your inner critic, judge your younger choices, and wonder *what if?* Or you can let go of the old questions, the ones that have already been answered, for better, for worse, and move on. Here, now, this is my life.

My last few months in the church I'd tried to listen more clearly to my inner voice and follow where it led. When I wrote a letter announcing my decision to leave, admitting that my call had changed, that I didn't know what came next but would spend a summer on the farm, it felt like I was getting closer to my authentic self. As I preached a farewell sermon that took its inspiration not from scripture but from Emily Dickinson's poem about Possibility, I noticed that there was no mention of the Bible or Jesus in my writing. This had been my trend in recent months, but I'd always felt a little guilty about neglecting the hallmarks of a Christian sermon. This time around, though, I decided to own it, admitting in my last sermon that while my words were less traditional than they used to be, I had learned the importance of speaking from my heart. As I look back on that farewell sermon, and all the ones before it, I realize now that no one ever criticized my style or suggested I ramp up the God-talk. I have a feeling that's *partly* because I come from a pretty liberal tradition, but more than that I think people can tell when you're being your authentic self, and it's more likely to resonate, whatever you're saying.

I had preached my last word and hung up my robe. In a final bow to who I was right now, I threw caution to the wind and, on our last official night together, invited the advisors into the back room at the cheese shop.

To drink beer.

* * *

By mid-June I'd been moonlighting at the cheese shop since March, but I still hadn't told anyone at the church about it. I didn't want it to appear that I was neglecting my responsibilities. What's more, working on a family farm had a certain wholesome appeal to it, but cashier in a store? Even a classy European-like shop staffed by gourmands? Well, my professional pride got in the way, and I had decided to keep this part of my life tucked away until I had a reason to do otherwise. Now I had found the reason: to thank the advisors for all their help with the youth group, and for making me laugh, I was treating them to a beer tasting at the shop, which sold a small but thoughtfully curated selection of drinks. Like introducing your best friend to your boyfriend, I was nervous but excited to bring together the old and new. The advisors knew me as their leader, and here in the cheese shop I was pretty much the stock girl, working a register among other things. But in spite of my "demotion," I was enthralled with this bustling setting and its fancy food. Would the advisors like it here too? Or at least understand what I saw in this place?

We all walked the ten minutes from my apartment to the store, and I smiled to myself as the group tried to guess where I was taking them. I've always loved the sense of anticipation that paves the way to a good surprise, and I knew that none of them had any idea where we'd end up. The shop was officially closed as we approached from the side, and while I could have taken everyone down to the main entrance and had someone unlock the front door for us, making it clear we were in a market, I decided to prolong the suspense.

"This way," I said, as I led the advisors through an unmarked employee entrance, emptying us into a small industrial kitchen where one of the night staff was washing dishes in a deep sink.

"Where *are* we?" one of my unsuspecting followers asked as I led the twelve of them out of that kitchen, through the cheese room where a few of the cheesemongers were putting rounds of tomme and blocks of cheddar into the case for the night, and into the baker's kitchen beyond. This was our makeshift tasting room for tonight: a large metal work surface had been set up with glasses, big bottles of small-batch European brews—Belgian ales, German wheats, English porters—and hunks of cheese to accompany our tasting.

"Is all of this for *us*?" Colin asked, eyes opened wide at the drinkable feast before us.

"Yes!" I smiled at the group, enjoying my role as hostess. I was pretty sure they liked it here. "This is a cheese shop which also sells beer, as you can see, and this is Tim, the beer buyer." I introduced them to a tall friendly guy who'd just walked into the kitchen. "Tim's organized this beer tasting for us. And the reason I know him, and the store, is because I work here."

"Wait, *you* work *here*?" Colin asked. "How did we not know that?"

"I think Amanda's pretty good at keeping secrets," Jen said, and she smiled over at me. She knew that I didn't reveal much personal stuff, but now that I was on my way out, the boundaries between work and personal were starting to blur, and I liked that I could share this part of my life with them. And I think they liked it too. Though everyone was quiet at first, their tongues loosened after a few sips, no surprise, and as we sampled one beer after another, and the advisors asked intelligent beer questions and made plenty of jokes, I felt my heart swell to be part of this group.

I remembered back to my first years at the church—how the advisors would go out for a pint on Monday nights after youth group meetings and I would rush home to Luke. I remembered back to our trip to South Dakota, when at the end of the week we'd toured the Coors brewery and I'd waited outside with the kids while the advisors sampled. Now here we were, in a cramped kitchen tasting beer all together. I didn't feel like an outsider watching other people have fun; instead I was in the midst of the fun, standing on a bridge between my old world and my new, and inviting the advisors to stand here with me.

The mood was jovial as we walked back to my apartment for a late dinner that I'd prepared ahead of time. And just when I thought the night was wrapping up, it was the advisors' turn to surprise me. It'd been my custom to pick out an individual gift for each of them, which I gave at our end-of-year dinner, wrapped in brown craft paper and tied up with pretty ribbons. This year, instead of individual gifts, I'd given everyone the beer tasting, but the advisors' surprise was that each of them had picked out an individual gift for *me*. What's more, each of them had wrapped my present in brown paper, tied with a pretty ribbon, just the way I usually did for them, and each little item was meant to celebrate my path ahead. I opened a pair of bright green gardening gloves, a vegetarian cookbook, a bottle of wine, stationery to keep in touch, and so on until I had a pile of presents beside me.

Common wisdom may say it's better to give than to receive, and in my young adulthood I'd internalized this belief, offering myself and not expecting much in return. But there is an art to receiving as well—to sitting back and letting goodness flow to you. That night I sat back and received with all my heart, as the tangible tokens piled up beside me, and the intangible ones of camaraderie and joy, wove their way around me.

I thought back to our first meeting, five summers earlier, on a sweaty July night when I'd been so intimidated by this boisterous group with their "secular" traditions and had resigned myself to enduring my work with them. If you had told me then that this was how my ministry would end—laughing in my living room, drinking beer with the advisors-turned-friends as they handed me presents tied up with dainty ribbons—I would have said, "*No way.*"

Even so, I like to believe that, if I'd really stopped to think about it back then, *something* about this final scene might have resonated, might have called out to me from up ahead, like a familiar tune you haven't heard in years. In college I'd loved entertaining, treasured the moments I was in the midst of laughter; later in my twenties, I yearned to be part of a big group of friends. In fact, what I'd always loved best about church was the sense of community, but when it became my profession, I got lost in the role and felt set apart. Now, on my way out, here I was in the heart of a fun-loving set of friends. I'd invited them into my home (not a big brick house, yet, but it *was* a big brick apartment building) and let them see that I was developing a taste for beer and digging in the dirt on Sunday.

"*No way,*" I imagined my younger self saying about this final scene, weighed down by feelings of obligation after her first official meeting with the advisors. But from where I sat now, surrounded by a pile of presents and waves of laughter, I was so grateful for the unexpected ways that life works out.

As I closed the door behind my friends at the end of the night, a flash of metal caught my eye. On the floor, behind the door, was the first present they'd given me, back when I was married and living in my old house, the Tibetan prayer bells that I'd put in my trunk and heard singing the day I moved to Cambridge. I bent down, picked up the tiny mallet and hit each bell, from low to high:

Ding, dang, dong!

They were meant to be meditative, and on that drive to Cambridge their tinkling had been a comforting reminder that I wasn't alone. Tonight, I *knew* that I wasn't alone, and the bells sounded like joy.

✳ ✳ ✳

The earliest memory I have of church, somewhere around age four, is climbing up to the belfry to help ring the bell before a Sunday service. In turn, as a minister, I'd led wide-eyed children up the ladder and into the tower to ring the bell for themselves. Bell song often spoke to me. Like the time I heard the church bells ring after officiating a summer wedding, just a few weeks past my own divorce. The ceremony itself had flowed seamlessly; it wasn't until the couple recessed down the aisle arm in arm and the bells began to ring that I felt something stir in my own heart and I sank onto a bench in the hallway and cried for my own connection so recently dissolved.

There in the field on that hot summer Sunday, out of context completely, I heard the bells ringing from outside the church, and I felt free. I had shed a layer: trading in my heavy black robe and heels for an old tank top and boots, but even more than that, I was shedding the *shoulds* and growing a new skin of *anything can be.*

My congregation had sent me on my way with their blessing, and my cousins had welcomed me to the farm with theirs. Finally, I felt that I was right where I wanted to be. Had I found it, then? Would this summer job turn into the next Big Thing? Would my contentment pulling weeds and feasting on sun-warmed black-berries last for years and years, until eventually I'd take over the farm? Marry again, a man who liked to drive tractors, and we'd build a house in the empty field out back, raise our children to love dirt, live happily ever after on love and vegetables, the end?

Maybe.

Or maybe not.

The Sufi mystic Rumi said, "Let the beauty be what we do. There are hundreds of ways to kneel and kiss the ground." In my early twenties, I'd assumed that there was just one way for me to kneel, one Big Thing, and that once I found it, we would be part-ners for life. But now here I was, ten years later, doing something completely different.

How long would this last?

I knew better than to try and figure out my forever in this moment. "Forever is composed of nows." So I stopped thinking of anything but right now and felt the warm sun shining down upon my head like a blessing from above. Over the past few years I'd lost a sense of the divine in my work, but standing here in a field in my muddy boots, I felt such a sense of rightness that I could only describe it as divine, and I offered a silent word of gratitude, not in advance, not looking back, but for the right now that was my life that Sunday morning outside on a small farm.

Then I knelt down on the ground, let my knees sink into the warm dirt, and filled my bucket with greens.

Coda

About a year later . . .

Barbara hit the bell three times, and on cue my friends began to drift in from the field carrying jugs of flowers and glasses of beer, ready to eat.

"Is someone going to say a blessing?" she asked.

"I have a plan, don't worry," I assured her. After two seasons on the farm, I'd already anticipated my cousin's attention to grace.

It was mid-September, a year and few months since I'd left the church. I'd loved my first season at small farm so much that one summer had turned into a second, and I was planning to come back again next year. My work at the cheese shop had carried me through my first year out of the church and had come to a natural close in May, when I started back to the farm full-time. Come November, when the farm closed down for the winter, I would start exploring other interests—cooking, teaching, writing. Who knew where they might lead, but I was grateful for all of these possibilities outside of the church. Occasionally I still preached a sermon at Pilgrim or officiated a friend's wedding, but that was the extent of my church life these days, and I liked it that way. One day up ahead, when I had a family of my own, I might feel a pull toward church again, but for now I was right where I wanted to be.

Tonight I'd invited fifty friends to have supper at small farm, something that had become an annual tradition, a chance for my friends to travel out to the country and wander around the fields, and for me to show off this place where I felt so proud to work. As the last person drifted in from the field and we stood in a big circle beside the farm stand, I asked my cousins to tell everyone the story of the farm: how it began with one tractor and a field of pumpkins and had grown into seven tractors and twenty-four acres, but more than that, a labor of love.

As Barbara and Dwight finished up, I look around at all the familiar faces.

"Supper is ready, but before we eat, I thought everyone could say something they're grateful for."

As my friends started to speak, a little hand tugged at mine, and I looked down to a toddler in a blue sundress. Kelley had finally had the baby she'd been longing for and was expecting another. I picked up my little friend and listened as my big friends shared the ordinary everyday things they were grateful for right now.

"My kids," said my mom.

"My furry brother," Silas said, his arm around Argos, the family dog.

"Beer!" said my dad, raising his Mason jar.

"The bounty of the Lord," Barbara said.

"Tractors," said her husband.

"A night off!" said Matt, who loved his job at the music club but was enjoying a rare evening in the country.

"Adventures!" said Jesse, just back from a trek in the Pyrenees.

"Amanda's dinner parties," said Jen, my advisor friend.

Around the circle the thanks continued: *"Farms like this." "Vegetables!" "My children." "My husband." "My wife." "Second chances. . . ."* And on and on, until all fifty people had flung their thanks into our circle.

After the last one spoke, there was a pause.

Though there was nothing explicitly religious about our blessing, it had been a beautiful offering of thanks in the here and now, said with our eyes wide open to the beauty before us. In my old life I might have offered an "Amen," but tonight all I wanted to say was "Thank you" to my friends around me and to the world beyond, feeling so grateful that I'd landed in this moment.

Ten minutes later, our big circle was seated at one long table—covered in mismatched china plates full of salads I'd made from vegetables on the farm. If you looked carefully, you'd see that the white tablecloths were actually bed sheets, the silverware didn't match, and some of the Mason jars were still dusty from years in my cousins' basement, but this imperfect spread looked perfect to me: almost everyone I loved best in the world was sitting right here, shoulder to shoulder at one long table, alongside flowers I loved to weed, eating food I helped to grow and prepared myself—piles of greens, red and golden beet salad, white beans with sungold cherry tomatoes, pasta with pesto made from basil I'd weeded over countless hours all summer long, stacks of sliced heirloom tomatoes, small jars of gazpacho, my mom's deviled eggs sprinkled with parsley, crusty bread from the bakery, and homemade butter sprinkled with chives and sea salt.

Julia Child said, "The pleasures of the table, and of life, are infinite," and tonight I couldn't agree more.

I looked down the table lined with flowers and friends, ones I'd known for years, like Deric, sitting beside his new fiancée, and Laura, the willowy gospel singer from divinity school, and new ones too: down at the end was Mitch, the silver lining from Matt's fortieth birthday party, the same gray-haired hip forty-some-thing-year-old who'd asked, "What do you do?" Exactly a year after we met the first time, Mitch and I had re-met at Matt's for-ty-first birthday party back in February; this time around, I was feeling much better about myself and my life, and when I sent him an email after the party—my dating hiatus now over—he'd asked me out for a drink. That was six months ago, and we were still having fun for now. It's surprising how life works out; in my twenties I'd imagined that every man I dated, all three of them, that is, would become my husband, but now in my mid-thirties, when most of my peers were settling down and having children, I was eager to live in the moment and have fun without getting stuck in the *what-ifs*.

I finished the last few bites on my plate, full but never too full for dessert, and got up to scoop some ice cream.

"Look!" someone shouted, and everyone got quiet; I turned and saw a procession of one: my sister, walking up from the red barn, carrying a cake full of light.

It was just a few days after my birthday, and though I hadn't been planning to celebrate here, it was a happy coda to the night.

Emily held her gift out to me: chocolate cake topped with buttercream, a pile of berries on top, and enough candles to mark each year of my life so far—thirty-five, plus one for good luck.

"Make a wish!" she said.

What do you have to wish for when nearly everyone you love best is gathered up in your favorite place on a beautiful late-summer's eve?

Even though I'd never imagined my life would look exactly like this, I'd always imagined it would *feel* like this: at home in the moment, surrounded by love.

The candles on my cake fluttered as the ones I loved waited expectantly for me to make a wish.

So I closed my eyes, and I dwelled in Possibility.

Then I took a deep breath and blew.

A Thank You Note

When you're writing a book, with no one to answer to but yourself, encouragement from others is priceless. To every friend and stranger who asked about my book over the past four years, your questions meant more than you'll know! They were the bridge that carried me over.

To my writing coach and publishing expert, Brooke Warner, the only person I've ever listened to without question, and whose wisdom steered *The Do-Over* across the sea and into port, a thousand thanks.

If you look for it, inspiration is all around, even in the briefest of encounters. Several writers offered inspiration in a few hours that's stuck much longer. Thank you to Marianne Jacobbi for her early advice to try writing a couple days a week and see if I actually enjoyed it (I did!); to the novelist Nancy Thayer, of Nantucket, whose warm welcome one magical October afternoon showed me the sort of writer I'd like to become; and to the prolific Joan Walsh Anglund, whose picture books my mom read to me as a girl and who, years later, over champagne and lobster, in a cottage by the sea, told me to always carry a pen and notebook to catch "thoughts like butterflies" before they fly away. I hope that, like Joan, I'm still catching butterflies when I'm ninety.

Thank you to all the friends who gave me the key to their home and a peaceful place to write: the Dwyers in Allihies, County Cork; the Sibley-Groves in Totnes (twinned with Narnia), Devon; Darlington in London; the McElroy-Poux family in Seattle; the Stratfords in Bozeman, Montana; the Ruddocks in Harwich on Cape Cod; and Lelia Evans, the chicest farmgirl in Stowe, Vermont. And a shout-out to the coziest writer's cabin imaginable, Foxglove Cabin, in the woods on Whidbey Island, Washington. Worth *every* penny.

A heart full of gratitude to all the ones I'm blessed to call friends and family, most especially thank you . . .

To my dearest friends and most enthusiastic cheerleaders, each in her own unique way: Kelley, Molly, Theresa, Beth, Becky, and Lelia.

To the former advisors, now friends, still making me laugh twelve years in: Jen, Shannon, Ben, Jon, Kristin, JKU, John, Mike, and Kim.

To Matt, of Club Passim, for the gift of music, hugs, and humor.

To my sister's London friends who've become family friends and who offered much-appreciated company and brainstorming of book titles one memorable summer across the pond: Kate, Jeremy, Eleanor, Joe, Cat, Ben, and baby Arthur.

To the Dicks, my book group, who turned me on to Emily and her poetry, and who appreciate eating as much as reading. (And who graciously lent their editing expertise to this book in the final stretch.)

To the congregation of Pilgrim Church in whose sanctuary I've only ever felt love, and to all the other churches who've shared their Sunday mornings with me—most especially the first one, in Cambridge, where my parents met singing in the choir; without it I wouldn't be!

To my grandparents—Jinny, Beau, Sally, and John—for your genes and gifts which have shaped my life in invaluable ways.

To Jane, Bob, Emily, Brian, Eliza, and Babe, for sharing your family and your porch.

To my cousin, Dwight, the most kind-hearted, commendable farmer I know, and to Barbara, for teaching me to love the flowers almost as much she did, and to love my neighbor too. And to their small farm, a peaceable kingdom, as close to heaven on earth as I've ever come.

To my sister and brother, Emily Darlington and Silas, the greatest gifts in my life, in whose company I always feel at home, inspired, better about myself and the world. To Silas, for making me laugh, wisdom beyond his years, and leading me toward the best version of myself. And to Em, sister extraordinaire, who has had my heart from the beginning, and who excels at being true to herself and greeting every day full of grace; thank you for being the one who always gets it.

To my parents, Mac and Priscilla, for creating a family full of love, giving me roots, wings, and a home I can always return to.

And to Argos, wheaten terrier, just for being you.

It's family tradition that, before the first sip, we all raise our glass to someone we know, if only in the loosest sense of the word. And so I raise an overflowing flute of something sparkly to the Prime Minister, as played by Hugh Grant, who said that whenever he gets gloomy with the state of the world, he remembers:

Love actually IS all around.

In the company of all the stars above, I know it's true.

Made in the USA
Middletown, DE
09 June 2017